THE HISTORY OF CIVILIZATION

THE PEOPLES OF ASIA

THE HISTORY OF CIVILIZATION

General Editor C. K. Ogden

The *History of Civilization* is a landmark in early twentieth Century publishing. The aim of the general editor, C. K. Ogden, was to "summarise in one comprehensive synthesis the most recent findings and theories of historians, anthropologists, archaeologists, sociologists and all conscientious students of civilization." The *History,* which includes titles in the French series *L'Evolution de l'Humanite*, was published at a formative time in the development of the social sciences, and during a period of significant historical discoveries.

A list of the titles in the series can be found at the end of this book.

PLATE I

CHINESE MOSLEM
(Original home probably Samarqand)

[front.

THE PEOPLES OF ASIA

L. H. Dudley Buxton

Routledge
Taylor & Francis Group

LONDON AND NEW YORK

First published in 1925 by Routledge, Trench, Trubner
Reprinted in 1996, 1998 by Routledge

2 Park Square, Milton Park,
Abingdon, Oxfordshire OX14 4RN
&
711 Third Avenue,
New York, NY 10017

Routledge is an imprint of the Taylor & Francis Group, an informa business

Transferred to Digital Printing 2008

First issued in paperback 2013

British Cataloguing in Publication Data

ISBN 13: 978-0-415-15587-8 (hbk)
ISBN 13: 978-0-415-86972-0 (pbk)
ISBN Eastern Civilization (10 volume set): 978-0-415-15613-4
ISBN History of Civilization (50 volume set): 978-0-415-14380-6

Publisher's Note
The publisher has gone to great lengths to ensure the quality
of this reprint but points out that some
imperfections in the original may be apparent

PREFACE

HE who attempts to collect the information which is available on the races of Asia is confronted almost more than in any other study by the many languages in which his authorities have written. The vast mass of Chinese literature which bears on the ethnology of Eastern Asia must perforce remain unexplored by the ordinary anthropologist, and though Western scholars have made a beginning of translating it into more familiar tongues it will probably remain for Chinese scholars of the future, versed in " barbarian " as well as their native learning to unlock the closed book. A beginning has already been made by the collaboration of Chinese and foreigners in the very interesting ethnological publications of the Chinese Geological Survey. Most of their publications, as well as many Japanese publications, are written both in the native tongue and in some European language, and are therefore addressed to a wide public, while the practice of quoting tribal and place-names both in character and in transliteration avoids the confusion which may easily occur where only transliterations, often on different systems, are given.

Even in Western languages, however, the literature on the subject is vast and ever increasing. I have tried in the bibliography to indicate those books which I have found of the greatest service to me in my own work, and the student by referring to them will be enabled to trace at least a large part of the specialized literature on various parts of Asia. Considerable prominence has been given to easily-accessible books and publications, the advanced student will know his own way about the big libraries ; and from my own experience I believe that there is no more annoying experience for the more elementary student than to find that the library he frequents does not possess the work *which he is told is the most useful one on the subject he is studying, or if it does possess it, when the book arrives, it turns out to be written in a language which is imperfectly understood. In many cases, therefore, I have referred to a summary in English, French or German, as well as the original article. The summary will give the elementary student all he requires, the advanced student can then go on to the full work in a less-known language.*

It is difficult for me to express adequately my debt to very many scholars both here and abroad. My friend and chief, Professor Arthur Thomson, Dr. Lee's Professor of Human Anatomy in the University of Oxford, has never ceased to offer every assistance in his power to further my work, and to his advice and kindly criticism, never grudged on the busiest of busy mornings, I owe more than I can ever acknowledge. Mr. Henry Balfour, F.R.S., Keeper of the Pitt Rivers Museum, has continuously and generously helped me in many matters with his extensive knowledge and wide experience, and this volume owes much to him. Professor Myres first introduced me to Asia and, more important still, to field work; he has not failed to see that I did not neglect the introduction which he had given. To Dr. Marett I owe an especial debt in regard to the technique of anthropological writing. Abroad my especial thanks are due to Dr. Black, of the Rockefeller Institute in Peking, and to the Director of that Institute for admitting me as a temporary member of their staff and giving me the use of their laboratories. Professor Adachi allowed me to examine at leisure, under his guidance, the magnificent collections of the Imperial University at Kyoto, and Dr. Nieuwenhuis escorted me in person and by deputy through Java. The opportunity to undertake this extensive travel was given me by the generous Fellowship endowed by M. Kahn. I feel that thanks are also due to a series of Chinese and Mongol scholars in Peking, some of whose photographs have been utilized in this volume for demonstrating on their own persons and on those of their friends —dwellers in the remoter parts of Asia—some of the different racial types of that vast continent.

I feel sure that these scholars would consider that one whose beard is not yet grey is guilty of filial impiety in attempting to discuss so vast a subject. No one is more conscious than I am that this is but a vindematio prima *of the harvest-fields of Asia. I have written in the hope that even such a scanty gleaning may help to attract others better equipped to reap the treasures which are to be found in abundance. In so short a space it is impossible to do more than indicate the general trend of the published work on the subject, and to incorporate here and there the little bits of actual original work which I have been able to do in one or two places.*

My father, Dr. Dudley Buxton, and Mr. G. R. Carline have been kind enough to read through the typescript, and I owe very much to their careful and thorough revision. Mr. Charles Henderson, I.C.S., read through the chapter on India in typescript and proof, and Mr. Ernest Thomas, the chapter on the Near East. My pupil, Mr. Fraser of Queen's College, rendered invaluable help with the index. Mr. Chesterman, Assistant in the Department of Human Anatomy, Oxford, has prepared the prints for publication from my own negatives.

To all these gentlemen and to many others who have assisted me at various times, I owe a deep debt of gratitude.

L. H. D. B.

Oxford, June, 1925.

CONTENTS

		PAGE
PREFACE	. . . .	V

CHAPTER
I.	INTRODUCTION	1
II.	THE RACES OF ASIA	32
III.	THE ORIGIN OF THE ASIATIC RACES	71
IV.	WESTERN ASIA	84
V.	INDIA	115
VI.	CHINA	148
VII.	THE FRINGING LANDS OF CHINA	167
VIII.	ARCTIC ASIA	192
IX.	JAPAN	205
X.	SOUTH-EASTERN ASIA AND INDONESIA . . .	220
XI.	SUMMARY AND CONCLUSIONS	245
	BIBLIOGRAPHY	250
	INDEX OF TRIBAL NAMES	261
	GENERAL INDEX	265

LIST OF ILLUSTRATIONS

PLATE

I. CHINESE MOSLEM . . . . . *Frontispiece*

II. A MONGOL . . . . *Facing page* 58

III. CYPRIOT PEASANT . . . . . ,, ,, 94

IV. TAMIL WOMAN . . . . . . ,, ,, 126

V. A VEDDA . . . . ,, ,, 144

VI. A KHAMS TIBETAN . . . . . ,, ,, 172

VII. A MANCHU . . . . . . ,, ,, 188

VIII. A PEASANT WOMAN FROM SOUTH JAPAN . ,, ,, 216

NOTE

THE references have been serially arranged by chapters. The first figure refers to the chapter, the second figure to the serial number of the reference within the chapter, and the third figure is to page of the work quoted, if it has been found necessary to add this. Where the work quoted deals entirely with the subject quoted I have not usually added the page. II. 12, 24 means page 24 of the twelfth reference in Chapter II; reference to the bibliography at the end of the volume will show that this is A. C. Haddon : *The Wanderings of Peoples*.

THE PEOPLES OF ASIA

CHAPTER I

INTRODUCTION

ONE of the greatest difficulties which the student of anthropology has to face is the selection of criteria which he is to adopt in order to distinguish the various peoples he is describing. Many such criteria have been suggested in the past and have been variously accepted. Most books therefore which deal with any country, other than a restricted area, are apt to be very confusing because the same basis of classification has not been adhered to throughout. In some cases the authors, although consistent, have used criteria which have not won general acceptance, and therefore their works have proved less useful because it has been hardly possible to compare them with other investigations in the same field.

The divisions of mankind, which have become traditional, are based either on physique or culture. Herodotus is one of the earliest ethnologists to suggest the former. He says that it was possible on a certain battlefield to distinguish between the crania of the Egyptians and the Persians because the former were less easily broken. This statement, which has been widely accepted even in modern textbooks, is unfortunately not correct. Aristotle also would apparently accept a physical criterion when he says that the Greeks differ ($\phi\upsilon\sigma\epsilon\hat{\iota}$) from the barbarians. He seems however to mean a psychological rather than an anatomical difference, as he is not concerned with what he would no doubt have considered a branch of medicine.

Language as a test of race was also widely accepted by the Greeks, and even as early as Homer the Carians are classified as speaking a " barbarian " tongue. This form of classification has been very widely accepted by ethnologists, owing, no doubt, to the rapid advances made at the beginning of the last century by the comparative philologists, and we still speak in the same breath of Semitic and Mongoloid races when in the latter case we mean a physical type and in the former people speaking kindred languages. Nationality has also formed a frequent test for race, although this criterion has been less widely accepted than the linguistic test. In this volume the basis of classification will be physique, and as far as possible all linguistic and national terms will be avoided. It is not possible at present however to adopt a terminology which entirely eliminates such words except by coining an entirely new set of names, a procedure which is only likely to lead to confusion. We can hardly avoid words like " Turk " or " Arab," although these two words have rather a linguistic and a cultural than a physical connotation.

The history of the classification of mankind is not without great significance at the present juncture, describing as it does the reason for the modern acceptance of certain terms as well as explaining their exact significance which otherwise is often apt to be confusing.

The work of Herodotus and Aristotle has already been mentioned. It was not till the beginning of the seventeenth century that Western Europe seriously began to reconsider the problems of ethnology which had been bequeathed to her by the ancient world. In the meantime much material for comparison had been accumulating owing to the voyages of the Elizabethan mariners, many of whom brought back succinct accounts of new types of " barbarians " which had been unknown to the ancient world.

It is unnecessary to consider in detail the many classifications of mankind which have been suggested since the Renaissance. The reader will find them fully described in Keane's *Ethnology* (I. 1). Some of the more important may however be mentioned in so far as they relate to Asia. Bernier who died in 1688 suggests that there are four main divisions of mankind: Europeans, who are white, Africans, who are black, Asiatics, who are yellow, and Lapps. Linnæus (I. 2), writing nearly a century later (he died in 1783), still adopts the three same main groups but includes hair and eye colour, so that the Asiatics are classed as yellow with brown eyes and black hair. He also includes the Americans as a fourth class, but removes the Lapps from their solitary eminence.

It is to Blumenbach (I. 3) however that we really owe the foundations of modern anthropology and some of his terms have survived until to-day. His contributions to racial study are summarized by Duckworth (I. 4, 4) as follows. He first employed the term " anthropology " in descriptive morphological studies. He recognized the fact that no sharp lines demarcate the several varieties of mankind, and realized that the transition from type to type is imperceptible. Further, he clearly enunciated a classificatory scheme of the varieties of mankind, admittedly arbitrary but with the object of facilitating study, the classification being based on the characters of the skin, hair and skull. Finally, he recognized the influence of external causes in producing and perpetuating variation in animals, including man ; he also recognized the origin of varieties through degeneration and very nearly anticipated Darwin.[1]

His terms have survived until to-day ; he called the White races " Caucasic," because in trying to obtain a non-terri-torial name he was struck by some fine Georgian skulls among some skulls he happened to be examining and so called the race " Caucasic " after them. His term for African Ethiopic has not survived, but Mongolic (or the variety Mongolian) is still in use. Modern anthropology has not accepted his separate classification for Malay.

An immense amount of work was done in the next eighty years, but this need not be discussed here ; it is of great interest however to note Huxley's classification, published in the *Journal of the Ethnological Society* in 1870 (I. 5). Here we find that further exploration has borne fruit in a more elaborate classification, although the main lines are not different. Asiatic peoples are included in all Huxley's

[1] As Keane somewhat inaccurately states Blumenbach's position the following note, which I owe to my colleague, Miss Blackwood, is of interest. In his first edition (*De generis humani varietate nativa* 1775, p. 99) he follows Linnæus and divides mankind into four varieties. In the second edition, 1781, he alters the four to five, adding the group Malay " after I had more accurately investigated the different nations of Eastern Asia." This later division he elaborates in the third edition in 1795.

groups. Under the Negroes he includes the Negritos, but unlike modern observers he groups together under that name the Andamanese, the Papuans and the Tasmanians. His second classification, the Australoid, is also of interest for our purpose; these include the Australian aborigines, the hill tribes of the Deccan (Dravidians) and the Egyptians. His Mongoloid group comprises the Mongols, from Lappland to Siam, the Malays, the Indonesians and Polynesians, and the Eskimo and American Indians. His group of fair Whites do not enter into the present consideration, but under the dark Whites or Melanocroid he includes the inhabitants of Syria, Arabia, Persia, and " Hindostan."

The writers of the next thirty years put forward various classifications most of which differed from Huxley in minor points. It is important to note that in some cases different criteria were used. Colour and hair form had on the whole been the criteria adopted by the older writers, some of the more modern have preferred to rely on hair alone. Topinard (I. 6) introduced the combination of colour and the nasal index and classed the Yellow races of Asia as " Yellow Mesorrhine." His classification has been generally followed.

Sergi's work (I. 7) is of importance because he suggested an entirely original form of classification, that of head form. He considered that the brachycephalic element which has penetrated into Europe was essentially Asiatic in origin as opposed to the Eurafrican longheads. His classification is therefore in many ways a greater challenge to students of Africa than to those of Asia. Dependence on skull form is however a new method. It has not received wide acceptance owing to the difficulties which are encountered in understanding the various subgroups suggested by him.

The classification indicated by Duckworth in his *Morphology and Anthropology* (I. 4, ch. xvi.) is one of the most important of modern attempts. It depends on criteria which, although they have been much used by anthropologists for many years, have not, so far as I am aware, been employed to any great extent for general classifications. He has introduced a method which is not dissimilar in principle to that used by many morphologists for classifying other animals, and his results, although they naturally agree in many cases with the work of previous observers, have certain differences,

which if proved to be true will profoundly alter many of our
views on the population of Asia.

He takes three main criteria and divides mankind on the
basis provided by these criteria. They are: cranial capacity,
cephalic index, and the projection of the face. Thus his
Group I includes men of small cranial capacity, dolichocephalic heads and prognathous faces, the type being called
the Australian. Group II have similar characters but differ
in other morphological details, the type being the African
Negro. Of the Asiatic peoples he has made a classification
as follows: the first, Group IV which he describes as
Eurasiatic, all have a large cranial capacity and are orthognathous. They are divided into a dolichocephalic and a
brachycephalic subgroup; this type includes the inhabitants
of Europe, part of North Africa, all of Asia, with small
exceptions, and most of the continent of America. In the
other Asiatic group are the Andamanese, who have small
capacity, are brachycephalic and orthognathous. The contrast in size and importance between the two groups is very
striking and brings out clearly the distinguishing point
between Duckworth's classification and that of previous
authors. He appears to hold the view that the greater part
of mankind belongs to the same group, but that a few varieties
have specialized either in response to environmental or other
conditions. These varieties include the peoples who are most
generally conceded to be backward races, and include not
only those very clearly specialized peoples, the Andamanese
and the Eskimo, but also the Negro, the Bushman, the
Australian aborigines and the Polynesians.

Most classifications have considered that the differences
between the Yellow races and the White are sufficient to
justify their being included in the two great varieties of
mankind; Duckworth, however, insisting on their resemblances rather than on their differences, refuses to separate
them by as wide a gap as that which divides them both
from, say, the Negro. His subdivision is also of fundamental
importance as it links up the brachycephals of Europe with
the Yellow peoples of Asia more closely than with their long-
headed European neighbours, in much the same way that
some authors, notably the Italian School of Anthropologists,
are inclined to link up the Mediterranean race with the Negro.

An examination of the crania of, say, Chinese and of the round heads of Western Asia must reveal the similarity of cranial form; indeed, it is often difficult if not impossible on an examination of the calvaria alone to distinguish between the two. The difference in the bony framework of the face and of the rest of the skeleton however suggests that there is considerable difference between the two. Duckworth's criteria however are based in two cases on the calvarial form, and therefore tend to mask the differences. The exact degree of relationship between the different groups of mankind is still so uncertain that this particular classification deserves greater recognition than it has received by most writers on the classification of mankind, many of whom have been content to follow the more traditional and at first sight clearer classifications.

Ripley (I. 8) who, unlike most of the authors we have been considering, did not discuss the population of the whole world, but limited himself to one continent, Europe, adopted three criteria, the cephalic index, that is the percentage ratio of the head breadth to the head length, stature, and colour. On this basis the inhabitants of Europe instead of forming six races, as they do according to the criteria adopted by Deniker (I. 9), are divided into three. In the north there is a fair, tall long-headed race called the Nordic, on the central massif is found a round-headed race of medium colouring and stature, " Alpine," and on the shores of the Mediterranean a short, long-headed *brunet* race, which coincides with Sergi's Mediterranean race. Although there are certain objections to Ripley's theories, especially his views on the Negroes and his treatment of the round-headed races of Central Europe, his views may be said to dominate the field of anthropology at the present time, even where they are not accepted in full, and any student of the ethnology of Europe or Asia must delve deeply into the material collected in his brilliant and exhaustive monograph.

The majority of the workers who have been quoted above were by training and interests anatomists. Following the lead of Quetelet (I. 20) and Retzius (I. 21) they had been in the habit of taking certain measurements, but being for the most part not interested in the mathematical aspects of the problem they failed to make the full use of their figures or to follow the path indicated by Quetelet. To Professor Pearson (I. 10) is due the introduction of the scientific study of numerical data into anthropology. He saw that there were ready to hand a series of methods, many of which were in general use by statisticians and astronomers, which could be applied with every hope of success to biological problems. Of the original workers in this field, of whom the most distinguished were Galton and Weldon, Pearson is the only survivor, and he has gathered round him a school of "Biometricians," many of whom have devoted considerable attention to anthropology.[1] Although the members of this school published their earliest papers nearly thirty years ago, their views have not met with universal acceptance, partly perhaps owing to the fact that many anthropologists are unacquainted with the comparatively obscure method of writing which has characterized some of their publications and partly also because many of the Biometricians, owing, no doubt, to an early specialization in the principles of applied mathematics, sometimes showed a lack of anatomical training. In considering the work of this school it must always be remembered that the mathematical treatment of data is merely mechanical and that nothing can emerge from the machine which was not originally put into it. It is however possible to grade by mathematical methods great quantities of data which might otherwise be very unwieldy if not impossible to handle.

The older anthropologists had been content to take measurements and to work out "averages" by rule-of-thumb methods without considering at all accurately how far these averages could really be taken as typical measurements of the group from which the original measurements were obtained. To the Biometric School we owe the introduction into anthropology of certain concepts of great practical value. These may be conveniently grouped under three headings : measures of dispersion, probable errors, and the theory of contingency and correlation. It must not be supposed that these ideas originated with or were even introduced into anthropology by this school, their use in anthropological work had previously been suggested with a

---

[1] A special periodical, *Biometrika*, is published devoted to biometric research.

slightly different terminology by Quetelet. The Biometric School, however, popularized them and extended their scope far beyond what had been done by any previous workers, and the debt which anthropology owes to Pearson, both for developing old methods and for devising new ones, is even now hardly sufficiently recognized.

It had been recognized by all writers from Herodotus onwards that certain races were more mixed than others, in other words that the component stocks from which certain tribes had originated presented similar features, while in the case of other tribes their origin had to be sought in less closely related stocks which had mixed together and produced a hybrid people. By the use of the standard deviation and the coefficient of variation Pearson has shown that it is possible to measure the comparative pureness of various peoples.

The standard deviation is found by taking the square root of the mean square deviation from the mean. It should be noted that " mean " is the technical term for what is called, in popular language, the " average." It would, of course, be possible to take the mean of a series of measurements and then to take the average deviation of the measurements from that mean. It has been found in practice, however, that greater accuracy is obtained by taking not the actual deviation but the square of those deviations, and then taking the average of those squares and finally the square root of this average. The figure thus obtained is called a measure of dispersion, because it shows how far the various individuals of the series which is being examined are " dispersed " or scattered in relation to the central point or average. If the standard deviation is small, that is, if the dispersion is not great, the mean will be typical of the group, but if it is widely scattered then obviously but few individuals in one group will have measurements which approximate to the mean. In other words, our mean will be a less reliable indication of the racial type. The matter may be understood more simply if we compare anthropological measurements with cricket scores. If one batsman makes in three innings 0, 15, and 30, and another 13, 15, and 17, we should say that, though both have the same average, one was a more steady player than the other, although, of course, we should want his score for more than three innings before we could pass a definite judgment, a point which we shall return to later. The steadier player we may suppose was always good to make about 15 runs, or, in other words, his average closely approximated to the score we might expect him to make. With so few figures this can be seen at a glance. If both had played fifty innings it would be less easy. Let us therefore work out their standard deviations. The mean in both cases is 15, the first player's first innings deviates from the mean by 15, the square of which is 225, his second innings is equal to the mean and the third innings has the same deviation as the first. The total square deviation is therefore 450. To get the mean or average of this we must divide by the total number of innings, three. The mean square deviation is therefore 150, i.e. $\frac{450}{3}$. The square root is just over 12, which represents the standard deviation of his score. Using the same method the mean square deviation of the second player's score is $\frac{8}{3}$, i.e. 1·67, the square root of which is under 1·3. This example will serve to show in an exaggerated form how the standard deviation may be used, but we can hardly apply the theory of mixed races to a single player's scores.

It will be clear that if we mix two series, say one in which the heads are short and another in which the heads are long, the average measurement will represent not a typical member of the series, but a compromise between the two. The standard deviation will be great, because the short-headed series will extend on one side and the long-headed on the other. In some cases, no doubt, this would be revealed by a graph, but there are many cases when the use of a measure of dispersion is more convenient and for comparative purposes it is infinitely less unwieldy. It will happen sometimes that we may wish to compare measurements whose means differ very much. We might wish to know whether a certain race had a more variable head length or stature. In order to do this we must have some common factor. This is to be found by the " coefficient of variation," which is obtained by multiplying the standard deviation by a hundred and dividing the product by the mean. To return to our cricket analogy, on examining A's scores at the end of the season a member of the club decides that he is a more reliable bat than bowler, another member takes an opposite view. If the club possessed a biometrician he might suggest that by comparing the coefficients of variation of A's batting and bowling averages the matter could easily be settled. All that has to be done is to work out his batting average, say 15, with its standard deviation, say 9, the coefficient of variation will be $\frac{900}{15}$, i.e. 60, and to do the same for his bowling average, and we can compare the two figures and decide which member of the club was right.

The great value of such methods will be seen where we have reason to suspect that a race is the result of the mixture of two races which present some features in common, but which differ in other respects. We should expect the hybrid to show little variation in those characters in which the two alleged original stocks are alike, and to have a wide measure of dispersion where they differed. This suggestion could be measured by comparing the coefficients of variation.

While it is possible by using familiar analogies to illustrate the meaning of the standard deviation, it is less easy to explain that of probable errors. It will be clear that if I take a series of measurements on a savage tribe and at a subsequent date take another series, I shall not by the law of chance which, as Laplace says, is common sense reduced to calculation, get exactly similar results on both occasions. It will also appear that the larger the number of individuals in my series the more likely the two are to agree. Now, although it would be better to work out my averages from as large a series as possible, it is convenient to know how far my average does really represent the population under review. This will depend on two things, first, how variable the population is and, secondly, the number of individuals measured. The more I measure and the lower my standard deviation the more likely is my series to approximate to the true mean of the population. The value of the probable error is estimated from these two factors, it therefore supplies a method of showing in a convenient way the reliability of the data. If the probable error is great the mean value calculated must be accepted with caution, if small, then the calculated value probably approximates to the true mean value. The probable error can be calculated for mean standard deviations, coefficients of variation of correlation and so on. The name is perhaps unfortunate, as it does not signify the error that is likely to have occurred in the calculation owing to personal equation or any other cause.

The theories of contingency and correlation are different aspects of the same problem, the former deals with characters which cannot and the latter with those that can be measured. It is of the greatest importance in anthropology. A coefficient has been constructed, the actual methods of calculation of which need not concern us here. If two variables vary exactly in relation to one another, such as mass and weight, they are exactly correlated and the coefficient if calculated would be one. If there is no relationship between the variables the coefficient is in the neighbourhood of zero. In anthropological work we seldom or never get either unity or zero, owing to many accidental features, but the varying size of the coefficients serve to show that two features are closely connected, either as cause and effect or else both as effects of the same cause. It is unnecessary to give examples here, as there will be numerous occasions when various coefficients will be quoted in the sequel.

I have considered at some length these aspects, perhaps the simplest but, at the same time, not the least important of Pearson's work, because a proper understanding of them is necessary if we are to make use of much of the data on the peoples of Asia which have been collected by workers in the field.[1]

Biometricians have been for the most part interested in method. They have seldom therefore, with one or two exceptions, applied themselves to wide ethnological problems. Recently however an attempt based on the study of certain Asiatic peoples has been made to supersede the older methods of analysis by the construction of a provisional " Coefficient of Racial Likeness " (I. 14). This coefficient attempts to give a numerical value to the combined characters of a race.

It has been felt by many anthropologists that reliance on a single character or index or even on two or three arbitrarily selected criteria, as for instance stature, the cephalic index and so on, is not a sufficient method of gauging racial differences. In some cases also it is found that the apparent evidence is very contradictory, Groups A and B, let us say, differing from one another but little in two criteria selected and much in two others, the reverse being the case between A and C. It is not then an easy task to decide on the relationship between B and C who may differ in a different way from one another.

The suggested coefficient gets over this difficulty by combining all the characters and indices together and reducing them to a single index figure. It is well known that the significant difference between the mean values of the same character in two different races can be estimated by dividing this difference by its probable error. When the quotient of this division is more than three the difference is said to be significant.[2] The probable error of any mean depends on two things, the standard deviation and the number of cases used to obtain the mean, and the constant ·6745. The coefficient of racial likeness is found by dividing the difference be-

---

[1] The biometric aspect of anthropology has a bibliography of its own. The student may most profitably study the papers quoted in later chapters. For general works see I. 10, 11, 12. A very clear statement of *method* will be found in I. 14.

[2] For a further discussion of this point see my paper on Cyprus (I. 13, 194).

tween the means of the two people under discussion divided by the sum of the two standard deviations divided each by the number of cases on which the constants were based. For greater accuracy in the same way that we take not the mean deviation from the mean, but the mean square deviation, the figures are squared before we divide. The figure so obtained must, of course, be divided by the number of characters we have selected. We get then what practially amounts to a mean significant difference, or rather the value of the mean significant difference divided by ·6745.

Symbolically the significant difference is found where, say, M_1 is the mean cephalic index of the first race and M_2 the mean cephalic index of the second by the following :

$$\frac{M_1-M_2}{\sqrt{\epsilon_2^1 - \epsilon_2^2}} = \frac{M_1-M_2}{\sqrt{\left(\frac{·6745\sigma_1}{\sqrt{n_2}}\right)^2 - \left(\frac{·6745\sigma_2}{\sqrt{n_2}}\right)^2}}$$

whereas the coefficient of racial likeness is found by the following formula

$$\frac{1}{k}\Sigma\frac{(M_1-M_2)}{\frac{\sigma_2^1}{n_1}+\frac{\sigma_2^1}{n_2}} - 1$$ where k is the number of characters considered, ϵ the probable error and σ the standard deviation.

It will be seen at once that whereas in dealing with significant differences we are at once aware whether the first or the second race is bigger in respect to certain characters and possibly smaller in respect to others, we are here avoiding the difficulty of plus or minus signs by squaring the differences between the means. Whether this is a disadvantage or an advantage will be seen when the method has been put to a further test. It would seem, however, to be an advantage to consider differences apart from their signs, and to obtain an average value it would, of course, be necessary to have some means of preventing the plus and minus differences cancelling out.

The objection to the assumption of a similar standard deviation for different races, an assumption which is discussed by Morant in his paper, need not concern us here, as we are dealing with numbers which are at least sufficient to assure us of a standard deviation with a comparatively low probable error, and much greater numbers than have been used in the previous papers where this coefficient has been employed.

The difficulty that some characters may give greater weight than others may be suggested, but the method of using the standard deviations and expressing the differences in these terms overcomes this difficulty from the technical point of view. It does not however overcome it from the practical. Clearly if we were to take characters which were closely correlated we should not be giving a fair weight to our measurements. Suppose we had ten characters of which three were closely correlated and the other seven were only slightly correlated to one another. Under those circumstances it would not be fair to divide by ten to get our mean coefficient, and yet as the correlation is not likely to be complete it would be wrong to treat the three closely correlated characters as a unit and divide by one. This difficulty is overcome in practice by choosing characters which are known to be correlated in only a slight degree to one another, so slight a degree that the correlation can be neglected. This difficulty is one which always deserves consideration.

A further objection is that the measurements which we select are necessarily of an arbitrary character, and with the present state of our knowledge it would seem as if some were of greater racial significance than others. By racial I mean less affected by environment and more by heredity. The selection of characters to form the coefficient must then be an arbitrary affair and the value of the result will depend on the skill with which the selection is made. Anthropologists are at present by no means agreed on what the best characters are, and in the present state of our knowledge the matter must be considered to be purely in the experimental stage.

A further objection that may be raised is that we are reducing definite measurements, whose significance is easily understood although they may be differently interpreted, to a purely arbitrary figure. If the same measurements were selected in all cases this figure would be of great value; when the selection is different in each author's paper, the value of the coefficient is thereby much impaired. The amount of computation necessary is such that it is unlikely that a single author would be able in the limited time at his disposal to cover more than a comparative restricted field.

A scientific method must however be judged by its results, and it is clear that at present the coefficient is in an experimental stage. It has however seemed worth while to consider it here in some detail, because it has been used so far in the elucidation of problems which are entirely Asiatic and because owing to its comparative obscurity it does no seem to be well known to ethnologists. At present the method has not shown anything which could not have been discovered by less complicated means, except for the association of the peoples of South Indian with the Yellow races, a statement which is not likely to meet with general acceptance, but this will be considered in a later chapter. It is more than possible, however, that biometricians may succeed in developing this or a similar method. Such a method if it were devised and proved to be satisfactory would be one of their greatest contributions to science.

I have dealt at some length with the work of the Biometric School because I shall have numerous occasions to make use of their methods in the chapters which follow. They have been for the most part ignored by the general textbooks on ethnology, such as those of Keane, Deniker, and Ripley, and many modern monographs while quoting the standard deviations and so on of the figures with which they are dealing neglect to make an adequate use of the very convenient, if sometimes complicated, machinery which has been constructed by the Biometric School.

So far they have not attempted to publish a general classification of mankind, but seem to have been working towards a goal which resembles that suggested by Quetelet.

The most recent classification which has been published is that of Haddon (I. 19). He has adopted three characters, skin, hair, and nose. The scheme, he says, " is not a classification as that word is understood by zoological and botanical systematists, as it includes geographical considerations. All those who have attempted to make a systematic classification of mankind have found themselves in difficulties and have frequently fallen back on geographical groupings."

Haddon has on the whole followed, with considerable modifications, the classification suggested by Topinard. He differs in some respects from many of the views put forward by the Biometric School, notably in the suggestion that wide variations may be found not only in mixed races but also in undifferentiated pure ones. His criteria do not cause him to suggest any divisions which differ widely from those which have been generally accepted, although he seems to take a somewhat different view of relationships. Indeed, it becomes abundantly clear from a study of the various attempts which have been made to classify mankind that, except in the case of a few authors who have very unconventional views, which do not seem likely to receive wide acceptance, there are certain divisions of mankind which appear whatever criteria are used.

Writers who have approached the problem from very different standpoints have on the whole come to opinions which, however diverse they may seem at first sight, are found on subsequent investigation to agree in fundamentals although they may differ widely in detail. The divisions are however for the most part artificial, and it will be seen in the sequel that a difference of opinion does exist in regard to some peoples as to whether they should be placed in the White or Yellow group of mankind, even though the authors who admit the difficulty are perfectly convinced that the White and Yellow groups represent distinguishable divisions of mankind. Border-line cases are so frequent that the ethnologist has either to admit undifferentiated peoples or to suggest racial admixture. The adherents of mathematical methods, as I understand them, would make variation the supreme test and declare that where there is much variation we have evidence of racial admixture. Haddon on the other hand seems, as I have said, to believe that a lack of differentiation can also be the cause of wide variation. Again, some of the Biometric School believe that racial mixture can eventually proceed to the pitch where the mixture becomes a compound and the two or more stocks become so blended that the final race shows as much and as little variation as a " pure " race.

But not only is the difficulty confined to the main racial stocks. The subdivisions of the main groups are almost infinite in number, and the subject for endless controversy and vast columns of figures and infinite measurements which appear often to be but imperfectly understood. There are few criteria which are generally accepted and the student is left to wander disconsolate in a welter of conflicting literature.

The fundamental problem seems to concern the question of racial fixity. In the days before the acceptance of the doctrine of evolution this problem had been seen by anthropologists such as Blumenbach, who suggested that the solution might be seen in degeneration, for the fall of man seems to have fired imaginations more strongly than his rise.

To-day the problem is discussed on a wider footing. In general terms the question is limited to the discussion whether environment can ever effect mankind in such a way as to produce heritable characters. The opinion of most biologists appears to be that man like other animals is the carrier of germ plasm (I. 37). His mortal body is not capable of transmitting the effect of stimuli, which it has received, to the immortal and precious matter which it holds in trust for future generations. The bearers of the torch of life may stumble or may scale the mountain heights, they may extinguish the torch which they are carrying, but they cannot alter the nature of the divine fire.

There are however certain varieties of the human race which, although capable of producing fertile hybrids, appear to represent more or less true strains. Some of the differences are constant and others are less easily capable of exact observation and measurement. The origin of these differences has been the subject of considerable discussion ever since the acceptance of the doctrine of evolution. Two points of view have been expressed. One school, which on the whole has not met with much support, is inclined to put forward the multiple origin of man from different apes or ape-like ancestors, a view which is made untenable by the close resemblances of the different groups of mankind. The second school suggests that man has become modified owing to the effect of environment. Here again there seems to be two ways in which this modification may have taken place. The varieties of man may be due either to sports or mutants, those which have survived being the ones which were most suited to the conditions to which they were subjected, or to the gradual modification of various organs owing to the response to certain environmental stimuli. Haddon suggests that it is possible that at one time man was less differentiated than he is at present and therefore more capable of responding to the effects of environment. Keith (I. 40) has suggested that this progressive evolution has not yet ceased to operate, and that civilization is having an effect on the physical form of certain members of the human race.

The effect of the mixing of different types, once the types have become specialized, has been pointed out as the possible origin of certain racial types; such a suggestion does not however get over the original difficulty of the specialization of type.

The actual mechanism of the change does not concern us here. The evidence does however seem to suggest that certain human types are associated with certain environmental conditions. It would however seem as if there were potentialities in the human race and that so long as these potentialities were allowed their full play response to environment was possible, but that after specialization had taken place in a particular direction the line of evolution must be forward, not backward; that is to say, that if for some reason or other a particular type had developed a broad nose, the stimuli which might make another type have a narrow nose would not cause the broad nose which had in the course of ages been getting broader to turn back and narrow itself again.

It must also be remembered that although for purposes of study we isolate certain features, yet in actual fact man is a complex organism whose existence depends not on individual functions of various organs but rather on the mutual function of a most complicated series of organs. In the paragraphs which follow I shall try and show very briefly how far it would seem that certain features, some of them often considered of racial importance, do seem to respond to environment. What I have said at the beginning of the paragraph must however be always borne in mind. The relationship of the whole series of organs to environment is really the most important feature. To discuss this relationship would however be a study of greater complication than can be attempted in this book. Professor Arthur Thomson (I. 15) has suggested that environment plays an important part in moulding certain features of the human frame. Most of his views are based on what may be called mechanical considerations. He would see in the stresses to which the head, for instance, is subjected the most important

c

influences which mould its form. At the same time he has not expressed any opinion on the length of time which it takes for such mechanical influences to become effective, nor exactly how far they may be considered racial or individual characters. The importance of this work will be seen when we come to estimate in detail those characters which have usually been considered to be good criteria of race. If these can be proved to be the direct result of the influence of environment, whether on the group or on the individual, it is clear that though they may serve to distinguish a particular tribe, so long as it remains in a particular environment, they will not serve to show the actual kinship of various peoples who may have certain features in common. This matter is of special importance, since it is clear that race if it is to have any meaning must follow the connotation which is given it by Broca when he says:[1] "The varieties of mankind have received the name of races, which gives the idea of a more or less direct relationship between individuals of the same variety, but does not decide either affirmatively or negatively the question of the relationship between individuals of different varieties."

When we are faced with the problem of the effect of environment on the human frame we are in a position to make especial use of the theories of correlation and contingency, the details of which have been outlined above. They enable us to test in a very exact way the extent to which a certain character in the human body varies in relation either to another character or else to outside influences. They cannot always be used, but where possible their employment is of the utmost importance.

The most generally accepted criterion of race in the past has been the cephalic index. Thomson (I. 15) has shown that there are several factors which determine the shape of the head. The most important is the size of the brain. There can be little doubt that on the whole there is a correlation between brain size and body size, but at present we do not know how far different brain sizes are correlated with different races. If we did it might be possible to find in this an important indication of racial differences.

---

[1] Article, "Anthropologie," in *Dict. Encycl. des Sciences Médic.*, vol. V, quoted by Topinard, *Anthropology*, English Edition, p. 198.

Secondly, the size of the cranial base as measured from the root of the nose, the nasion, to the basion, the midpoint on the anterior margin of the foramen magnum, is of great importance. This length which forms part morphologically of the vertebral column is correlated with its length, as although the length of the column varies considerably, its component parts seem to retain consistently the same proportions. Thomson holds that if a small brain be imposed on a long base then the skull will be dolichocephalic, whereas the skull will be increasingly brachycephalic as the size of the brain is increased or the length of the base decreased.

Thomson has also shown that the temporal muscles are relatively long in the long-headed races, and that there is a definite correlation between the size of the head and the length of the temporal muscles, combined with the associated shape and mechanism of the jaw. In the round-headed races, for instance, the masseter muscles tend to be more developed and the jaw is relatively wider and shorter than among the long heads who have a narrow long jaw. Keith (I. 16, 131) has objected to these theories on the ground that the muscles of mastication and of the neck undergo their greatest development between the twelfth and twenty-eighth years, before which time the brain has almost completely attained its adult size and shape, and that all the evidence obtained from measurements in the living indicates that the changes in cranial form which take place then affect only its external contour, leaving the shape of the cranial cavity unaffected.

While admitting that the association of head-form with muscular development is at present non-proven, and that there are many difficulties in the theory, at the same time there seems to be sufficient evidence to suggest an actual correlation, and the question of causal relationship is the matter which is at present in doubt.

Whatever doubts then may exist in relation to the actual factors which determine head-form there can be little doubt that up to the present it forms the most convenient way of grouping the various types of man. In the first place, abundant data on the cephalic index have been collected by competent observers from probably more groups of people than on any other character. This in itself is of advantage when we are dealing with a large area. Secondly, among all the indices which are in frequent use the cephalic is the least variable. The mean is therefore most likely to represent the true mean of the race. Thirdly, in spite of narrow variations within the race, among mankind in general the mean cephalic index of various groups has a variation of about twenty per cent, a sufficiently wide variation to enable the observer to make groups which will not shade too much into one another. On the other hand, in certain respects the cephalic index is an unsatisfactory guide, because similarity of index is by no means an evidence of racial kinship, and races which are obviously related may have indices which differ very widely. The broad-headed German and the long-headed Scandinavian appear to belong to the same division of humanity yet they have a head shape which differs widely. According to the list given by Deniker at the end of his *Races of Man* the natives of the New Britain Archipelago, the Kanarese of Mysore, the Bashilanges of the Kasai (a tributary of the Congo), the Eskimo of Greenland, the Botocudos from South America and the Spaniards of Valencia all have a cephalic index which only differs by 0·1 per cent (that is, are identical), yet it could hardly be suggested that these peoples who include representatives of what are generally conceded to be the most widely divergent races, are in any sense akin to one another in a closer way than others who have a different cephalic index. Reicher has shown that the head-form of the Chinese does not differentiate them from the Dissentis type, whereas the facial measurements serve markedly to distinguish the two.

It is clear then that in spite of its value and the general acceptance which it has received that the cephalic index is not a guide on which absolute reliance can be placed. It is possible that under certain circumstances it may be affected by the muscular development of the individual and other features which appear to be singularly sensitive to environment. Individuals who are of very different racial stocks may have the same cephalic index, and what is more important large groups of stocks which differ may have the same mean cephalic index. Conversely it seems not improbable that a difference in cephalic index does not necessarily mean a difference of race. Against this we place the convenience of the cephalic index, the fact that it often does prove an undoubtedly good criterion of race and that it is of the measurements commonly taken the least variable.

We have seen that the nasal index has by some writers been considered to be a good indication of race. Here again we find that races which appear for many other reasons to be unrelated to one another have identical indices. In conjunction with Professor Thomson I have discussed this problem elsewhere (I. 18). Thomson had already suggested, in reference especially to the two Americas, that it could be demonstrated that the nasal index was correlated with certain climatic conditions, and that high indices were to be found in a damp hot climate and low in a cold dry climate, with an intermediate series corresponding to the different degree of these extremes. In the later paper evidence was brought from the whole world, which suggested that temperature was the most important influence and relative humidity the lesser. A survey of many nations however showed that although of course many exceptions do occur, it is possible to predict, with a fair degree of accuracy, the nasal index from a knowledge of the temperature and the relative humidity of the country in which the people live whose nasal index is under discussion. The Eskimo living in the Arctic have the narrowest noses, whereas a band of broad noses stretches across the world in the region of the tropics. Thomson has suggested that this distribution has resulted from the necessity that the air before being admitted to the lungs should be warmed and moistened so as to avoid injury to the delicate tissues of the lungs. In the conditions which prevail in tropical forest the air is both warm and moist and can be admitted to the lungs without the necessity of and the muscular energy involved in passing it through narrow channels.

The correlation between the nasal index and climatic conditions is so high that some explanation must necessarily be found for the phenomenon. The exceptions which occur seem very probably to be due to over specialization or to the fact that the peoples investigated have not been subject to the conditions in which they now live for them to be affected by the climatic conditions; such an example may probably be found in the Australians and the Tasmanians, who have much broader noses than the environment would lead one to expect.

At present however we do not know how long it is required for environment to act on the human body, and it is not impossible that when the matter is more fully understood we shall find in the nasal index a valuable guide to the movements of peoples, especially when we find that a certain people have an index which seems to be at variance with their present surroundings but which is correlated with climatic conditions in an area from which it is suggested on other grounds that they may have migrated. It seems improbable that the nasal index will provide us with the original evidence, although even that is not impossible, but rather that from this source we shall obtain confirmation of what might otherwise remain merely an hypothesis.

Stature has been considered by some writers to be a fair indication of race. It has been discussed with great lucidity by Ripley (I. 8, 96) who sums up: ". . . it would appear that stature is rather an irresponsible witness in the matter of race. A physical trait so liable to disturbance by circumstances outside the human body is correspondingly invalidated as an indication of hereditary tendencies which lie within." The environmental features which appear to have an effect on stature may be grouped under several headings, climate, locality, food which is naturally related to the two first, health in relation to the group, and the influence of social selection.

The effect of the direct influence of climate is at present uncertain, some of the tallest races of men live under most diverse climatic conditions. There are tall groups in Northwestern Europe, among those peoples whom Ripley has called Nordics; the Nilotic Negroes living in the swampy region which surrounds the course of the Upper Nile have also great stature. The northern Chinese are markedly taller than their neighbours and their kinsfolk. The Patagonians of South America have become proverbial for their stature. The pygmy races, on the other hand, are for the most part confined to the tropics. Here they live side by side with other and taller races, and it seems difficult to correlate their stature with purely climatic conditions. As a general rule it would appear as though extreme conditions rather tended to be associated with shorter stature, but there is at present no reason to suggest that this is the effect of climate other than by indirectly affecting the food supply.

Locality seems to have both a direct and an indirect effect. The latter is due to the different food supply which groups living under different conditions can obtain, and this is correlated both with the climate and the position of residence of the people, the seashore in northern lands, the depths of a tropical forest, coral islands in the centre of the ocean and so forth. It has however been claimed that the stature of mountaineers tends to be shorter than that of the lowlanders. Here again the testimony is very conflicting, and it is possible that the influence here is not the direct result of altitude so much as the effect either of different climatic conditions, the highlands being relatively colder, or of food supply which is usually more scanty on the hills than on the plain. Owing to the elevated position of much of Asia we shall have considerable opportunities of testing this theory when we come to deal with various peoples in detail.

There can be little doubt that food has an important effect on stature. As a general rule those races whose food supply is scanty or unsatisfactory are shorter than their neighbours. It is not impossible that the pygmies of the tropical forests may be the result of a racial starvation of this sort. A tropical forest is an unpleasant place to live in and the inhabitants are often hard put to it for food. How far however the continued effect of generations of starvation can influence the race is uncertain, and the evidence at our disposal would suggest that the influence is more likely to be individual than racial. As far as I am aware the anthropological significance of vitamins has not yet been fully worked out, but it seems possible that some of the diets of savages are lacking in these necessities. On the other hand, I am informed that the diet of some primitive peoples of small stature, the Veddas of Ceylon for instance, contains all the component parts of a well-balanced diet.

Collignon and after him Ripley have drawn attention to the presence of so-called "misery spots" where, owing to inclement surroundings and a condition of semi-starvation, the people are of a noticeably lower stature than their more fortunately situated neighbours. I have reason to believe that such misery spots exist in certain parts of Asia. During a short journey in the Fukien Province in South China I was very much impressed by the short stature of certain villagers, who seemed to be living on a totally inadequate diet. The European evidence suggests that when people migrate from the misery spots to the plains the stature of children regains the normal; we have unfortunately no evidence to say whether this does or does not occur in China. It seems however not unlikely that this may occur. Under such circumstances the misery spot would necessarily be considered as a non-racial phenomenon affecting not the stock but those members of it who happened to be subjected to such unfortunate conditions. We are at present hardly in a position to distinguish between conditions which may be called "individual" and those which are "racial," as we have little data extending over many generations where conditions of food supply are known to have changed, or where we know that the same stock has changed its habitat.

There seems to be good reason to believe that the stature of a stock is affected by the general conditions of health which prevail, and it has been suggested that such diseases as malaria may cause the average stature to deteriorate. Here again it would appear that such weakened vitality was to be considered rather as part of the individual than of the stock.

Selection may no doubt play a great part in the development of stature; although, as Pearson has shown, where the descendants of tall individuals tend to approach the racial mean there are many complicated factors which play a part. In dealing with Asia we are faced with rather a different problem from that of Europe, because among the majority of the population the desire for children is very great and there is therefore a great prejudice in favour of fertility. Sterile marriages are the result of physical disability not of social causes, and owing to the prevalence of polygamy, sterility on the part of the female does not operate in the same way that it would in Europe. Vigorous strains have therefore every chance of surviving, and it seems that not infrequently stature, which is not excessively abnormal, is correlated with a vigorous strain. There would therefore be a tendency for selection to increase the stature. Another way in which selection may have affected the population of Asia is even more difficult to verify at present. Certain parts of that continent have been subjected to great catastrophes which have destroyed millions. Usually the original catastrophe destroys both the strong and the weak. It is however not infrequently followed by a famine in which the strongest, who tend to have a stature above the average, survive. The great loss of life leaves the area less densely populated, and therefore the stature of the race, other things being equal, tends to increase slightly.

I have sketched five of the ways in which environment may have a direct or indirect effect on stature. It will be seen that in many cases we are quite uncertain whether these effects are limited to the individual or whether they extend to the race. The data on which we base our anthropological conclusions are however collected from individuals, and it is seldom that we are in a position to estimate other than in a general way whether the characteristic stature which our measurements would assign to a particular group is really characteristic of the stock to which the individuals belong, or whether the village or town in which the observations were taken imposes some special restriction on stature. Different stocks may be differently affected, so that under certain circumstances we shall get the convergence of characters under different conditions; or again, similar conditions but different racial potentialities may produce different results. It would seem therefore that at present we must take stature as we find it, remembering these difficulties and only eliminating it when we can definitely trace the direct effect of environment.

The characters which I have so far been considering admit of definite measurement, and therefore although different individuals may obtain results which differ slightly from one another, on the whole their disagreement will not be considerable. There remain however a number of characters which are less easy to observe. For descriptive purposes they may be considered as qualities rather than as quantities. Such features include hair, eye, and skin colour, and the form of the hair. Now we may say that a man has a cephalic index of 82, a definite number, but when we describe a man's eyes as blue it is clear at once that we are open to misconception because there are many shades of blue. Even if the observer provides himself with coloured glass, leather, or hair, he is still likely to make very grave errors, because it is notoriously a difficult matter to match shades, even when they are in the same medium. However, the difference of hair colour is less momentous in Asia than in Europe, as in the former continent the hair is, in the majority of peoples, black, and the eyes are usually brown. The texture of the hair varies, but, as in the majority of cases it is straight, the exceptions are all the more noticeable. The colour of the skin is a great problem in dealing with Asiatic peoples. It varies from an almost complete black to a white, which is hardly, if at all, darker than the skin-colour of Southern Europe. The skin-colour differs in different individuals of the same race, and on different parts of the body of the same individual. When we are dealing with quantities, we can conveniently get over this difficulty by working out the mean value of the quantity for the group. With qualities this is more difficult, and though several suggestions have been made, no satisfactory method has yet been evolved. This is all the more to be regretted, because undoubtedly skin-colour provides a convenient method of distinguishing some of the peoples of Asia.

There can be little doubt that these characters, like those we have previously enumerated, can be affected by environment. It is notorious that, on the whole, black colour is associated with a tropical climate. On the other hand, there are dwellers in the tropics who are by no means black, and the Negro in North America, who has been removed from his tropical home and has lived for generations in a more temperate climate, is still clearly differentiated by his dark skin from his fairer neighbours. Here again, then, as in the case of the nasal index, we have a character that would appear to be correlated with climatic conditions, but which persists even when those conditions are changed.[1] The

---

[1] The following very remarkable observation is quoted by Grimble (I. 34, 42). He states that in the Gilbert Islands " a girl is bleached before marriage, she lives in a small thatched house in a cubicle in which the deepest gloom prevails. She is rubbed with coco-nut juice and massaged. After a few months of such treatment in a seclusion which no sunray ever pierced, the rich and dusky olive tint left her skin and she became pale with the dark

pigmentation of the eye seems to be correlated with that of the skin, to which that part which carries the pigment is closely connected. The matter is, however, more difficult in this case, as although it is comparatively easy to recognize the different shades of skin and eye colour, when once the comparatively limited blue and hazel eyes are eliminated, are all classed as brown, although it would appear that the amount of pigment present varies very considerably. It is therefore almost impossible with the data at present available to come to any definite conclusion on this point.

The colour of the hair is also a difficult matter. The prevailing colour in Asia being black, it would appear at first sight as though environmental conditions were but little connected with this colour; on the other hand, in Europe, we find that fair hair decreases, at least along the western seaboard, as we progress southwards.

The texture of the hair does, however, differ very considerably in Asia. Apart from the curly-haired Negritos, whose hair differs from that of the majority of the inhabitants of Asia both in form and in texture, the straight-haired races differ very much, especially if the individual hairs be examined; the Ainu, for instance, have hair which is very much greater in transverse diameter than that of their neighbours, the Chinese and the Japanese.

With these difficulties before us, we must make a selection of those criteria which are to guide us in distinguishing between the different peoples of Asia. It is clear that we can adopt no such simple classification as Ripley has adopted for Europe. In the first place, we possess less data than he had at his disposal. In the second, it will be found that though, no doubt, the cephalic index is of value in distinguishing the various races, its importance is local rather than general; we can use it to distinguish one tribe from its neighbours, but by this character alone we can hardly place

paleness of some Spanish lady who never leaves her house until sunset. One still has the chance of judging what her appearance may have been because though the formalities of the Ko (this initiatory rite) have long been abandoned, many Gilbert women to this day continue to bleach themselves in private. The constant massage leaves the skin silken in texture and the beauty of the subject, though no longer of a merry and full-blooded type, is certainly enhanced by etiolation." I have not been able so far to find other observations on this curious practice, which almost amounts to an experiment on the nature of the pigmentation of the human skin.

any tribe in its true place, phylogenically, among the peoples of Asia. The data, however, on the cephalic index is, perhaps, more abundant than for any other character, and therefore it must play an important part.

Hair and eye colour, features of such value in Europe, can serve us but little in Asia, where the hair is almost universally black and the eyes brown; where, however, exceptions to this universal rule occur, they are of particular value. Differences in the nature of the hair, where variations from the straight variety occur, are similarly most instructive, and form a very clear basis for classification.

Skin colour is hardly taken into account by Ripley, although his terms, blond and *brunet*, must naturally be taken to include the colour of the skin as well as that of the hair and eyes. In Asia, in spite of the fact that, as has been seen, skin-colour is a feature which is liable to be affected by environment, we have in it a guide which often serves to distinguish the broader grouping of races, even though, owing to its infinite gradations, it may fail when we are dealing with more local problems.

Stature has appeared to be an uncertain guide, although, in spite of its uncertainty, we must remember that there is a close relationship between the stature of parents and that of children, and therefore even here we shall be able to rely, at least to a certain extent, on the evidence of stature.

We have seen that the nasal index is related particularly closely to the climatic conditions under which people live. There can be little doubt, however, that the nasal index of adult offspring is correlated with that of their parents, although no exact data is available on the subject. Where we have different groups, more or less, in the same environment, the nasal index may sometimes serve to distinguish them, and may even provide a guide or a suggestion as to their origin.

It seems not improbable that we should find in Asia a valuable guide to race in the dimensions of the face, if a method could be devised which would show adequately the peculiar flattening which is so characteristic of some of these peoples. At present, however, no such method is in general use, and the ordinary measurements quite fail to show these remarkable characters.

I have, so far, been considering the effect of environment on the human frame from what may be described as the static aspect. Such a method has, however, the obvious disadvantage that the races of man can by no means be considered as static. In all the continents there have been movements to and fro, and though it is possible to trace the effects of cultural migrations, it is more difficult, if not impossible, to trace the exact way in which physical migrations have advanced. It is clear that when we study the effect of environment in Asia to-day, we are acting on the presumption that the people we are studying have been in their present habitat sufficiently long for them to have the characters which that environment requires from their innate potentialities, or else that, as may in some cases be happening, each generation is responding inevitably to its surroundings, and the characters which are called racial are merely individual characters, but which are acquired by each individual owing to his response to his environment.

If there is no correlation between environment and those characters which are accepted as racial, we shall find that migrations will affect the population of given areas. Yet there have been innumerable invasions into China, especially from the north, and it has been alleged that these invasions have not altered the population of China, because the latter " absorbed " their conquerors. We do not know whether this is a fact. If it is true, there remain two possibilities at least. The invaders may have been too few or of a recessive strain, and so may not have been biologically strong enough really to affect the population into whose midst they introduced themselves, or they may have changed in response to the effect of the new environment in which they found themselves. Parts of Asia do seem to have changed profoundly since we are first able to trace their history. Other parts, as far back as we can go, not very far it is true, do not seem to have had a population very different from the present. The history of Cyprus has been one of invasion after invasion ; masters from the East and from the West have ruled the island ; there are marked changes in culture at various periods. On the other hand, the inhabitants of a little Bronze Age village on the north coast,

Lapithos, had a population in the main hardly different from the population of the village built near by to-day. A selection of skulls of all sorts of dates from all over the island did not present any great differences at different periods. On the other hand, there did seem to be slight local differences in the proportion of Armenoid and Mediterranean blood between some villages and others. The two stocks had remained constant for over four thousand years. Whether there were slight differences between the villages in ancient times or not could not be determined from the material at hand. It did, however, seem that no essential change had taken place. The exact explanation of this problem is far to seek.

We know that many races have met and mingled in Western Asia. The two stocks were Armenoid and Brown, and were both there in very early times. They were apparently present side by side even then. But at that time the long heads seem possibly to have been in the majority in the Mesopotamian region. The environmental effect can hardly have been to drive out the original inhabitants.

While, therefore, strong arguments can be put forward which suggest that environment may be an important factor in shaping races, and the more or less staple form of most populations is the strongest argument in favour of this hypothesis, we do know that migrations have occurred in sufficient strength to change the population of a certain district, either by mixing with the aboriginal population, or it would appear in certain places apparently ousting them. It seems probable that those peoples who have mixed least with others show the least variation. Are we therefore justified in believing that they are in greater and more perfect equilibrium with their surroundings, or are we to consider that environment must be left out of count ? The arguments in favour of the effect of environment are, in some characters at least, too strong to be disregarded, but, on the other hand, migrations do appear not infrequently to introduce an alien strain, which coming from a different area should be out of harmony with the new surroundings. If environment were a potent factor, the new strain ought to change or die out ; sometimes it does disappear, at other times it does not. It may be that we are dealing with too short a period in human history for us to look at this problem in the proper perspective, but that when we have more examples of fossil and sub-fossil man we shall be able to approach the difficulties with more certain steps.

CHAPTER II

THE RACES OF ASIA

A. RACIAL GEOGRAPHY

IN the last chapter I have been considering the different races of man, the relation which exists between any race, and the environment in which that race lives. I have only dealt with environmental conditions and their relation to mankind in very general terms, and it is now necessary to discuss in broad outline, first, the actual environmental conditions in Asia, and secondly, the races which inhabit that continent, and to see how far, if at all, the two are correlated, with special relation to somatic rather than to cultural features.

Ethnologically Asia cannot be separated from Europe, a point which has been made abundantly clear by Ripley in his monograph on the races of Europe. The northern part of Asia, together with all Europe except the Mediterranean seaboard, forms one biological area, and in the opinion of some anthropologists a single anthropological area. The Ural Mountains, although they form a prominent feature on most maps, do not impede the migrations of peoples, and to the south die away altogether. The real ethnological boundaries run east and west, and therefore only serve to divide peoples within the continents, and for the most part have emphasized the ethnological unity of the great Eurasiatic continent.

But not only is Asia intimately connected with Europe. It has also a close connection with the other continents ; Africa may be said almost to be peripheral to it ; America, though contact is only close at one point, is ethnologically closely bound up with Asia. The Aleutian Islands form a bridge, or rather a series of stepping-stones, but they include big gaps filled by the stormiest seas in the world. The gap across the Bering Strait forms the closest link with America, a link which is made the easier by the presence of ice. Man almost certainly reached America from Asia by this route, and it is held by some anthropologists that there have been migrations back from America into Asia by this route. This connection is, however, one which has raised considerable controversy, and it is hardly necessary for our present purpose to do more than state that man has passed over the Bering Strait at least once, and possibly many times.

The Pacific islands lie for the most part to the east and south-east of the great continental mass. They cover an immense area, but the land surface is relatively small ; they are widely scattered, but the gaps between islands are often not great. Although the nearest island to the American coast is Easter Island (I am speaking here, of course, of the Oceanic islands, not those which organically form part of the American continent), they are separated from Valparaiso by a thousand miles of sea ; Europe first knew of the Pacific from its eastern shore, yet the islands have always had a closer connection with Asia than America.

In general terms the islands may be described as spreading fanwise from the great archipelago of South-eastern Asia. It is by the route which follows these great islands, some of which probably formed part of the mainland at the time when man first lived in them, that most of the inhabitants of the Pacific started on their journeys to their distant homes.

Professor Elliot Smith believes that the islands have actually formed a bridge over which culture has been carried to America, and although his conclusions have not been accepted by many anthropologists, there can be little doubt that in recent times a certain amount of Asiatic blood has been infused into America over the great breadth of the Pacific, although how far this has affected the population is a point yet to be studied.

Although Oceania proper has probably been separated from the rest of the world for a long period, man and his companion, the dog, established themselves in the largest of the islands, Australia, at an early period, and also had his home on some of the land in the neighbourhood of this vast sub-continent. It seems likely that Asia has played its part in influencing the peopling of Australia ; this event is so

D

remote in time that at present this island and Tasmania, and a few other islands, can be treated with little reference to what was almost certainly their mother-land. On the other hand, the connection of Asia with the seemingly more distant islands of Polynesia is recent and practically historical.

Many anthropologists from Huxley (I. 5) onwards have believed that there survive in Asia peoples who are closely related to the Australian aborigines. It has been suggested by those who uphold these theories that the Australian aborigines are the last surviving descendants of peoples who once formed an important element in the population of Asia, until they were overwhelmed by races better equipped for the battle of life.

Africa, from an ethnological point of view, may be described as almost peripheral to Asia. It has been influenced by, rather than has influenced, Asia. The connecting links are three. First, and probably most important, are the shores of the Mediterranean and the Mediterranean Sea itself. If it can be proved that in early times man was actually living in the Mediterranean basin while the land bridges between Europe and Africa were still in existence, and the work which has been done by Dr. Zammit in Malta suggests that this was the case, then the gap between Asia and Africa at this time was non-existent. Asia dominates the Eastern Mediterranean, and the narrow strip through which the Suez Canal is cut forms a means whereby many of the races inhabiting North Africa to-day reached that continent.

The second link between the two continents is found at the Straits of Bab-el-Mandeb. It is questionable how far people have passed that way. At present the hinterland on the Asiatic side is not suitable for racial migrations, but it is more than possible that since man has been in possession of this area the climate may have been less severe.

At first sight it would seem somewhat of a paradox to suggest that the Indian Ocean had ever formed a means of connecting the two continents, and the third link in our chain. How far the actual mainland of Africa has been affected ethnologically by peoples passing over the sea is not clear. Apart, however, from a substratum consisting of an aboriginal Negro population, the majority of the inhabitants of Madagascar belong ethnologically to Asia rather than to Africa (II. 2, 245), a feature which man shares with the flora, although the two can hardly be connected.

Asia then, from her geographical position, has played an important part in the peopling of the other continents; indeed, it may have been the original centre of dispersion of mankind, a point which will be discussed at greater length in the following chapter. Her seaboard is not relatively so extensive as that of Europe, but the eastern side of the continent looks out upon an ocean which, unlike the Atlantic, contains many islands which have formed the home of man. The Indian Ocean, which washes the southern aspect of the continent, has not, with the exception noted above, played an important part in the spread of mankind.

The importance to ethnological history of the Mediterranean can hardly be exaggerated, but here it seems likely that it has enabled the peoples of Western Asia to spread westwards, and that on the whole the sea has not affected the actual distribution of the Asiatic peoples as much as it has affected the distribution of the European peoples. The Arctic Ocean washes the northern shore of the continent, but at least for our present purpose it may be disregarded, as it does not afford a means of communication.

In later chapters I shall describe in greater detail the main features of the different parts of Asia and their relationship to mankind. Here it is more important to consider from a wider outlook those features in relation to the continent as a whole. Asia is divided by a series of mountain ranges. Centering from the Pamirs there are a series of uplifts which form high plateaux. They stretch through the great desert of Iran and are extended to the far-away mountains of Armenia and Anatolia. Eastwards there are a series of ranges which have had a profound effect on the history of mankind; they reach as far as the Pacific and are prolonged into the great islands of the archipelago. To the north lies the great plateau of Tibet and the Tarim basin, from which there radiate two great series of mountains, the Kun Lun, which eventually die down into the plain in Central China and form the escarpment on which the Great Wall of China is built; but physiographically the southern mountains of Japan form a continuation of that group.

The Gobi is bounded on the north-west by a very large series of ranges which form the nursery for the headwaters of the great rivers of Siberia. Starting with the Altai Mountains in the west, the southern Altai run south-eastwards, and other ranges extend to the east and north-east, terminating in the Yablonoi Mountains. The great gaps in these ranges, which form easy passages from the Mongolian plateau to the great plains of Siberia, have contributed to ethnological history, as they have allowed the passage of the Mongol hordes from their upland homes into the west.

About two-fifths of the continent is built up of plateaux, and these ranges and plateaux, which separate the plains from one another, have provided nurseries for the development of peoples. Some of the plateaux are true or half-desert, and in places a true oasis type of culture has developed which has been followed usually by large migrations when, owing to some slight geographical or other changes, the delicate balance which makes an oasis possible has been disturbed. These plateaux and plains, which are of the greatest interest for our present study, are first the great tundra of the north, in which life is only possible under specialized conditions, but which have served as an ethnological link with North America. The Gobi, separated on the north and west from this last-named area by mountains and forests, and on the south by an escarpment which, even when surmounted by a wall, has not always proved an efficient boundary, is a second plateau area of great interest in ethnological history. In the great basin between the Tien Shan and the Kun Lun Mountains, there sprung up an oasis culture, but important as this area has been in the history of Asia, ethnologically it is of less significance. The great alluvial plain of China, separated from the Gobi by the escarpments of the Khingan Mountains, and from the Tarim basin by the Kun Lun, and from the south by an elaborate series of folded mountains, forms the delta of two great rivers, the Hwang Ho and the Yangtze. Just as structurally it is for the most part covered with material brought down from the uplands, so ethnologically it consists of a people who have absorbed into their midst the overflow from all the surrounding areas, and in spite of this has developed a type which, as we shall see, is one of extraordinary distinctiveness. The great plains of India, in spite of the approaches, are shut off effectually from the rest of the continent and especially from the north-east, so that it has happened that most of the immigrants into that area have come from the west. Western Asia includes the great plateau of Iran, politically divided into Persia, Baluchistan and Afghanistan and Anatolia, which is connected with the former plateau by the bridge-land formed by the highlands of Armenia and Kurdistan, and separated from the plateau of Arabia by the great Mesopotamian region. North of this highland bridge-land the Iranian plateau stretches a plain which merges to the north-east into the great plain of Siberia, and ultimately into the frozen tundra of the north.

Many of these uplands are continued out to sea in the form of islands. Those which fringe the Asiatic continent are some of the largest and in certain cases the most densely populated in the world. For our present purpose they may be divided into five groups, the Aleutian islands have already been mentioned in regard to their relation to America. The Japanese islands in the widest sense include a fringing line of islands from Kamscatka to Formosa. We may include in them, first, the Kuriles and Saghalien; secondly, Japan proper, although ethnologically Hokkaido (the northern island of Japan) belongs more properly to Saghalien than to Japan; thirdly, the Ryukyu Islands, and lastly Formosa (Taiwan). The third great group of islands differs in many ways from the last, and forms a distinct group, namely, the Philippines. The East Indian Archipelago, " Insulinde," as it is usually called by Dutch and German writers, consists of a series of islands, some of great size, which have formed a bridge-land leading from Asia to the islands of the Pacific, on the one hand, and to Australasia on the other. The fifth series of islands form a less definite group, but may be conveniently called the Indian islands. They include Ceylon, which is closely connected with the mainland, and the more isolated groups of Andaman and Nicobar.

A continent of the vast size of Asia naturally contains many rivers, some of them of great length. Not all of these, however, have played an equally important part in the history of mankind, and for our present purpose the following four groups are of the greatest importance : first, the

Tigris and the Euphrates, the streams which made possible the great civilization of Mesopotamia ; secondly, the Yangtze and the Hwang Ho, which, and especially the latter, formed the cradle of the Chinese people; thirdly, the rivers of India, and lastly, the great rivers of the north. These four groups have played different parts in the ethnological history of the continent. The first two together form an oasis in which life was concentrated, and thus, by its fertility in contrast to the neighbouring lands, constituted a place where different types of peoples have met from the earliest times of which at present we have any records. The area affected directly by these rivers is comparatively small, but owing to its favoured geographical position is of immense importance in early history. The Hwang Ho has played a very different part. Intimately associated as it is with the history of the Chinese, it has often been the destroyer as well as the life-giver. The river brings down immense quantities of silt, and gradually raises itself, so that it flows on the plain rather than through the plain. At intervals it breaks through its banks, and spreads over immense areas, causing great destruction of life. It has changed its course very con-siderably within historic times. The Hwang Ho, therefore, falls into a very different category from the rivers mentioned above. Together with the Yangtze it has built up an enormous fertile plain. While depending for its origin on the rivers, the great plain of China bears a different relation to them from that which Mesopotamia bears to its rivers. In the former case the plain is so vast that, ethnologically at least, its fluviatile origin may be said to have been for-gotten. The whole of the great flood plain is inhabited, and though owing its fertility to the rivers has spread far beyond a narrow river valley.

The great rivers of India have again played a very different part in the history of the people from that taken by the rivers of China. In the north the influence of the Indus is closely parallel to that of the Nile. To the east the Gangetic valley forms a hot, extremely fertile area of great length in proportion to its breadth. Owing to conditions which favour the extreme growth of vegetation, the density of the population has become great, and owing to the possible

communications of this valley with the south-eastern part
of Asia, it has in many ways a different ethnographic
history from the rest of India. In Southern India, separated
as it is from the north by the Narbada, rivers exercise a
different function. The only important streams which flow
to the west are the Narbada and the Tapti. Elsewhere the
Western Ghats render the coast difficult of access, and the
population has become concentrated, where concentration
has occurred, in the deltas which look towards the east.
None of the rivers have, however, so great an ethnological
importance as those that have been mentioned before.

In spite of their great length and size, the rivers of the
north have not played a very important part in the ethnological history of the great plains of the north. An examination, however, of any map which shows the distribution of
Russian settlements, will make it very clear how these
streams serve as means of communication along which alien
culture and physique may pass. The distribution charts of
the Russians show long extensions along the course of the
Obi, the Yenesei, the Lena, and the Amur river, to mention
the most important. Although most of the country has been
penetrated, the foreign concentration has been quite clearly
along the river lines, just as the early posts in North America
stretched along the chain of the Great Lakes and up the
Mississippi.

Owing to its vast size Asia includes the greatest extremes
of climate, from the very great cold of the north to the
extreme heat of the south and south-east. It also varies in
dampness from the moist supersaturated air of the tropical
forests to the dryness of parts of the desert region. In the
neighbourhood of the equator the climate is comparatively
equable, elsewhere both the daily and annual ranges are
very great. At present we know very little about the anthropological effect of a varying temperature, but it seems
not improbable that it is considerable.

The extreme coldness of the north is due to the fact that
the low-lying plains of Turan and Siberia are cut off from the
warm influence of southerly winds by a very high mountain
barrier. The winters are, therefore, much more extreme
than in the corresponding area in America, where, owing
to the general north and south trend of the mountains, the

great plains are open alike to the influence of arctic and of tropical or sub-tropical weather.

From the point of view of the study of mankind, it is most convenient to consider the climatic and the vegetational zones together, as the vegetation to a large extent reflects the climatic conditions in a concrete form. In the extreme north the country is tundra, the northern limit of which is the Polar Sea, and the southern boundary is the 50° F. isotherm in the hottest month, a limit which in very general terms is the northern boundary of the forest zone. Practically the whole of the extreme eastern corner of the continent is tundra, and tundra conditions are, at least to a large extent, reproduced in certain parts of Tibet. There is little precipitation in winter, and the subsoil never thaws. Owing to the prevalence of high winds the snow does not lie deeply on the ground. The cold of winter, however, makes it necessarily a waiting period, and most tundra peoples retire to the forests to avoid the rigors of the climate. With the end of the winter there is a sudden bourgeoning of life, the vegetation begins to grow and the inhabitants of the tundra leave the forests and retrace their way to the north. The country is characterized by its extreme barrenness and monotony ; there are no trees, only shrubs and dwarf bushes, in the more sheltered spots berry-bearing bushes grow, and the most characteristic fauna consists of the reindeer and various species of rodents.

South of the tundra there are found great northern coniferous forests, characterized by such trees as *larix siberica* and *abies siberica*. These gradually give place to deciduous forests, which are made up for the most part of the familiar forest trees of Britain to-day ; they also contain forest meadows with a flora like our meadows and hedgerows. The forest and meadow gradually changes to steppe. The boundary in very general terms may be considered to be south of the Irtish, the Altai Mountains and the Yablonoi range, though the steppes hardly extend very far east of the Khingan Mountains.

The steppes may be conveniently divided into two types, depending very largely on the annual amount of rainfall. There are first of all the rich grass steppes. These are the great steppes of Siberia, which extend between the 50° and

55° parallels north latitude as far east as the Obi, and there are similar steppes south of the Altai and Yablonoi Mountains, and also in the upper valleys of the rivers which rise on the Tibetan plateau, in part of Turan, and on the southwest of the Iran.

There are five regions which may be described as poor steppe, which often pass into true desert. First, there is the Turanian region, which includes the Caspian-Aral-Balkhas area and the Turkoman desert; secondly, the Taklamakan desert in the Tarim basin. To the north-east of this area stretches the Gobi, which is made up of a central core of poor steppe, with grass steppe round it. The Arabian desert is practically a continuation of the Sahara, with characteristic date-palm oases. The people in this region also show a marked similarity with the peoples of North Africa without, apparently, any Negroid affinities (but see page 104). Finally, we may include in the poor steppe and deserts certain parts of the Iranian and Anatolian plateau. Practically all these regions have an annual rainfall which hardly exceeds ten inches.

South of this region we have a sub-tropical area which is conveniently divided into the Western "Mediterranean area," which has winter rains, and of which the most typical trees are the myrtle, the olive, the fig, the pomegranate, and the evergreen oak, and an eastern region with summer rains, usually known as the "Sino-Japanese area." Here the flora and types of mankind differ very much from that which has become so familiar to us as typical of the Mediterranean. In spite of these differences, however, it is important to remember that both belong to a sub-tropical habitat, and in studying their differences the general similarity of the environment must not be forgotten, even though the size of the areas and their general relation to the great land masses are very different. Further to the south we find a great savanna region, a land of tropical meadows. It includes parts of Southern Arabia, India, Indo-China, and the more lofty parts of Ceylon and the Malay archipelago. The first-named is more closely connected with the African than with the Asiatic savanna.

Much, though not all, of this savanna region has a very high rainfall, and like the temperate meadow is characterized by the presence of many species of gramineæ. Much as in Western Europe, the meadow and deciduous forest has been the birthplace of culture, so in South-eastern Asia man has found the tropical savanna the place where he could best develop. This matter is of great importance, because whereas in the former continent we find such a large proportion of the people have apparently become physically adapted to the climatic conditions which prevail in the deciduous forest meadows, a very large proportion of the inhabitants of Asia appear to be more closely *en rapport* with the climatic conditions of tropical savannas.

South of the savannas and on the lowlands we find the extreme type of tropical climate which makes for the growth of tropical forests. Here we have a high temperature, though often not so high as in some deserts, a very heavy rainfall and a high relative humidity. Owing to the high temperature this must necessarily mean also a high absolute humidity. The great growth of the forest trees and the denseness of the forest produce conditions which are very different from those prevailing in the other areas. There can be little doubt that these conditions have had a very great effect on mankind, and though the typical inhabitant of the equatorial rain-forest belongs to Africa rather than Asia, yet certain of the peoples in the forest belt of the latter continent appear to possess characters which seem to be closely correlated to the very special conditions under which they live.

B.   THE " WHITE " AND " BROWN " RACES

The races of Asia have been very differently classified by the systematic anthropologists, the difference in classification depending partly on the criteria which have been adopted (although in that there is now a fairly general agreement), and partly in the different use of the nomenclature. In some cases the same terms have been used to mean different things, and equally frequently it will be found that a different nomenclature really conceals a similarity of race. Before giving them the nomenclature which I propose to adopt, it may be convenient to give some of the classifications which have been generally adopted in the textbooks at present current.

Deniker (I. 9, 365) suggests that there are eleven races, of which five are peculiar to Asia, namely, the Dravidian, the Assyroid, the Indo-Afghan, the Ainu, and the Mongolian. Six are met with in other parts of the world, namely, the Negrito, the Indonesian, the Arab, the Ugrian, the Turkish, and the Eskimo. Their distribution he defines as follows : " The Eskimo in the north-east of the continent, the Ainu in Saghalien, Yezo, and perhaps in Northern Japan. The Ugrian race is represented by its Yeneseian variety. The Mongolian race, with two secondary races, northern and southern, is found almost all over Asia. The Turkish race is limited to the inland regions of Central Asia. The Indonesians are numerous in Indo-China and in the islands from Japan to the Asiatic Archipelago, while the Dravidians and Indo-Afghans abound in India. The latter are also met with in anterior Asia side by side with Assyroids and Arabs. Some representatives of the Negrito race inhabit the Malay peninsula and the Andaman Islands ; the elements of this race are also found among the inhabitants of Indo-China and perhaps India."

The difficulty about this classification, comprehensive and convenient as it is, may be found if we study the terms which are used. Some of them are essentially linguistic. Turkish, Ugrian, and Dravidian connote certain known languages, or groups of languages, and the use of these terms is unsatisfactory when applied to physical anthropology, since physical and linguistic types are by no means correlated. It would also appear that Deniker himself recognized the difficulties of his classification, either from a linguistic or physical point of view, as he appears for the most part to abandon it in his detailed treatment of the peoples of Asia.

Joyce (II. 2) has stated that : " The Mongolians are roughly divided into two great groups, the northern and the southern, the former including the Manchu, Coreans, Mongols, Turkomans, Turko-Finns, and Magyars ; the latter, the Japanese, Indo-Chinese, Tibetans, and some of the inhabitants of Malaysia." The minor divisions within the groups he describes as " ethnical families," without further defining exactly what he means by these terms. It will be seen, however, that his use of the term " Mongolian " is very different from that of Deniker.

Haddon (II. 12) has a classification which differs very considerably from those which I have outlined above. He admits the following : first, the Mongoloid peoples. Beyond stating that they are brachycephalic, he does not describe them further, but distinguishes them from his second group, the "Alpines," of whom he sees the presence in Asia of both short and tall varieties. Thirdly, he mentions "two main brachycephalic" peoples, the Turki and the Ugrians, who were doubtless of more or less common origin ; usually they are stated to be a very early cross between Proto-Nordics and Alpines, with, in places, occasional Mongol mixture. On the other hand, they may be descendants of an intermediate variety between the two former types. We have then four different races, all of whom are said to be physically distinct, but who all have the common trait of brachycephaly. The two latter are suggested to have found their origin in the Altai and the upper waters of the Yenesei respectively, and possibly to have been the ancestors of the ancient Sumerians. Haddon's next race he describes as "brunet dolichocephals." They are, he says, scattered in South-east Asia as, for example, the Man-tse of South China, and an essential element in the Indonesians, and possibly also of the Dravidians. They appear to coincide with the people whom Elliot Smith terms "the Brown race," but have a somewhat wider distribution.

Haddon is very careful to define the Proto-Malays as Mongoloid brachycephals, a definition of great importance. Most authorities agree with him on this point, and it would be of great advantage if the undoubted Mongolian element among the peoples of the Archipelago and Malaysia were definitely called by this name. Hrdlicka (II. 13), however, seems to confuse them with Indonesians, the confusion, of course, being purely verbal, and the same difference of terminology appears, as far as I can understand, in the excellent monograph of De Zwaan (II. 14) on the island of Nias, although in this case it is difficult to disentangle the author's own views from those of the authorities whom he quotes. The Ainu are considered by Haddon to be an outlier of the Alpine race, a theory that he appears to have modified in his last book. Finally, there is a "black woolly-haired race, of which the Pygmy representatives, Negritos, the Andamanese, the Semang of the Malay Peninsula, the Aeta of the Philippines, and the pygmies of New Guinea; the taller varieties are the recently extinct Tasmanians who walked from New Guinea to Tasmania, the Papuans proper, and the ground stock of the Melanesians."

It is difficult in a résumé to do justice to the many brilliant suggestions of Haddon's small volume, and recently he has suggested another classification. This new grouping was originally put forward by Giuffrida-Ruggeri (II. 15), but Haddon has adopted it with some modifications in the last edition of his book on the *Races of Man* (I. 19).

The grouping has the advantage that it is simple and direct, and by the use of Latin words it avoids much of the confusion arising from different meanings being attached to the same terms. Apart from the Negritos, the inhabitants of Asia are divided into Leucoderms and Xanthoderms, White and Yellow man. The Leucoderms are divided into two groups, Dolichomesocephals and Brachycephals. The former are divided again into three sub-groups, Indo-Afghanus, Irano-Mediterraneus, and Indo-Iranus. The *Indo-Afghanus* is dolichocephalic, leptorrhine, and of medium to tall stature; they include such peoples as the Afghan, the Balti, Kashmiri, Dardi, Rajput, Panjabi, Sikh,[1] etc. It is suggested that their area of characterization was between the Hindu Kush and the Sulaiman Mountains, whence they spread into North India, and possibly eastwards also. This type appears to correspond closely to Risley's Indo-Aryan type, which will be discussed on page 137. The Irano-Mediterraneus is described by Haddon as a somewhat indefinite group, it is mesocephalic, leptomesorrhine, and from medium to very tall stature. It appears to correspond in part to Ripley's Iranian type (I. 8, 443 ff.),[2] and includes the Persians and various other peoples in the Near and Middle East. " There is no reason to doubt that there is a

---

[1] This is an oversight on Haddon's part, the Sikhs are a religious not an ethnic group.

[2] The word Iranian is unfortunately open to considerable confusion, Ripley, l.c., clearly expresses his view that the Iranian physical type is akin to the Mediterranean, and by accepting the term Irano-Mediterraneus, Haddon apparently does lip service to the same idea, but elsewhere he uses Iranian as a synonym of Pamiri, a very different racial group. The latter use of the term is the most general one, but many authors have followed Ripley. The question is more fully discussed on page 112.

substratum of population in this group with a C.I. of about
76, a N.I. of about 61–63, and a stature of about 1·633 m.
(64¼ in.), which may very well be termed Mediterranean,
as other characters conform to that type; these may be
regarded as the laggard representatives of a group that
wandered mainly westwards."

The *Indo-Iranus* includes the Baluchi, Dehwar, and Brahui,
who are on the border-line between meso- and brachycephaly
and leptomesorrhincy; the stature is from medium to tall.
"They may be regarded as an intermediate or mixed
type."

The White brachycephals are divided into two groups,
Georgianus and *Armeno-Pamiriensis*. The first class includes
the Grussini, Svani, Mingreli, and Imeri. "This type shows
slight brachycephaly, strong leptorrhiny, and medium
stature." The second group is divided by Haddon, who
differs slightly from Giuffrida-Ruggeri into two divisions:
the first Pamiri or Iranian,[1] is strongly brachycephalic,
leptorrhine, and medium to tall in stature. The second
subdivision, Armenian, is characterized by very high heads,
a vertical occiput, an extremely prominent and characteristic
nose, and seem to be slightly taller.

The Asiatic Xanthoderms are grouped into three main
divisions, *Mesocephals*, *Brachycephals*, and a second group
of *Brachycephals*. The first include *Protomorphus*, *Palæarcticus*, *Tibetanus*, and *Sinicus*. The first subgroup includes
the so-called "aboriginal tribes" of China and Assam.
Haddon adds that they are probably more closely allied to
the Leucoderms than to the Xanthoderms. If we are to fit
them into Giuffrida-Ruggeri's scheme, we must either widen
the Irano-Mediterraneus, so as to include small statures, or
give them a separate class. The Palæarcticus only belongs
in part to this group; as some of the Palæarctic peoples are
round-headed, it is, as we shall see, more a cultural than a
physical classification. It is said to be distinguished by
platycephaly, which, however, occurs among other peoples
not in this group. Only part of Tibetanus is included among
the Mesocephals, the typical peoples being such tribes as the
Lepcha and the Eastern Tibetans. The fourth subgroup is
Sinicus, and includes the Chinese.

[1] See previous footnote on use of the word "Iranian."

The first group of Brachycephals includes Altaicus and Nearcticus among its subgroups. The first includes many of the Altaian folk, and the latter the Chukchee.

The second group of Brachycephals has four subgroups, *Meridionalis*, confined to Burma and Assam, the "brachymorphus" branch of Palæarcticus and Tibetanus, and Centralis, including Manchu, Southern Tungus, Buriat and other Mongol tribes, such as Torgut and Taranchi, and the Hazara in Afghanistan.

On this scheme Haddon's comment is of interest, and may be quoted: "The foregoing arrangement is based mainly on the cephalic index, nasal index, and stature, and I have borrowed it with modifications from Giuffrida-Ruggeri, as it is an interesting attempt to reduce the chaos of Asiatic racial anthropology by adhering closely to anatomical data, but even so there are several unclassified groups. A consideration of other characters, doubtless, will lead to a modification of the scheme."

This criticism draws attention to the weakest points in the scheme, which are serious omissions, and too great an attention to certain limited characters, especially the cephalic index, which leads to serious difficulties when followed too closely. The author has also failed to pay any attention to biometric work, as an indication of the reliability of an index figure.

The comparatively minute division is one which is especially open to serious objection. Although it is, no doubt, possible to recognize what appear to be local divisions, the narrower subdivisions of mankind seem to run so closely into one another that it is to be doubted often whether they may not be considered as strains, due to in-breeding, or other local or environmental causes. The minute subdivision masks the merging of groups into one another, and often fails to take account of the mixing of different races. If we are, for instance, to follow out logically the suggestions which Giuffrida-Ruggeri puts forward, we must have a group which is half White and half Yellow, for certainly some of the people he mentions might be placed in either group.

If we approach the classification of the peoples of Asia from the purely physical standpoint, and we must remember that the majority of the authors we have been considering took other criteria into consideration, we may, provisionally at least, adopt three main stocks, although so much mixing has taken place that it is difficult always to find pure examples of any of them. Races have mixed, and the resulting mixture has blended so closely together that it has become a compound, and instead of a high degree of dispersion we have the low one that is normally found in pure races. In spite of this fact, however, it seems clearer for systematic purposes to adhere to the larger divisions, and to disregard, at least for the moment, those separate divisions which appear to have been evolved from the hybridization of the main stocks.

The three main stocks are, first, a very large group of peoples who are akin to the races of Europe, the type which has often since Blumenbach's time been called Caucasian, and which very frequently is known as " White." The second group are conveniently known as the Yellow race ; they are often known as Mongolians, or Mongoloid, a name that I shall have occasion to criticize in the sequel. Thirdly, there is a stock which is probably more widely divided from the other two than they are from one another, namely, the Negrito. It is possible, as will appear, that we should also include in our survey of the peoples of Asia the fourth great group of humanity, the Red man, for there are undoubtedly tribes in Asia who are closely allied to the aboriginal inhabitants of North America, but probably we may include them as a specialized branch of Yellow man.

The stocks akin to the races of Europe can be distinguished from the other races most clearly by the following characters : Fair, or brown hair, where it occurs, may be said to be a certain guide, but over most of Asia the hair is black and the eyes brown, in spite of different racial affinities. The cephalic index, though sometimes providing a useful guide, is not always of value, as the stocks which we are discussing include tribes which possess the extreme variations in this index of the human race. On the other hand, it seems probable, as far as we know at present, that long heads do not occur among the representatives of Yellow man, except as individual cases, and that the means of groups always tend to meso- or brachycephaly. Where, therefore, we are uncertain whether a particular group belongs to that race or not, the cephalic index may sometimes form a useful, although not an absolute, guide.

The texture of the hair, while again not forming an invariably good criterion, will often serve to distinguish our first and second classes. The races akin to those of Europe often, but not invariably, have wavy or curly hair, and though sometimes a mixture between the straight hair and the woolly Negrito may cause a type of wavy hair, this latter is usually quite distinct from the normal wave of the European, or of his kinsmen in Asia.

Skin-colour would appear at first sight to be a good guide, but we shall find people who seem to be akin to the White races who have a very black skin, and there are innumerable shades of brown which link up the gaps in between. The absence of any yellowish tinge in the skin is, however, a criterion which will usually distinguish our first and second classes. Stature, nasal index, and other measurements, though often of value in the discrimination of local races, hardly serve when we generalize. If we are really to distinguish the two races we must take a complex of characters, a complex that could doubtless be easily multiplied, but which usually makes itself clear enough, if we consider those which have been enumerated.

The stocks which I have described by the somewhat cumbrous title of races akin to the inhabitants of Europe may be divided into several groups; we have already seen that Ripley has three such divisions, Nordic, Alpine, and Mediterranean. We shall see that later observers have to a certain extent assailed his position, especially in regard to the two latter "races." Representatives of all three races occur, as Ripley himself showed in Asia. They must therefore be discussed in comparative detail. The Nordics are tall with long heads and fair hair. These are the chief characters on which Ripley relies. They are usually of a muscular build, with well-marked ridges over the brows among the males, and big bones in both sexes. The cranial capacity is large, and the skull tends to be well filled and of an even curve when viewed in profile (*norma lateralis*). The nose is usually comparatively narrow and long, both relatively and absolutely. The orbits are large. The jaws are

E

often, especially in early specimens, heavy, and the ascending ramus is usually high.

It has become usual to speak nowadays of Pre-Nordics and Proto-Nordics. These are suppositions based, for the most part, on the evidence of the distribution of the present Nordic race; we cannot, at present, describe the anatomy of the Proto-Nordics in the same way that we can describe the anatomy of the Proto-Egyptians.

The present area of characterization of the Nordics is the Scandinavian peninsula. Their original home is discussed on page 77. They are found in Western Europe in diminishing number as we leave the Baltic area. At one time they appear to have penetrated far to the south, and some authors suggest that they formed an appreciable portion of the leaders of the Sumerian population. At present, however, we have no definite evidence on this point. Among the ancient crania from the Thebaid in the collection in the Department of Human Anatomy in Oxford, there are specimens which must unhesitatingly be considered to be those of Nordic type. If this is so, it would seem that they probably entered Egypt with the other alien elements which began to filter in from Asia in early dynastic times.

How far the Nordics ever formed any appreciable element in the population is doubtful, but these specimens prove their existence. It is of particular interest to find this long-headed type on the shores of the Mediterranean in early times, because some authors, notably Giuffrida-Ruggeri and Fleure (II. 16, 97), have believed that there is no ultimate distinction between them and the Mediterranean race, except that the Nordics have specialized, possibly owing to a colder environment.

The two races, or sub-races, have little in common except their cephalic index. The Nordics have been in possession of the northern part of the North Sea area since the melting of ice permitted them to enter that region. It is curious, however, that they have sometimes advanced over the domain of the Mediterraneans, and sometimes have receded before them. For instance, in England to-day some observers are inclined to believe that the Nordics, who originally drove the Mediterranean population from these islands, are now in turn being swamped by them. This has been put forward

as an additional argument that they are both varieties of
the same stock; this, on the whole, though possible, seems
unlikely (the matter is further discussed on page 77).

That the Nordics occur in Asia is, as I have said, probable,
but there does not at present seem to be a good case for their
occurrence, except mixed with other elements, and the writers
who suggest, for instance, their presence among the Sumerians,
do not seem to have any cranial evidence to support their
arguments. There is, however, as we shall see, a large population which is probably alien to the " Proto-Nordics."

As we advance south-eastwards from the Mediterranean
west of the high plateau which forms the eastern boundary
of the land of the rivers, and so into the great sub-continental
area of India, south, that is to say, of what appears to have
been the glaciated zone in glacial times, and for the most
part south of boundaries which have remained some of the
greatest obstacles to the migration of man throughout the
historic period, we find that the bulk of the population,
though by no means everyone, belongs to the same race.
In this area few or none of the people are actually white
of skin, most are brown. They are slenderly built, have
rather small noses and long heads, which vary considerably in
their dimensions; their hair is straight or curly, and their
eyes are brown. They have but little hair on the face or
body. If we look at them in profile, the most striking character is the great bulge of the skull at the occiput. The
forehead is smooth and rather prominent and, owing to the
poor development of the brow ridges, it lacks that powerful
appearance which has become famous under the name of
the " bar of Michael Angelo." This absence of brow ridges
is no doubt due to the lack of muscularity which is characteristic of these peoples. It is further borne out when we
examine their skulls, for we find that the jaw is lightly made,
that there is a slender development of the zygomatic arches,
and that there is a general absence of those ridges which are
prominent on very muscular individuals of many races. As
we advance further to the east we find that the skin gradually
grows darker. In Southern India and Ceylon people who
have a skin-colour that is almost black still appear to have
a skull form which in its essentials does not differ from that
which has been described above, and which might serve as

a generalized description alike of the majority of the inhabitants of Egypt, whose traits have been brilliantly described by Elliot Smith in his book on the *Ancient Egyptians* (II. 17), for many of the dwellers on the eastern shores of the Mediterranean, and for a greater part of the population of Mesopotamia, although, as we shall see later, they are intensive in part of that area. In India, and elsewhere in the tropical zone, the character which especially distinguishes the men of this type from those who live more to the north-west is, apart from their colour, the great size of the nasal index. This, I have explained in a previous chapter, is possibly due to environmental conditions. There are, no doubt, sub-races of this type, especially in India. Further to the east a final extension of this Brown race appears in the Nesiots ("Indonesians"), whose physical characters will be discussed at greater length in a later chapter. All these various peoples seem to have sufficient in common to warrant our classing them as one branch of humanity. Their differences within themselves are also great, but for the most part are concerned with three types of character, first skin-colour, secondly stature, and thirdly nasal index, all of which have been seen to be singularly responsive to environment, and therefore convenient for distinguishing groups within the race, but of little value in dealing with the great racial divisions of mankind.

It would seem then that, if the assumptions which have been detailed are correct, we have several branches of a race, which so far we have been considering as the Brown race, fringing the south-western aspect of the Asiatic continent. In the West it is known as the Mediterranean race, in the centre as Brown, in India there is no definite name which has been applied to it, although, as we shall see in the chapter dealing with that country (see page 137), probably most of the Dravidian tribes can claim kinship with this same race. It has been called Oriental by Fischer (II. 18 and II. 19, 456), but this term is open to confusion, as Deniker uses it in a different sense, and recently Morant has used it in yet another significance. The most easterly extension of this race I have termed *Nesiot* in order to avoid the confusion which has arisen from the use of the linguistic term Indonesian to mean also a physical type.

There remains a further branch of the European stock. This is termed "Alpine" by Ripley. Recent work has suggested that possibly, even in Europe, it should be sub-divided into Alpine and Dinaric (see especially II. 19, 101), the latter being distinguished from the former, especially by the greater stature which is usually found among its members. It seems probable that both Alpine and Dinaric are represented in Asia. There remains a third branch of this race, generally known as the "Armenoid," which is one of the most important elements in Western Asia. This branch has also been called West "*Asiatische Rasse*," and Hittite, and by many authors has not been distinguished from the Alpine branch.

All the members of this group of races differ from the Mediterranean and Nordic in having round heads. Associated with this the general architecture of the skull is very different. The jaw, instead of being comparatively long, and often relatively feeble, is broad, and often, though by no means invariably, well developed. This breadth of the jaw may no doubt be associated with a broad cranial base. The nose is sometimes very well developed, and among certain branches is noticeably large. The cheeks tend to be broad and often slightly flattened, the brow-ridges, without being large, are well developed. The pilous system is more abundant than in the first group, and there is plenty of hair on the face and often on the body.

Elliot Smith has described these peoples in his work on the *Ancient Egyptians*. He calls attention first to the fact that, although these people may even have dolichocephalic heads, they universally have a large cranial capacity. That some cases may be found even with dolichocephalic heads should cause no astonishment, for, especially in cases where a certain amount of racial admixture has taken place, the normal variation of the group is always large, and he has clearly shown that we are dealing with a group of crania which in Egypt, at least, is much more variable than the Proto-Egyptians. Generally, however, these people, else-where than in Egypt, and anywhere where they are found in a relatively pure state, are markedly round-headed. In many cases the head is distinctly high and has a flattened occiput, in great contrast to the bulging occiput which is found in Mediterranean man. It is probable that these differences may be correlated with the difference in the bulk of the brain. Mediterranean man tends to have a small brain; Alpine man, on the other hand, tends to have a large one. In order to accommodate this increase in size, he will tend to have, as has been shown above, a rounder head. Where, however, the base of the skull is long, even the increase of the size of the brain will not serve entirely to secure a round form.

But as we are dealing in three dimensions, not only will the cephalic index be affected, but also the height of the skull, which is, as would be expected, greater than in the Mediterranean peoples. The form of the forehead is also different. Where the top of the skull is high-domed the forehead tends to be vertical, but where the top is flattened the forehead tends to be sloping. Such a difference is, no doubt, to be expected from the different architectural necessities of the individual skull in the two cases.

The form of the jaw among the Alpine peoples is usually a very distinctive trait. In the Mediterraneans the jaw is usually small. The ascending ramus is broad, both relatively and absolutely, and the sigmoid notch is shallow. This type of jaw is frequently correlated with dolichocephalic skulls and resembles in general form, though not in detail, the jaws of many primitive dolichocephalic peoples. The jaw of the Alpines, on the other hand, has a long and narrow ascending ramus. The sigmoid notch is deep, and the coronoid process is long. It is, in fact, the type of jaw which is built rather for rapid movement than for slow, forceful action. Elliot Smith, in discussing the difference between the jaws of these two races, draws attention to the features which I have described, and lays stress on the fact that they are racial and not environmental features. Although there can be little doubt that as racial features they are of the greatest value in distinguishing between the two groups, yet the arguments put forward so forcibly by Thomson suggest that environment and habit may have played an important part in moulding the features which have afterwards, as it were, become crystallized into " racial " characters.

The form of the orbit is, as Elliot Smith has pointed out, another convenient method of distinguishing between these two minor groups of mankind. In the Alpine type they are slanting, in the Mediterranean straight, that is to say that in the latter a line drawn along the upper margins of one orbit would, if produced, follow the upper margin of the other, but in the Alpine race would pass above in at an angle. It seems not improbable that this different form of orbit is correlated, partly with the form of the jaw and partly with the architecture of the nose, which differs considerably in the two groups. In the Alpine, apart from the nasal index, which has been shown to be correlated with environment, the Alpine peoples normally have a much bigger and more prominent nose, and not infrequently considerable thickening of the integument in the neighbourhood of the nostrils.

There are other characters which could be selected to distinguish these peoples, but those which I have enumerated are some of the most important. I have used the word "Alpine" in referring to the broad-headed peoples, whom Elliot Smith, speaking from the point of view of an Egyptologist, terms Aliens. This term has been used for want of a better, for these peoples include not only those whom Ripley calls Alpines, but other sub-races which are undoubtedly akin to them.

In Europe these include the true Alpines, described by Ripley as having broad heads, medium stature, and eyes that are hazel or brown. These people have a wide distribution in Asia. In certain parts of Europe, notably the east coast of the Adriatic, but extending into Hungary, a type occurs which some authorities, notably Deniker, believe to be a definite variety of the Alpine; they have termed it Dinaric, and notice, as a principal character, that the stature is greater than in the normal Alpine. Ripley, who considers stature to be an uncertain guide, does not believe that this type is worthy of subdivision. As far as our knowledge goes at present there does not seem to be any direct evidence for the occurrence of this type in Asia, although there is every possibility that further analysis may show that it exists.

A more important type is that which has been termed Armenoid. In the pure Armenoids it would seem as if the stature were medium to short, the hair almost invariably

black, or black-brown, and eyes but seldom hazel and usually
brown. The nose is very large, and differs considerably in
index. The head is flattened behind, and usually very high,
sloping to a point well behind the bregma. Often the brow-
ridges are largely developed, a character which Duckworth
(II. 20) found in a skull he examined from Syria, and a
feature which I observed very frequently in a large series
of Bronze Age skulls which I excavated at Lapithos in Cyprus.
This type is found in Eastern Europe, it forms a very important element, and perhaps the aboriginal stock of the
population of Western Asia. It occurred in ancient Kish, and
is to be found in Mesopotamia to-day, and extends into
India. It probably also forms part of the population of
Central Asia. It does not appear to occur in the north of
Asia, where the true Alpine stock is well represented.

Although it is often possible to recognize with absolute
certainty these different branches of the Alpine race, and
possibly one or two other sub-branches, it seems very doubtful
as to their exact value in ethnology. There is hardly, at
present, sufficient data for us to be quite certain whether
we are dealing with local varieties whose differences are due
to particular environmental conditions, or whether isolation
or other causes have differentiated them for sufficiently long
periods to give them the rank of a definite variety of the
human race.

C.   THE YELLOW RACES

The second great racial stock with which we meet in Asia
I have called provisionally " Yellow Man." They are usually
called Mongolian or Mongoloid, and sometimes even are
loosely spoken of as Mongols. This terminology is extremely
unsatisfactory. It is really a tribal name which, owing to
great military genius of certain of its chieftains, notably
Ghenghis Khan and his more famous grandson Kublai Khan,
became transferred to a wide group of peoples, including the
Kalmucks, the Buriats, and the people to whom the great
Khans belonged. Owing to the fact that Kublai was ruling
over China when that country was visited by Marco Polo,
the name was also associated closely with China. It has
therefore come about that the Chinese over whom Kublai
ruled are often referred to as being the most typical of the

Mongolic people. It would appear, however, that some of the peoples who speak Mongolian languages, that is, Buriats, Mongols, and Kalmucks, are allied to the great races of Eastern Asia, while others are most closely akin to the races of Europe. Owing, no doubt, to the nomadic habits and the warlike propensities of these steppe dwellers, a great deal of mixing has taken place, and the tribal names and language clash with physical characters, as Ripley has shown so clearly that they do in Europe. When therefore we describe the Asiatic type, of which some of the Chinese are the typical representatives, as being Mongoloid, we are using a dynastic and tribal name, and are obscuring the fact that although many of the tribes who can historically and linguistically claim the proud name of Mongol are physically " Mongoloid," on the other hand many of them have only a slight admixture of this blood. The name has, however, received a definite connotation, and it would seem difficult to avoid using it entirely, even if it does tend to obscure the issue. The whole question will become simpler when the actual racial characters of the Mongols are discussed.

This second great race of Asia may truly be called Asiatic in contrast to the races which I have been discussing. This is the type which is in many ways most typical of Asia. It seems to have penetrated into Europe ; recently, in examining a number of skulls in the magnificent local collection of Budapest, I was struck by the fact that so many crania possessed features which are usually associated with the Asiatic rather than the European type, and these contrasted strongly with those which came from Western Europe.

As a general rule skulls belonging to the Yellow race are brachycephalic, often markedly so. A careful study made by Reicher failed to show any marked difference in the cranial form of the Asiatic brachycephals which he examined and the Dissentis skulls belonging to the Alpine type which he selected as his standard of comparison. Some of his Asiatic skulls, however, are certainly those of men belonging more closely to European than to the Yellow race. On the other hand, his Chinese skulls are certainly good representatives of the latter race. This resemblance in cranial form between the two great stocks is doubtless the reason why

many observers have been inclined to class the two together
in much the same way that, on the basis of cranial form, the
Negro and Mediterranean man have been classed together.

If facial form is taken as a standard of comparison, however, there is at once a striking difference. Among most of
the Yellow men, though by no means all, the bizygomatic
width is not greater than in the average European, although
those who live in the extreme north of Asia often have a
breadth which is both absolutely and relatively great. The
breadth of the face is therefore more apparent than real.
This appearance is due to the very great flatness which is a
marked character of so many Chinese faces. The malar
bones, which form part of the upper framework of the cheeks,
are developed in such a way as to have a great depth and
strength. Instead of presenting a rather small slightly
convex surface, which slopes backwards towards the zygomatic arches, they are much flattened, and form a bony
framework, which instead of transmitting the stresses of the
jaw to the cranial vault, appears to be able to withstand
much of them. There is therefore little need for the massing
of bone at the glabella, which is such a characteristic feature
of the skulls I have been discussing in the previous pages.

The general architecture of the jaw also seems to be different, and especially so from the Mediterranean type. In
the latter, most of the power depends on the temporal muscle
which takes its origin from the temporal fascia and fossa,
that is the side of the cranial vault. It is inserted on the
internal surface and the forepart of the coronoid process of
the mandible as far as the last molar. This arrangement
gives great power to the up-and-down movement of the jaw.
It tends to compress the side of the cranial vault. In Yellow
man, and in some of the White races, the principal muscle of
mastication is the masseter. This muscle takes its origin
from the malar process of the maxilla, and is inserted into
the angle and lower part of the outer surface of the ramus
of the mandible. It will be seen that from their position
these two groups of muscle fibres are, to a large extent,
complementary, but it will usually be found that in certain
races one group is more developed than the other. Now it
is precisely the region in which the masseter takes its origin
which is most characteristically developed in Yellow man,

PLATE II

A MONGOL
(Probably with Chinese blood)

[face p. 58

The point of insertion in the lower jaw is also much developed in the same race, and the great development of the masseter muscles in the lower part of the face is easily observed in nearly every Chinese. In addition to the direct pull exerted by muscles on the points or areas of origin and insertion, which are, of course, mechanically equal, there are certain stresses set up by the working of the jaws, much in the same way that in addition to stresses in a blacksmith's arms and body as he wields his hammer, there are very considerable stresses set up in the anvil every time he hits it or any object placed on it.

The stress due to the temporal muscles is, as has been explained, more or less directly upwards. That due to the masseter is distributed over the face; a fact that can be tested experimentally on oneself, and very simply, by moving the jaw so as to put first greater strain on the temporal muscles, which can be felt contracting under the hair on either side of the face, and secondly, on the masseters which can be felt on either side of the jaw. Yellow man may be conveniently then described as a " masseter type " of man. Among certain specialized forms of Yellow man, notably the Eskimo, there is a combination both of the temporal and the masseter form of mastication to an equally high degree.[1]

The form of the nose is equally characteristic of Yellow man. In the European races the nasal bones either form a depression at their juncture with the frontal bone, or in the case of the Armenoids are continued directly into the frontal bone in such a way as not infrequently to produce what is known as the Grecian profile. In both cases the nasal bones are arranged at a comparatively acute angle to one another. Normally, but by no means invariably, in our typical Yellow man we shall find that the depression in the nose takes place slightly below the nasion, that is, the juncture of the nasal and fronto-nasal sutures. The nasal bones are also set at a much more open angle to one another, giving the top of the

---

[1] A good example of the great development of the masseter muscles can be seen in the portrait—opposite page, where the subject is in no sense particularly muscular, showing that the particular development is a definitely racial and not an individual character. Owing to the fact that the temporal muscle lies beneath the hair, it is impossible to show its extension in an ordinary portrait.

bridge of the nose a flatter appearance, not unlike that found in European children.

An examination of a fairly large number of Chinese bones in various parts of China revealed other characters which appear to be associated with this stock, notably the particular form of the astragalus, one of the bones of the ankle-joint, but these differences are too technical to be discussed here.[1] It would seem, however, that the differences are sufficiently great to warrant our allowing to Yellow man definite racial status on the evidence of bones alone. It must be remembered, however, that some of the characters show evidence that whatever may be the case to-day, they are ultimately variations of the human form which can be correlated with environmental conditions, possibly progressive, possibly, as Haddon seems inclined to suggest, impressed on the human frame at an earlier and undifferentiated period.

If we turn to the superficial characters, we find that Yellow man has many points which separate him from the stocks we have previously discussed. In the first place, his hair is practically universally straight in form and almost circular in section. It is comparatively sparse, but grows to a considerable length. It is black in colour. There is little hair on the body, and the beard, although present, is but poorly developed, being often limited to a few scattered hairs. Black hair, of course, is by no means limited to Yellow man, and straight-haired individuals occur also among many other peoples. The presence of curly hair, however, in Asia may be taken as a certain indication of blood which belongs to a different strain from Yellow man, and therefore may be of great convenience in identification. The hair is neither very fine nor very coarse, coming usually intermediately between the hair of some of the Mediterranean men and that of the Ainu, and this last is remarkable for the size of the cross-section of the individual hairs.

The skin-colour varies considerably. It practically always has some shade of yellow which may be almost white in some

[1] An account of the skeletal characters of the Chinese will be found in Dr. Black's account of human bones found in Honan and Fengtien, published in *Paleontologica Sinica*, which by Dr. Black's kindness I read in manuscript. I should like to take this opportunity of thanking Dr. Black for setting at my disposal for examination the collections in the Department of Human Anatomy in the Peking Union Medical College, and for the general hospitality which that Institution showed me during a visit to Peking.

of the high-born ladies of Northern China. The fairest men are usually of a very pale saffron, only a little more yellow than the tint which would be described as olive and often lighter in tone than olive. This tint may perhaps represent the true colouring of the " Sons of Han," but in a large collection of male Chinese it comes not very frequently. The complexion then varies through the various shades of yellow to a dusky yellow-brown, sometimes so dark that the yellow tinge is almost obscure, and among some of the tropical peoples the brown has almost a greenish hue. There is usually a great contrast between the parts of the body which are exposed to the sunlight and those which are not, in the latter the yellow shade is usually more apparent. The coolie who works exposed to extremes of weather is usually much darker than the upper classes who are more sheltered. The skin-colour is darker in the south than in the north. As far as my observations go, it is like so many of the characters of Yellow man, intermediate, that is to say, it is neither so black as the darkest of the inhabitants of Southern India and Ceylon, nor so light as the fairest Europeans.

The eyes are always brown, they vary considerably in the degree of brownness between a dark brown that is almost black and a much lighter brown. The sclerotic, that is, the white of the eye, is not infrequently pigmented, but never to the high degree which is found in the Negro.

The form of the eye presents two characteristics which are of great interest. First, not infrequently the eye-slit, instead of being horizontal, is oblique, giving the eye a slanting appearance, which is due to the superficial anatomy of the eye-slit, not to the orbit itself. This obliquity of the eyes is by no means universal, but it is a sufficiently marked character to have become classical in the artistic representation of the human face in the Far East. Native artists also have been usually careful, when representing men of other races, to draw them with straight eyes, showing that they were well aware of this racial characteristic in their own people.

The second character of the eye which is of importance is the so-called "Mongolian fold." This feature is due to a fold of skin covering the inner canthus of the eye. It may be variously developed. In some cases there is a large semi-lunar fold which covers the whole of the inner corner of the eye and joins the skin of the face several millimetres beneath the lower eyelid. In other cases the fold is reduced to a slit infolding which just covers the inner corner of the eye. It is frequently absent.

This fold occurs occasionally in European children, and sometimes even in adults, but its relative frequency among Yellow men give it the right to be regarded as a racial character. It is possible that it may be considered to be related to the peculiar nature of the nose, which has been shown to resemble in some cases that of European children. It was formerly suggested that the nasal index could be considered to be a good criterion of the Yellow race, but subsequent research has shown that this is not the case.

The divisions of the Yellow race are by no means so clearly defined as those of the stocks which we have considered previously. The cephalic index does not provide us with a satisfactory basis of classification. Among many of the peoples of Asia very high cephalic indices occur, but they can be shown practically always to be due to the influence of " Alpine " man and not to belong to true Yellow man as we have defined him. As a general rule, we find that the cephalic index is in the neighbourhood of 80, with a slight and surprisingly small variation on either side. From this it might be supposed that Yellow man is but little differentiated, a statement that is probably fairly true.

There are, however, two great subdivisions so great that possibly the division may be considered fundamental, namely, the cleavage which exists between the Yellow man, of which we have taken the Chinese as a typical example, and the division which was formerly called Red man, but which is now generally referred to as the Amerind race. There are various subdivisions of this people, which need not concern us here. What is, however, of importance for our present purpose is the theory so strongly put forward by the Jesup Expedition that some of the northern tribes of Siberia are definitely American in origin, representing probably a backwash of that stock, or stocks, which originally crossed from Asia into America.

These peoples, who include many of the northern tribes of the extreme east of the Asiatic continent, differ from the more southern examples, for whom Haddon has adopted the convenient term of " Parœan " in various ways, none of which, however, appear to be of fundamental importance. The most noticeable feature is the very great breadth of the face, measured across the zygomatic arches. Although this great width occurs in some of the Alpines, in the Palæasiatics it appears to be greater than in the Parœeans.

The true character of these northern peoples would be given by a measurement of the bimalar width, rather than by the bizygomatic, but the extreme difficulty which is experienced in measuring accurately the width across the check bones, owing to the absence of a fixed anatomical point, has led most anthropologists to abandon this measurement. The character then which serves most clearly to distinguish this group of peoples is hardly shown in the ordinary observations which are taken in the field, but which appears very clearly when seen either on the living individual or in photographs.

There is a second character which seems usually also to be associated with these northern peoples, namely, an extremely small stature. This hardly seems to be an invariable character, and is probably to be associated with the hard climatic conditions to which these people and their ancestors have been subjected for a long period. They also appear usually to have a low nasal index, a fact which, if the theory we have previously discussed is true, would be expected from their environment, and which would serve to class them as being a type of Yellow man which has specialized in response to Arctic conditions.

The skin, hair, and eye colour, and the form of the hair and eyes do not appear to differ from those of the Parœeans.

Although there are probably many sub-varieties in the vast population which inhabits China, it seems possible to distinguish two types. Whether again these deserve the name of races, in the sense which Ripley uses the word, is doubtful. In any case, until our knowledge of Chinese ethnology is greater, they serve at least as distinguishing marks which are convenient for identification. The terms which I propose to use are the Han type and the Sung type, suggesting, as these names do, North and South China. It must be remembered that I am only including those inhabitants of the Chinese Empire who can be considered to be true representatives of Yellow man. (The whole question is more fully discussed on pages 160 ff.)

The northern, or Han type, is most remarkable for its high stature. It has been suggested that this is due to admixture which has undoubtedly taken place with the more northerly tribes. This can, however, hardly be the case, as the northern Chinese are markedly taller than the neighbouring Mongol tribes. It is possible, however, that the great stature is a racial character, as some of the peoples to the west, who appear to be akin to the northern Chinese, also are reported to be of tall stature. The northern Chinese are slightly longer-headed than their southern neighbours, but it is at present uncertain how accurate the data are, and therefore the matter must remain open. This greater degree of dolichocephaly is what would be expected with a greater stature. They seem also to have rather broader faces, but again our data is insufficient to justify our putting this forward as a definite racial feature.

The southern Chinese are shorter, to a very marked degree, than the northern branch of the race. They are slightly darker, and usually have a very much higher nasal index. They also appear, as I have already stated, to be slightly more brachycephalic. As far as our data go at present, the stature and the nasal index form undoubtedly the most important points to distinguish the two. Both these features appear to be correlated with environment, but they would seem to be convenient methods of distinguishing the two great divisions of the Chinese people. It has often been stated in textbooks that the Chinese show a remarkable homogeneity of feature throughout the whole Empire. This, to a certain extent, undoubtedly is true. It seems not improbable that the Chinese have been able to absorb the different races which have at various times invaded China, owing to the way in which this general homogeneous type has been able to adapt itself in various ways to its environment. We find representatives of the two types widely scattered over Asia, but it will usually be found that in the more northerly parts the northern type predominates, whereas in the tropics the Sung or southern type prevails. This has happened in spite of the great movements of peoples which have been taking place for a very long period. During periods of flood, famine, pestilence, or war, whole provinces have been devastated. They have subsequently been occupied by immigrants from neighbouring provinces, till in the course of time a great deal of forward and backward movement has taken place. It will be found that in the south, among people who claim northern origin, the northern type is quite well represented. The subdivision into two types then must depend entirely on environmental conditions. In origin, apart from the border peoples of the periphery, there would appear to be little difference between the two groups. In their present appearance, however, they differ very considerably in certain features which have been considered of importance by anthropologists, and they may therefore be described as interesting local variations of one fundamental group.

The next group within the great family of Yellow man are those who have been described by Haddon as Proto-Malays, the present more specialized Malays, who arose in Menankerbau in Sumatra in the twelfth century, being a developed branch of this race. These peoples, who are widely spread in South-eastern Asia and in the Archipelago, are usually round-headed, they have noses which, though relatively broad, are narrower than those of their Nesiot neighbours. Their hair and eyes do not differ from those of the more northerly Chinese. They are usually of short stature, and have a skin which, though sometimes of a dull dark yellow, is more often of a dusky yellowish-brown. They have less prominent cheek-bones than the Chinese, and the face is less strongly developed. They are less muscular for the most part than their more northern neighbours, are generally more slender of habit, and have normally much smaller jaws, without that great development of the masseter muscles which is so characteristic of the Chinese.

The third great stock which is found in Asia is usually known as the Negrito (X. 47, App., and X. 38). These tribes are now found in a peripheral area, but it seems not improbable that at one time they occupied a much greater part of South-eastern Asia than they do at present. There

F

are certain slight differences between the local varieties which are, however, not sufficient to cause any more than a single division to be made in the group, although the geographical labels, according to the places of habitat, the Malay Peninsula, the Philippine Islands, and the Andaman Islands are convenient.   In Sumatra there are traces of Negrito blood, and a similar report has also been made in regard to the peoples of French Indo-China, but, except in the three places mentioned above, there are no longer any Negritos existing as groups in Asia.

The Negritos tend to be slightly brachycephalic, a character which is to be associated with their small stature. Neither of these two characters, however, serve absolutely to distinguish them from some of their neighbours, most of whom, among the more primitive tribes, are also of small stature.   The mesocephalic index is one which is also characteristic of so many of the Yellow-skinned races and their congeners.   The dark skin-colour, which would seem at first to be a good guide, is also of little service, as Martin states that among the primitive tribes of the interior of the Malay Peninsula there is, on the whole, but little difference in this feature.   No doubt the difference between the tribes in this area and their undoubted kinsmen to the north in the skin-colour is the direct result of climatic conditions.   These conditions have tended to cause a convergence between the different stocks in this as also in the nasal index, although in this feature there are certain differences.

In the Philippines, however, contrary to Martin's experience in the Malay Peninsula, both skin-colour and stature seem to mark out the Negritos from the rest of the population.   The Negritos are both darker and also considerably shorter in stature.   The evidence before us would then suggest that, although shortness is one of the characteristics of the Negritos, it does not serve absolutely to distinguish them from some of the Brown or Yellow races of South-eastern Asia, and that some of the Brown races may also have as dark a skin.

The nasal index (I. 18, 117) does not provide us with a certain criterion.   In this case the ranges are of great interest. Taken as a general rule, it would seem as if the Negritos tended to have the broadest noses, but that groups of the Nesiot peoples had noses which were often only slightly less broad. The Malayan peoples, who probably were the last immigrants into the area, have narrower noses, though the broadest groups often overlap with the narrowest of the Nesiots. If the hypothesis which is put forward earlier is correct, it may be suggested that the nasal index is gradually coming into equilibrium with the environment, but that this process of adaptation is a slow one, and that only those peoples who have for a very long time been exposed to extreme conditions of heat and moisture have the extreme index which appears to be truly associated with those conditions.

The most marked difference between the Negritos and all their neighbours, and one which serves very clearly to differentiate them from the rest, is the form of the hair. It is flat and ribbon-like in section, and curls tightly over the head instead of falling in long tresses as does that of so many Asiatics, or forming ringlets like some of the primitive tribes of India and Ceylon. They not infrequently have beards, which character is a marked contrast to many of their neighbours.

This latter character has been that from which they have obtained their name of Negritos—little Negroes. Although there are considerable variations in the features which are possessed by the different Negro groups, some of them shading into those possessed by other races, the particular type of Negro hair and the associated form of the skin appears to differentiate them entirely from the other stocks of mankind, and to associate the Negritos of Eastern Asia with the Negrillos of Central Africa.

The distribution of the two groups is a puzzling one. At present the Negritos occupy a fringing distribution within the area of their characterization. It seems probable that formerly they occupied a much bigger area, but it would seem as if their original home had been either in the centre of their present area, or possibly on the mainland of Asia, whence they, like their neighbours, may have spread. They do not, however, exist as groups on the mainland to-day, although traces of them are reported by Verneau. No traces have been found in Borneo, but this is not a matter of importance as the island is an outlier. Java has failed to give us well-substantiated reports. It is possible, however, that further information is yet to be gained from that island, as I have not been able to trace a full monograph on the physical anthropology. It seems not impossible that there may be traces of Negritos in Sumatra, an island which has only been studied in parts. West, however, of the Malay Peninsula, and of the islands in the Bay of Bengal, there are no traces of any types which can link up the Negritos and the African Negroes. At present, it is true, we are almost entirely deficient in specimens of subfossil man from this area, and it is always possible that further investigation or chance finds may enable us to establish a definite link. At present, however, the gap is a serious one. If we hold, on the other hand, that certain of the tribes of the Pacific are of the same stock as the Negro, and call them by the name of Oceanic Negroes, it is possible that we may find a connection between them and the Negritos. This being so, however, it is extremely difficult to find a link which shall connect these two great groups, supposing them both to have sprung from the same specialized branch of humanity. It is true that Joyce (II. 2) has lent the weight of his authority to the suggestion that the inhabitants of Madagascar are of the Oceanic Negroid stock in origin, apart from recent Malay immigrants. This, however, supposes a migration of these people from the East, a hypothesis which Joyce supports by the suggestion that the Oceanic Negroes are known to be daring seamen. It hardly is of any service in linking up the original two stocks.

Against this we must remember that our knowledge of the early races of man outside Europe is so small that we may be said at present to have practically no knowledge of where or how the Negro stock differentiated from the rest of mankind.

There is a further hypothesis which may be put forward, although at present there is insufficient evidence to justify it being considered as any more than a suggestion to be discarded when further information comes to hand. It has been said above that Martin considers that the most important difference between the Negritos in the Malay Peninsula and their neighbours is the difference in the form of the hair. We have been inclined to consider that hair-form is a good criterion of race, and in many cases it certainly does seem to be so. There are, however, very considerable differences between the hair of the different branches of the Brown race and of its allies and close kinsmen, the other European stocks. These differences seem for the most part to be associated with certain climatic conditions. It seems, therefore, at least possible that the resemblances in hair-form, which we find between the Negritos and the true Negroes, may be due not to kinship, but rather to the influence of a not dissimilar geographic environment. Professor Thomson has suggested to me that possibly the form of the Negro hair may be of special advantage in protecting the head from the excessive rays of a tropical sun The particular construction of the skin with its greater supply of sweat glands, may also be due to similar reasons and causes. No doubt all the dwellers in the tropics have not developed these peculiarities, but it seems not impossible that the Negro types in both Africa and elsewhere are specially adapted to their rigorous environment, and that we must look not to kinship for the cause of similar distinctive marks, but rather to the effect of a similar environment.

This is all the more possible in considering the races of Asia, because although the Negro in Africa does appear to present certain very distinctive features, though not sufficient for Sergi to dissociate him from the Mediterranean race, yet in Asia the difference between the Negritos and their neighbours is nowhere distinctive, except for the character of the hair.

The solution of the problem is still to seek, but it seems that those who would find kinship between the Negrito and the African Negro must search for fossil men which will provide a link between the two areas of characterization, whereas those who would support the convergence doctrine must trace out exactly how far the nature of human hair is correlated with environment. In view of the fact that we find that the tropics do appear to have some very definite effects on the human frame quite independent of race, it seems possible that the latter is the easiest working hypothesis to sustain.

Summarizing, then, the races of Asia, we have first the Nordic sporadically in Western Asia, with possibly an outlier of the same stock in the extreme east, the Ainu; secondly, various groups of the Brown race. The third group are the various sub-races akin to the Alpine race of Central Europe. Fourthly, we have a great group of peoples whose exact racial affinities have not been fully studied, namely, Yellow man. He may certainly be divided into two or three sub-types, possibly into more. Finally, we have the Negrito, with a small number of, for the most part, isolated tribes living in various localities in South-east Tropical Asia.

CHAPTER III

The Origin of the Asiatic Races

IN the last chapter I have been considering the form and distribution of the races of Asia at the present time. The origin of these races is a matter of the greatest interest to all students of ethnology, and is of particular interest in Asia, owing to the claims which that continent has to being the original home of large groups of mammalian forms. But owing to its vast extent and also to the inaccessibility of much of the continent, we have almost less exact information on this branch of the study of Asiatic peoples than of any other branch.

By far the most important of the fossil or sub-fossil finds is that of *Pithecanthropus erectus,* which was discovered by Dubois at Trinil in Java in 1891. The discovery of this specimen did much to stimulate research into the relationship of man and the higher apes, and the conclusion reached at the time was that a species was represented which was half-way between man and the apes. Concerned as we are with the more modern side of the ethnology of Asia, it is impossible here to discuss this find in the detail which it deserves. The following points, however, are worthy of special note. Boule (III. 1) believes that Pithecanthropus is really a gigantic gibbon. He considers that the man-like characters are due to convergence and believes that his suggestion is the best way to account for the intermediate character of the calvarium, the straight femur and the nature of the teeth which have simian roots and human crowns, that is to say, that they are broad rather than long. Unfortunately, the finds so far published are limited to these three parts of the skeleton, and repeated searches have failed to discover any more remains which might throw further light on the question.

Special attention may be drawn to the following details

The capacity of the calvaria, as far as it can be estimated, may be said to be of an intermediate character between man and the apes. Sir Arthur Keith believes that the fronto-malar region is simian rather than human. The occipital region is intermediate, but there is, generally speaking, a resemblance to that of the gibbons and the chimpanzees. Elliot Smith considers the endo-cranial cast to be human in character, but the frontal region is reduced, and here too the animal is probably intermediate in type.

There are abundant traces to prove that palæolithic man inhabited the continent of Asia. As long ago as 1864 Lartet reported that palæoliths were to be found in Syria. Since that time numerous further discoveries have been made in Western Asia, especially in Syria and Palestine. They have frequently been found in conjunction with a pleistocene fauna, which confirms the antiquity of the deposits. The forms of the implements coincides with those of Europe. Boule (III. 1, 354) reports that Chellean, Acheulean, Mouste-rian, Aurignacian, and even Magdalenian types occur. The glaciation, at the time when man was making these imple-ments, seems to have still extended to the higher mountain slopes and plateaux, as finds are very rare in Asia Minor and Persia. The plains, however, contain both palæolithic and neolithic deposits, and at Anau in Turkestan, Pumpelly (III. 2) has excavated a site which was inhabited continuously over a very long period from neolithic times onwards.

Numerous palæolithic deposits have been found in India from the Punjaub to Madras. They are associated with an ancient fauna, and the archæological problem in India is extremely similar to that of Western Europe. In Northern Asia it is also clear that man in a palæolithic stage of cul-ture at one time inhabited the valley of the Yenesei, where Russian archæologists have reported the presence of artefacts associated with the mammoth, the woolly rhinoceros, and the reindeer. The glaciation, however, appears to have been less extensive than in Europe, the most southerly palæolithic station being at Krasnoiarsk (III. 3 and III. 4).

The neolithic remains from the Irkutsk district are of interest because they have been covered with red ochre, as are some of the palæolithic skeletons. No special significance, however, can be attached at present to this curious coincidence.

The kitchen middens in Japan and other prehistoric remains in Ko, the neighbouring mainland, throw no light on our problem, because where it has been possible to link them up with known facts, they seem to have been made by people akin to the modern inhabitants of those areas. A discussion on their significance will be found in the chapter dealing with those peoples.

This brief résumé will show then that, at present, we have evidence of the presence of early man in Western, Northern, and Southern Asia. The cultural evidence from the Far East is at present either of doubtful value, or lacking. When we remember how very recent are most of the discoveries in Europe, and how prehistoric archæology has been re-written, even in the last twenty or less years, the doubtful nature of negative evidence is at once apparent.

Various ancient finds have been reported from the loess and elsewhere in China. The most important are described by Teilhard (III. 6) from the great Ordos bend of the Yellow River. Five different localities are said to contain palæo-lithic remains. These are Ning Hsia, in Northern Kansu, where the types are said to be Mousterian. Secondly, at Sjara Osso Gol, a fluviatile deposit, contemporary with the loess, is said to have contained similar implements, associated with forms which were similar to the *Elephas primigenius* and *Rhinoceros tichorhinus* of Europe. Yu fêng chiao deposits contained instruments which may have been of older date. King Yang is the fourth site mentioned. Further types were found at Shi tsui tze, in loess gravels, and in the desert at San tao Ho, which place is, however, on the Hwang Ho, the explorers summarize their finds by describing the area as a long band of palæolithic deposits, running from San tao Ho to King Yang, a distance of about 900 kilometres.

This find is of the greatest importance, but I have not been able to find a complete account of their journey, and it is hardly possible to accept their statements without a good deal of reserve. The exact condition of the *graviers du loess* as they describe them is extremely uncertain, and the action of the Hwang Ho is so capricious that except after long and careful study it is not always possible to ascertain certainly the age of the fluviatile deposits. To establish the definite geological position of palæolithic implements in so big a band of country as the great Ordos bend is hardly possible without many years of careful study. It is probable, and to be hoped that their finds are genuine.

I have had the opportunity, through the courtesy of Dr. Anderson and others, of examining a large number of so-called palæolithic implements in China. They could be described, typologically, not infrequently by the various names which are used in Europe. A careful examination, however, revealed that this description would be quite false. Those which could be dated, however, although often associated with extinct animals, clearly belonged to the Chalcolithic Period of China, whose pottery is clearly of the same type as that from Anau, and which possibly survived, at least in Fengtien, to as late as 1500 B.C. Some whose archæological position was uncertain were clearly what may be described as neolithic wasters, although it must be clearly understood that at present we have no data on the Neolithic Period in China, but only of the Chalcolithic. Others were uncertain both as to form and their horizon. In spite, therefore, of these isolated finds from the Ordos bend, there is no definite evidence of palæolithic man in China. The other finds which have been made makes the reported genuine implements seem very doubtful, especially since we know that early forms survived until what must be described as, geologically at least, a very recent period (III. 7 ; III. 8 ; III. 9).

The finds which are alleged to have been made in the south and in Indo-China are of an equally doubtful character. If we summarize the evidence it must be admitted that, although Boule has lent the great weight of his authority to the Siberian finds, and is apparently inclined even to accept the more than doubtful ones from Kansu, we still know nothing of early man north of the great uplift, and the reported finds make the problem if anything more difficult.

When evidence of man's handiwork is so doubtful, it is natural that his bones are likely to be even more rare. Apart from Pithecanthropus, two definite reports have been made of early man in Asia.

The first is said to be possibly of Aurignacean date. It was found by Zumoffen in a cave at Antelias in Phœnicia. No complete morphological report appears to have been published (III. 10).

The second is a sacrum, described by Matsumoto in 1915 (III. 11). The bone came from an ancient deposit in Honan. On the ground of its shape and curvature Matsumoto believes it to be Neanderthaloid. Considering the variations which occur in sacra, and judging from the published figures, it would seem exceedingly hazardous, even were its ancient date definitely established, to assert on morphological grounds that this sacrum belonged to a representative of Neanderthal man, and until Dr. Black's report is published we cannot say what was the exact form of early man in Honan during the Chalcolithic Period. Apart then from geologic evidence, the association is doubtful. The geologic evidence is, however, also extremely doubtful. Matsumoto publishes no data as to the way in which the finds were made, but only states how they came into his hands. He dates the sacrum by describing it as similar in condition and fossilization to the remains of what he has decided is *Elephas primigenius*, or a near relation. The remains of the elephant were, however, limited to a vertebra, which the author identifies, somewhat hesitatingly, as the ninth. It is described as very lightly fossilized. The evidence for the age of the sacrum is, therefore, doubtful in the extreme and can, until we have further bones from Honan in a definite stratum, be safely disregarded.

Our evidence, therefore, for early man in Asia becomes extremely meagre. Over the greater part of it we have at present nothing certain. Most of that part is little known, some is unknown. The negative evidence then counts for nothing. Many authors have, however, in spite of this doubtful position, confidently affirmed that man originated in Asia. Some schools of thought, especially Mathew (I. 28, 171), have suggested the central plateau. There is little evidence to confirm this attractive hypothesis beyond the fact that as the central plateau is remote and in a central position in Asia, the exploration of it is not likely to proceed rapidly. If early remains are found there, luck will favour the finders, and the finds will fit in with many enticing theories, but at present not even implements have rewarded the searchers in that region.

The Siwalik fossiliferous beds have suggested to others that the origin of man must be sought in this region. There does appear to have been what Boule describes as an extreme movement of life in that region towards the end of the Miocene and the beginning of the Pliocene, and the development of the higher primates is perhaps more marked than the other groups. But the evidence is limited to this general inference at present. The conclusions which can be drawn from the study of mammalian fauna cannot, however, always be applied successfully to man, and this hypothesis also remains an attractive and purely academic theory without any evidence to support it at present. The chance turning of a sod of earth may show that what has been written above is correct, or may entirely confound it, but at present that sod of earth has not yet been turned.

Wherever man originated, then, there is no reason particularly to suppose that he originated in any particular place.[1] No very primitive remains have been discovered in America, and it seems unlikely that there will be. Opinions are divided as to Asia, more perhaps incline towards it than against, but such theories can only be wild conjecture based on facts, which are not normally of value in dealing with mankind, though possibly they may be of value in dealing with him in a very rudimentary stage. The evidence at present throws most doubt on his antiquity in the north and favours his antiquity in the south. But all the evidence is such that it must date from a period long after man first became man, for he had already learnt to shape elaborate implements, and the evidence from Europe suggests that this relatively advanced stage of culture was only reached after a long apprenticeship. The relation of Asia to the modern races of man is also a hazardous territory and not less full of pitfalls than that we have been discussing, but there is more evidence. In Europe we have remains of man earlier geologically in every probability than anything from Asia at present found. This does not argue that Europe was

---

[1] Giuffrida-Ruggeri (III. 12 and III. 13) believes that man originated from a unique phylum, but that there were three cradles, not necessarily far apart, for the White, Yellow, and Black races.

necessarily the cradle of man, but it gives us a starting-point from which to work. Further, we have evidence of the movements of later man in Europe, and at least to a limited degree we can trace the history of the three great races of Europe, as they were described by the older anthropologists.

The situation is very clearly described by Boule. It is evident that the present centre of distribution of the Nordic race is Scandinavia; during palæolithic times Sweden was covered with ice and they must necessarily have developed elsewhere in an ice-free region. It seems probable on palæontogical grounds that this ice-free region is to be found in Russia, central, south, and east, and not impossibly in the Trans-Ural region. Here again we have no true evidence. Giuffrida-Ruggeri (III. 14), and a somewhat similar view is taken by Fleure (II. 16), suggested that the Nordics are a branch of Mediterranean man. This is by no means impossible; there is, however, no evidence to confirm this hypothesis, which has not met with general acceptance. Boule suggests that Nordics, or Pre-Nordics, existed in Magdalenian times.

It seems on the whole probable that the Nordics inclined to Europe and not to Asia. We do not know at present. We have suggestions, however, that in times which were sufficiently remote to antedate the modern inhabitants, there were spread over the northern steppe land forest and tundra of the Eurasiatic continent a people who differed very considerably from the modern inhabitants of those regions. We still have survivors of these long-heads belonging to the north at the two ends of the continent, the Nordics in Europe, the Ainu, and probably some of the Turkoman peoples in Asia. They differ profoundly from one another, but it is probable that they belong ultimately to the same stock. Unfortunately our methods of describing skulls differ so much that from the published accounts it is often difficult to be certain of the characters of some of the skulls; this is particularly to be regretted in the case of the early finds from Northern Siberia. It is clear that we have to do with a long-headed race, possibly more than one race, who at one period probably had a very wide distribution. Where their origin was it is impossible to say. We are by no means sure that they all are the same people. An examination of Ainu skulls and other prehistoric skulls from Japan, possibly of a remote age, possibly more recently, suggested to me that the kinship between the Nordics and the Ainu was by no means so remote as has often been suggested. The difference of pigment was great, but, as has already been seen, pigment is not a reliable guide to race.

It seems probable, then, that we had a centre of distribution, either in Eastern Europe or in Northern Asia, where the ice cap does not seem to have stretched so far to the south. The people dispersed from this centre in two directions and ultimately became in one case the tall, fair people of Northern Europe, and in the other the stocky, curly-haired Ainu with their *brunet* colouring and brown or auburn eyes.

It may even be that the Ainu are the relics, but little specialized of this early race. Their general characters are such, as we shall see in greater detail, as those of a primitive race, while it is not possible to avoid the suggestion, especially if one has lived among them, that their kinship with the peoples of Europe must always be borne in mind.

This suggestion would not necessarily shift the original cradle of the Nordic race further to the east than Boule suggests, especially since we have evidence of Proto-Nordic man on the Turkoman steppes. We must remember that to suggest kinship is by no means to affirm any particular home. Kinship means a common stock, but where that common stock originated is at present entirely uncertain, and I can only put forward the very tentative suggestion of common kinship while confessing that such kinship is as yet entirely unproven, and that even were it proved it would do nothing more than suggest what has been put forward on other grounds, namely, that Nordic man originated in the northern part of the Eurasiatic continent at a comparatively remote period, and that he migrated thence for some entirely unknown reason. It is to be noted that his migrations still continue, and at present he has succeeded in establishing, if not his pure type, at least strains with a fair proportion of his blood over most of the temperate zones.

In neolithic times it seems extremely probable that this migration was very active. That he or a kindred race sent further waves into the Far East is probable but by no means certain, and there is at present little direct evidence to support it. It is quite sure that at this time he overran the Scandinavian Peninsula, and so firmly established himself there as to give, as Boule says, the illusion that this was the place from which he originally sprung.

The Mediterranean race presents a different problem. While I have tried to suggest that the Nordics and those who resemble them, whether kinsmen or not, are at least specialized to live in northern conditions and on the whole have never succeeded in adapting themselves to southern conditions, it is clear that that branch of mankind which we call Mediterranean is a child of the south. It is possible that they may be two closely allied branches of the same race, the one adopted to tropical or sub-tropical conditions, the other to the north. We have no evidence to support or combat this theory. It has been shown, however, that while the association of the northern long-heads with one another is problematical, there are many reasons which suggest that the Mediterranean or Brown race has a wide distribution and probably a number of sub-races. These are distributed from the Dutch Indies to the Pillars of Hercules. They are found in Egypt in the comparatively early period which we call pre-dynastic, and they are represented in the earliest tombs which have so far been carefully examined in Mesopotamia. But this is all modern history. It carries us but back to yesterday in our search for origins. Some of the much earlier skulls from Europe apparently belong to this type. All we can say is that from remote times, as it would appear, almost since man in his modern and non-Neanderthaloid form was living on the earth, we find this type scattered along the western and southern seaboard of the great continent whose ethnological history we are considering. Where his cradle was we have no evidence to show us. As there probably were other races in occupation of the earth at the time that he was beginning, it seems not improbable that his birthplace was somewhere within the area of his present distribution, at a period sufficiently remote for him to become acclimatized to different conditions. At present it is impossible to be more precise.

One or two suggestions have been made about the origin of Mediterranean man which suggest a rather different origin from that which I have given above. Giuffrida-Ruggeri (III. 14), for instance, thinks that the race was produced by a cross between Cromagnon man and a type which he calls Proto-Ethiopic. The disadvantage of this theory is that we have very little evidence as to the true nature of the former type, and none in regard to the latter. In any case, this would not explain the present distribution of the Brown races, nor how they come to present such remarkable differences in pigmentation while preserving the same main features.

The great group of brachycephals, which I have divided into Alpine, Dinaric, and Armenoid, but which in this chapter I will refer to as Alpine for lack of a term which shall include the three branches, is generally admitted to have taken its origin in Asia. The precise relationship of this stock to Yellow man is one of the most important considerations in dealing with its origin. Some authors would hardly distinguish between the two, making them closely related. Others, again, seem to see in them closely related stocks, the Alpine being an offshoot from the Yellow. Boule suggests that the migration westwards probably began at the end of the glacial period, and that the Alpines gradually lost their Mongoloid characters as they advanced westwards. How this process took place he does not explain.

It seems probable that the early advances of Alpine man were not so much migrations as a series of infiltrations into other populations. In the Bronze Age, however, they certainly made a great influx into Western Europe (III. 15), but they had previously been filtering into the Near East at a time which can be definitely dated, approximately the beginning of the Dynastic Period in Egypt (II. 17, 114). They present in many ways a different problem from that which we have been discussing because, at least in Western Asia and in Europe, they are certainly not the earliest representatives of modern man, although as I shall show elsewhere they have been claimed as the earliest inhabitants of Asia Minor, a region which was not inhabited till neolithic times, possibly quite late therefore in man's history. Although to-day we find Alpine man widely distributed in Asia, on the whole where he appears in a fringing position it would seem as though his arrival was late. In Europe he is essentially the child of the mountains. That he originated in Asia seems almost the only conclusion that can be drawn from the evidence that we have at present. His relationship to Yellow man is not at present clearly understood in spite of many precise statements to the contrary. If we accept the supreme value of the cephalic index, and many anthropologists are very doubtful about its value, then we shall probably see a likeness. If not, then it is clear that there is no reason to suggest the closer linkage of Yellow man with Alpine than with the other races.

We have as yet no knowledge of the origin of Yellow man. The centre of Asia is a country which has not as yet been fully explored, and at present the earliest remains which have been discovered of this type do not appear to be of any very great antiquity. As has been explained above, we do not even know whether Alpine man is related in his origin to Yellow man. One point in regard to the early form of Yellow man which needs consideration here is his relation to the inhabitants of the New World.

The origin of the Amerind has been the cause of much discussion. Many anthropologists, notably Hrdlicka (III. 16 and 17), believe that there is not in the Americas any trace of early man. Hrdlicka's position seems to be that in most cases the evidence of antiquity breaks down, but that where it does seem that the geological evidence is difficult to assail, the character of the human remains is such that for the most part they do not differ from modern Indians, and therefore they are of no great antiquity (III. 18, 19, and 20). There are, it is true, one or two cases which seem at first sight not to fall within either of these two categories; they can, however, most of them be explained when the evidence is fully considered.

There is, however, no reason why the early remains of man in America should not be of some antiquity and at the same time bear considerable resemblance to the modern Indian. In North-eastern Asia to-day, as we shall see in a later chapter, there are peoples who bear a close resemblance to the modern Amerinds. This resemblance can probably be best explained by supposing that they had a common ancestor who did not differ very greatly from his modern descendants. It is true that the Amerinds to-day present certain differences, of head-form, colour, stature, and so on. These resemblances, however, are such that Hrdlicka believes that they may be

G

considered as belonging to the same race, while others suppose
that there are several racially distinct types in America. In
any case, it would seem to be generally admitted at present
that the resemblances between the Amerind and the Yellow
races are such that they must belong to the same racial stock.
There is no evidence which inclines one to believe that they
originated in America. It is therefore probable that they
originated in Asia. It does, however, seem probable that
there have been several movements of peoples in both
directions in the neighbourhood of the Behring Strait. Some
of the present people in Asia may therefore owe their origin
to the American continent, but only as a secondary racial
cradle.

The Asiatic Eskimo are not numerous in number, but
considerable attention has been drawn to this interesting
people. It would seem, as we shall show later, that the Asiatic
Eskimo are more closely related to their neighbours, who are
not Eskimo, than to the Eskimo of North America. It seems
that in any case we must associate the Eskimo people with
the Yellow race, while at the same time distinguishing them
from the Amerind. Possibly the differentiation may have
taken place at a comparatively remote period, but here again
we have no evidence on which to base any theories. The
cranium from Chancelade has been considered by many observers, from Testut (III. 21), who originally described it, to
Professor Sollas (III. 22), to be Eskimoid. Are we, therefore,
to find not in Asia but in Europe the original ancestors of
the inhabitants of the extreme north-east of the Asiatic
continent ?

Such a conclusion would be hazardous in the extreme.
In the first place, but little reliance can be placed on the
evidence of a single cranium. Secondly, we have at present
no means of judging whether the characters, which do seem
at first sight to resemble the characters of the Eskimo, are
really to be considered as such. The form of the nose has
been considered by some to be important evidence as proving
the relationship with the Eskimo. The narrowness which
appears in both the Chancelade specimen and in most Eskimo
skulls is certainly remarkable. It must be remembered, however, that both were subjected to extremely cold conditions,
and the narrowness of the nose may be a convergence, not

a matter of relationship. The form of the cranium, with its marked keeling when viewed from the front (in *norma facialis*), may also be accounted for in the same way. Professor Thomson has shown good reasons for supposing that the keeling in the Eskimo is not a racial character, but is due to the use which these people make of their masticatory apparatus. Here, again, we have no certain evidence and can only record the observed facts.

The conclusion warranted by our present evidence would be that the various peoples who can be grouped together as members of the Yellow race all probably originated in Asia, and it would appear in its northern part. The suggestions of Mongoloid man in Europe in palæolithic times have not as yet been substantiated.

We know nothing at present about the origin of the Negritos, and cannot say whether they came from Africa, which would seem unlikely, or whether, which is more probable, that they are Asiatic in origin. There is not at present any definite evidence, as far as I am aware, which would claim our belief that the Negro originated in Asia. Any theories that may be put forward on physical grounds must remain at present pure conjectures.

The outcome of this chapter, then, is for the most part purely negative. We cannot speak for lack of evidence of ultimate origins. It seems probable that the Yellow races, and at least one branch of the White races, have had their centre of dispersion in Asia, but in what locality it is impossible at present to specify. More generally, however, it seems not improbable that the earliest cradle of mankind was " somewhere in Asia."

CHAPTER IV

WESTERN ASIA

A. THE PEOPLES OF THE NEAR EAST

IN the previous chapters I have been considering in broad outline the general conditions to which man is subjected in Asia, and the groups into which the inhabitants of that area have been generally divided. In the chapters which follow I shall attempt to discuss in detail the general ethnology of the various parts of Asia. In spite of its disadvantages I have found it most convenient to follow the example of most of my predecessors, and to adopt the geographic method of grouping. This method has the obvious advantage that the greater part of the works referred to deal with particular small areas. It also makes the task of the reader simpler if he wishes to consult an atlas, as he will not be continually turning over pages. Such a division is, however, artificial when considered from the point of view of the classification of mankind, although geographical and other boundaries do seem to have played a definite part in the moulding of peoples.

The method which I have pursued is first to discuss as briefly as possible the geographical conditions in each area which seem to be of importance to the student of ethnology, and then to consider the affinities of the people themselves. I have added a number of references to other parts of the book from time to time in order to enable the reader to find a fuller discussion of some point which may be of equal importance in the ethnology of more than one area. The more general books have not been referred to more than once in the bibliography, but here again I have tried, by a system of cross references, to enable the student who may be particularly interested in one country to find papers which deal with the area in which he is interested, but which are more logically placed in the bibliography of another area.

The country which forms the subject of the present chapter includes roughly what is generally known as the " Near East " and the " Middle East," and part of South-East Russia. Much of it was formerly included in the old Turkish Empire, now divided under various groupings. As the older divisions are more familiar it may be convenient to adopt them ; they include, Anatolia, Cyprus, Mesopotamia, Syria, Arabia, all of which formed part of the Turkey in Asia, although Cyprus had been administered by Great Britain since 1878. Armenia now forms a separate province and Irak is included in Mesopotamia. Iran may be said to include Persia and Afghanistan. Finally, the northern part of this area is at present divided into the Turkoman and Uzbeg Republics.

The country has very diverse features, and does not form in any sense a unit, but it possesses certain ethnological features in common which are not shared by other parts of the Asiatic continent.

In this region and in this region only is there direct communication with two continents, and here the ethnological problem cannot be separated from that of Europe on the one hand, and that of Africa on the other. It would appear, however, that here as elsewhere Asia has had a greater influence on its neighbours than the other countries have had on Asia. The mountain ranges in general terms run parallel to the north and the south coasts of Anatolia. They then turn and run in two directions, one series parallel to the Syrian coast and the other east of the valley of the great rivers and finally parallel to the Persian Gulf. The Elburz Mountains are situated to the south of the Caspian Sea, and after curving to the south-east finally join the great massif of Afghanistan. The mountain ranges of Persia are separated from Afghanistan, first, by the depression of the Lut desert, and then after crossing a range which runs north-west and south-east by the desert of Seistan.

Arabia forms a province by itself, the highest portions, with one exception, lying on the west and forming a series of long-drawn-out steps to the Persian Gulf.

Owing to the diversity of the surface features there are considerable differences in climate. Except for the south-west corner of Arabia and the region between the Black Sea and the Caspian, the average rainfall in July is everywhere below one inch. In January the Mediterranean coastal region receives between four and eight inches. Apart from this coastal region and an area of small rainfall in Central-Western Anatolia, the country north-west of a line drawn from Suez to the south-east corner of the Caspian has an average rainfall of between two and four inches. The Mesopotamian region, and the Persian Gulf and the country lying south of the Caspian, between one and two inches, and the rest of the Arabian peninsula and the deserts of Iran less than an inch.

The January isothermal lines run roughly east and west. Anatolia and the region to the east is between the 40–50 degrees, Syria 10 degrees higher and Western and Southern Arabia between 70 degrees and 80 degrees. In July the central region, including the tableland of Arabia, the Mesopotamian plain, Kurdistan, and the Plateau of Iran have a temperature over the 90 degrees isotherm, and actually include some of the hottest inhabited towns of the earth. The extent of mountainous regions, of course, varies these generalizations to a large extent, and in many parts the winters are more extreme on the uplands than an enumeration of the isotherms would indicate.

The vegetation forms, perhaps, a better guide to the conditions under which man lives than a mere enumeration of climatic conditions. Corresponding to the main mountain chains there are large areas of Alpine vegetation; those proportionately largest are found in Armenia, but the longest stretches extend from Tabriz to Meshed, and from north of Kashan to south of Kerman.

There is an area of steppe between Angora and Konia, and south-west of Erzeroum. Otherwise the greater part of Anatolia consists either of cultivated land, or land which is capable of cultivation. The same is true of the Syrian coast and the Yemen. There is a long stretch of this country south-west, almost from Lake Van in Kurdistan. The edge of the mountain region south of the Caspian and the lower part of Mesopotamia is similar and there are areas of oasis in Syria, some of them of large extent. Much of Persia and the Tigris region is steppe, and elsewhere the country is either semi-desert or passes, in the Nefud and Dahna in Seistan and elsewhere in Iran, into true desert.

It will be seen from this that most of the movements must have been north-west or south-east, except along the Syrian coast. There are, however, reasons for believing that considerable changes may have taken place in this region and that roads may have become in some cases less hospitable than they were formerly, and regions once inhabited have now become desert. Most of the regions which seem to have changed appear to have been of an oasis type of culture, and this type is singularly sensitive to its environment; when once control is relaxed it is liable to change rapidly and considerably even without any general desiccation of the area.

The countries in the west which have been most closely connected ethnologically with this area are important. The Mediterranean offers a chain of islands which can be reached even by the most timid mariner. Cyprus and the high mountains near the Anatolian coast are always in sight of one another, and though the Lebanon is only visible at dawn from the island, a short distance at sea will make both lands visible to the mariner. Further to the west the chain of islands is even more continuous. It has happened, therefore, that owing to the biological law that surrounding areas are populated from large central areas, there has been a pressure of peoples from the Asiatic continent to the west. The round-headed peoples from the east have, within a period which we trace fairly exactly, that is since the end of the less well-known Mesolithic period and the earlier Neolithic Period, profoundly modified the population of Malta. This modification is so great that we may almost say that a different race occupies the island to-day from that which occupied it in chalcolithic times. They altered the population of Crete, in all probability during the Minoan Period. Of the other border lands at present we have little evidence to guide us, but there are suggestions that they have at least affected the population. In all this Mediterranean area there are indications that the aboriginal population was akin to the present Mediterranean race. The invaders from Asia changed the population at various times from the Neolithic Period onwards.

It would seem to be reasonable to ask the question whether the Mediterranean area made any return to the Asiatic. At present this question is difficult to answer. I have shown how the Mediterranean race spreads over much of Western Asia. On the other hand, it hardly seems probable that the origin of the Mediterranean race was in the Mediterranean region. Sergi and others believe that the Mediterranean race is akin to the Negro. There are, it is true, certain resemblances, but generally the Negro is so different that this connection can hardly be admitted.

Probably, then, the western road out of Asia has been used in one direction only by migrating peoples. On the outskirts it is true that there appear to have been many and various movements of peoples. The variations in some parts of Western Anatolia are so great that there must have been considerable admixture. The ancient historians also suggest that there were migrations in both directions. These later movements, however, appear to be of slight weight beside the greater racial trend which has been from east to west.

Undoubtedly, there has been at various times a close connection between Asia and Egypt. This country is a narrow trough, and one of the most convenient entrances to this trough is near its mouth. There is every probability that the background of the present and the former population of Egypt, Elliot Smith's Proto-Egyptians, have been in the country for a very long period. Within historic times, however, this type was overlaid by an invader of alien type who is closely akin to the Armenoid race. He appears earlier in the Delta than elsewhere, and there is every reason to believe that this invasion of a racial type into Egypt is exactly similar to the invasion of the same racial type into the Mediterranean islands, although they came earlier into Egypt.

Communications on the east are more difficult. It is one thing to travel in a caravan across a difficult country and quite another to migrate in sufficiently large numbers to change the type of the population. It is true that the pilgrims to Mecca are sufficiently numerous almost to be classed as a racial migration, but it seems as though the types of populations were established long before the Holy Cities were thronged by pious devotees.

The natural ways by which man can penetrate the land

of Iran from the east are restricted. There is a way to the north and north-east. To-day there is a caravan road which leads from Meshed westwards to Tcheran, south of the Elburz Mountains, and there divides, part of the road going to the south, where it divides again and serves Persia on the east and Mesopotamia on the west. The more northerly road runs west from Tcheran to Anatolia, through Azerbaijan. It seems probable that it was through the country traversed by this road between the Turkoman desert and the desert regions of Khorassan that the round-heads came into Western Asia. There runs a road from Meshed to Kerman, skirting the mountains to the south of the former place, but it is unlikely that this is a route which was followed by migrating peoples. Indeed, it is difficult to account for the present distribution of the short-heads in this part of the world under existing geographical conditions. On the whole the great mountain barrier seems to divide the two groups of peoples which mingle in places especially, as we shall see, in the area we are discussing. They must at one time have passed right across Asia, but under what circumstances can hardly be determined at present. If they took the more northerly route, as seems to-day the most likely, we should have expected to find more traces of them than we do in the region north of the Hindu Kush. On the other hand, it is by no means impossible that the period during which the Mediterranean race was distributing itself is so remote and so close to the age of extreme glaciation that the communications, even in Seistan, were open for man to pass without the elaborate organization and specialization which are necessitated by desert travel.

The whole of this area is concerned with the rise and gradual development of the culture on which our Western civilization is based. It is of little concern for our present purpose whether the original mother of our arts was the Nile valley or the valley of the twin rivers, for, as we shall see, their population was fundamentally not different in origin, though the Sumerians were of a different stock. In any case we have the interesting problem to consider as to whether the physical characters of the inhabitants of this area were of the greatest importance in making the beginnings of this civilization possible, or whether geographical or other factors were in the main responsible. It is of interest to note that, on the whole, the Greeks were of the same stock, but that probably the mixture, which made the population of the Near East such a curious blend, took place in Greece later than in the more eastern countries. We must also remember that Egypt had advanced far in her arts before the Armenoid peoples entered into her population, and the Mesopotamian people also contained a large blend of the Mediterranean race. We are, therefore, open to believe, if we consider that racial stock is an important element in contributing to the success of nations, either that the Mediterranean stock was the most important or alternatively the Armenoid, or finally a mixture of the two. It has even been further suggested that there was a Nordic strain at least among the ruling classes. At present we have not sufficient evidence on which to base any theories. It is, however, of interest to call attention to the early racial stocks of the peoples to whom Europe is so profoundly indebted for the beginnings of her culture, and it is the more important because some authorities have advanced very strongly the view that the potentialities of quite other races are really greater than these.

With such general considerations before us we may consider the inhabitants of the Near East in greater detail, always remembering that possibly the geographical conditions to-day may not be quite the same as when man first inhabited the area, and that the region has always been one of considerable turmoil; but that the populations to-day are not very different from those in ancient times of whom unfortunately we have so few relics.

Although for descriptive purposes it is convenient to consider the races which inhabit it as two groups, the inhabitants of Mediterranean Asia and the inhabitants of Iranian Asia, it must be remembered that on the whole the type of population is the same. There are two main stocks, Mediterranean man and Armenoid man; sometimes they are found in a pure state, more often they are mixed. The earlier inhabitants of this area have been found by different authors in one or other of these two types.

The most distinguished writer on this subject in recent years is von Luschan. In a paper published many years ago

(IV. 7), and subsequently elaborated in his Huxley Lecture (IV. 2), he put forward the suggestion that the earliest inhabitants of Asia Minor belonged to the type which he called Armenoid, a name that has now passed into anthropological literature. He supposed that Mediterranean man was a later comer. Von Luschan was inclined to see in these round-headed peoples the tribes who were responsible for the *issos* and *andros* terminations in place names, which are associated with many parts of the mainland of Asia and Greece.

He connected these peoples with the various heterodox sects which are found not only in Anatolia but also in North Syria and Mesopotamia. All these sects are remarkably homogeneous in their composition, and the statistical treatment of von Luschan's figures confirms his statement that we are dealing with a remarkably homogeneous race in an area where most of the peoples are extremely mixed.[1] Most of these communities are endogamous, and have by continual intermarriage succeeded in avoiding the excessive mixing which all the peoples in their neighbourhood have acquired. How far this endogamous condition has been enduring it is impossible to say, but it presumably must date from comparatively early times.

It is possible that these strange communities may have been endogamous before the advent of Christianity, and heretics before the days of heresy. Otherwise it is difficult to see how they could have kept their purity of type. Von Luschan would see in them the scattered relics of the earliest inhabitants. He believes that the later comers were of Mediterranean stock and that they mixed for the most part with the population, and these communities alone remained of the old stock.

If this is so, the original formation of these communities must be of very ancient date. Already in the Bronze Age it seems that both stocks were present in parts of Anatolia. The earliest inhabitants of Cyprus, of whom we have any definite traces, are almost certainly a mixed stock, formed of the elements of Mediterranean and Armenoid man. Although it seems not improbable that there was a Neolithic

---

[1] The standard deviations of the cephalic indices calculated from von Luschan's figures for Lycia are: Turks 5·2, Greeks 6·9, Bektasch and Tadchadsky 2·8.

Age in Cyprus, no relics of this age in the form of human skeletons have been discovered up to the present. I examined a number belonging to various periods in the Bronze Age. They seemed to me to differ in no essentials from the modern inhabitants of the island. If then the aborigines had already been swamped by Mediterranean man at this comparatively early date, the formation of the homogeneous communities must already have begun, a difficulty which it is hard to overcome. Both races were existing more or less side by side at Kish at a very early date. It seems, however, not improbable that the Sumerians belonged to the Armenoid race, and the view which traces the Sumerians from the Turkestan region may possibly be confirmed when we have further definite evidence from the excavators. (See page 103.)

It seems, therefore, on the evidence which we have at present, difficult not to believe that the aborigines, at least in Western Asia, were of Mediterranean stock. There seems to have been a movement of Armenoid peoples in early times towards the west. They reached Malta in the Bronze Age, ousting the Mediterranean stock who were there in chalcolithic times. It seems probable that there are also traces of these same people as far west as Anghelu Rhu in Sardinia. Their further extension to the west, which seems probable, need not be further discussed here. Colonies appear still to survive on the North African coast. They are there surrounded with people from a different stock. In Malta, however, I was impressed by the fact that they had definitely ousted the previous population and, in spite of a continuous influx of Mediterranean man throughout historic times, had maintained their racial features, in some districts even with a fair degree of purity. In one village (Siggewe) the standard deviation of the cephalic index of 80 males was only 2·95.

Hasluck (IV. 8) appears to be of opinion that much of the racial admixture and the present distribution of the racial types in Western Asia are of comparatively recent origin. After discussing the identification by von Luschan of the coincidence of religious beliefs and anthropological types, he continues: "The locality in which this anthropological type [the Armenoid,] is most frequent is the mountainous bridge-land which lies between the fertile countries of Anatolia, Persia, Mesopotamia, and Syria. This bridge-land has never been civilized, though it has been penetrated at various times by missionaries—religious, political, and military; in particular, being the old border land between Turkey and Persia, it was naturally the resort of Persian emissaries during the long wars of the two nations. The result of the presumed religious propaganda carried on from the side of Persia among still pagan nomads, Kurdish or Turkish, possibly also among Armenian Christians, is a patch-work of religious compromises of which the outwardly pre-dominating elements are Shia Islam, and Armenian Chris-tianity, among a people of marked physical homogeneity. A certain proportion of these peoples have migrated west-wards, as probably in other directions, either from natural causes or under pressure of artificial transplantation which was carried out in the sixteenth century by the Ottoman Government as a means of breaking up the solidarity of the border tribes known to be Shia in religion and consequently in sympathy with Persia. The emigration processes have gone on for centuries, the emigrants from the mountainous bridge-land sometimes amalgamating with the men of the plains under the influence of a prevalent civilization, some-times keeping themselves aloof owing to religious and other differences. The bridge-land type when found in the west may thus represent immigrations of widely different date, ranging from remote antiquity to comparatively modern times."

While not denying that there have been comparatively recent immigrations, it seems probable that the bulk of the population was in ancient times not unlike what it is at present. It is, however, more than likely that some of the homogeneous groups, some of which von Luschan pre-sumably considered to be the aborigines may, on the contrary, be the last-comers.

Many have suggested that there is a third element in the population, Nordic. The latest supporter of this theory appears to be Peake (IV. 9), who in an interesting paper on the racial elements at the first siege of Troy, suggests that about 2000 B.C. there was an invasion from the north-west of xanthochrous, long-headed tribes like the modern Kurds, i.e. Nordics. He suggests that some of these steppe folk sacked Hissarlik and proceeded to the grassy plains of Central Anatolia, while the remainder skirting the coast of the Ægean found their way to Thessaly and settled in the plains of Larissa. He says that one skull from Thessaly described by Duckworth in *Man*, "judged by the illustration, might well be Nordic." In this view he has followed von Luschan also, who saw in the Kurds representatives of the Nordic race.

Whatever their origin may have been, we find at present in Asia Minor several different types of population. There are first, a mixed type, with an extremely high standard deviation, especially of the cephalic index. This suggests that they are a compound of a long and a short-headed type of population. This mixed population is found especially in towns and on the sea-coast, where in some cases there is a definite tendency towards dolichocephaly. The pure round-headed type is found in the mountains and swampy districts. Cyprus (I. 13) has a mixed population in which the two types are blended. The standard deviation of the cephalic index in Cyprus is on the living about 4·1, while that for Crete is 4·24 ; as a strong contrast in the Lycian gypsies measured by von Luschan it is 2·83. It is of interest to note that within the former island there is evidence of local types. This variation is, no doubt, due to different mixings having taken place. I found that by crossing the mountains in Cyprus and travelling from the Bay of Salamis to the north coast, a leisurely day's journey, that the two populations were dissimilar. They were, however, closer to one another than to groups outside the island.

It is probable, therefore, that when we come to have exact data for the mainland we shall find there also a series of local types in addition to the religious sects of whose physical type we have already a few accurate measurements.

In Cyprus there is no appreciable difference between the Bronze Age people and the moderns, although the data is scanty. Here, again, it seems reasonable to argue from the island to the mainland, but at present we can do no more than say that the odds seem to be in favour of a similar population having existed in early times, as is found in Cyprus to-day.

There remain to be considered the three nations of this

PLATE III

CYPRIOT PEASANT
(A typical Armenoid)

[face p. 94

region which have, owing to their historical importance, become very familiar to the West : the Armenians, the Jews, and the Arabs. We have already seen how with our present knowledge it would appear that there is a mixed population in Western Asia. This mixed population clearly is independent of nationality, including as it does Greeks and Turks, and other peoples. In spite of this fact, however, it must be remembered that our data is very scanty, and that there is among the Turkish peasants a type which it seems possible sometimes to recognize, but which, so far, has not been classified by anthropologists. It is possible that there may be traces of eastern or Tatar blood among the Turks. The Turks in Cyprus are certainly physically not distinct from their Greek neighbours, whether they are in the mainland yet remains to be seen; so far no observer appears to have been able to make this distinction.

The case of the other nationalities is equally difficult. It is of course easy to detect racial traits, but it is more difficult to decide whether they are of fundamental importance. There can be little doubt that among the true Armenians there is at least an admixture of blood which must be classified as Mediterranean. An Armenian skull which was recently presented to the Anatomy Department in Oxford, with complete data as to its provenance, is certainly of this type. It would appear, however, that this is not the normal type. The mean Armenian type has a head which has a length of about 182 mm. on the living, and is absolutely and relatively short. The breadth is both absolutely and relatively great, the mean being certainly over 150 mm., and some authors would make it as high as 159 mm. The cephalic index is therefore very great, the means of different authors running from 83 or 84 to as much as 87. The head is a large one, and is high as well as broad. The bizygomatic breadth, which in Cyprus was found to be one of the most constant characters, is 136 mm., a measurement which is almost identical with that which I obtained in Cyprus. I also found that on the whole the bizygomatic breadth did not serve to distinguish the different local races in Cyprus. It is clearly then a character which will be of little service in distinguishing types in this area. The nose is high and relatively narrow, although there is evidence to suggest that the absolute breadth may be great. The nasal index is low and the nose itself is very prominent. The stature is sometimes high, but is usually between 165 and 167 cms. mean value. Although on the whole the type is *brunet* there is often what Weissenberg has described as an appearance of blondness. The eyes are usually brown, but hazel occurs, although somewhat rarely.

In general terms it will be seen that the type coincides closely with what we have described as Armenoid; von Luschan, therefore, appears to have been justified in his use of the term, although we must make the proviso that, certainly among Armenians, the Armenoid physical type is by no means universal. I have not been able to find any data which could be reduced to statistical form, so we cannot say at present how far they are mixed. There are, of course, Armenians scattered well outside the province which bears their name and which has been a thorn in the flesh to so many administrations from the Roman times onwards, but the question here is of the true inhabitants of Armenia, calling themselves Armenians.

In this country also we find the same type of brachycephalic religious communities, to which allusion has been made already.

If we are justified on the whole in speaking with certain provisos of an Armenian national type, are we equally so in dealing with the Jews? Data concerning the Jews has been collected from many different sources, and they may be said to be, anthropologically, well known. The question is naturally a vexed one, and has been the occasion for many controversies and many different opinions. Most observers profess to see in the Jewish type one of the most persistent varieties of the human race. Others, again, consider that the Jewish type varies in different places, the head-form accommodating itself to the local variety of head-form. "They have," says Ripley, "unconsciously taken on to a large extent the physical traits of the people among whom their lot has been thrown." Boas has affirmed even more strongly that the head-form of Jewish immigrants into the United States alters in conformity with American standards, even in the first generation of immigrants; the physical effects of detention at Ellis Island apparently having a permanent result on the population. Deniker divides the Jews into two types, one approximating to the Arab type, the other to the Assyroid. He admits that the types have been modified to a certain extent by elements from the populations among whom they dwell, but he adds: "Even in these cases, many traits, such as the convex nose, vivacity of eye, frequency of erythrism, frizzy hair, thick under-lip, inferiority of the thoracic perimeter, etc., show a remarkable persistence."

These two views are then totally opposed, and some form of reconciliation is necessary if the evidence can be interpreted in such totally different ways. Up to the present no evidence has been forthcoming to support Professor Boas' interesting hypothesis, and it has been strongly combated on other grounds. The evidence so far adduced by recent writers confirms the stability and importance of the cephalic index without, perhaps, giving it the pride of place that the ardent followers of Retzius would have granted it. With comparatively few exceptions, for exceptions do occur, the Jews from various parts of the world usually retain the characteristic brachycephalic head-form, their mean cephalic index being about 81. What, perhaps, is still more remarkable is they all have a very similar standard deviation of that index, usually between 3 and 4. Few cases occur below that limit, and rare cases above. This constant variation is not a little remarkable. It suggests that these communities which tend to be endogamous remain in about the same state of ethnic equilibrium, although they are placed in extremely different environmental conditions. But not only do the Jews retain their head-form in the majority of cases, they also preserve the other characters which Deniker has mentioned, the most noticeable of which is the form of the nose.

For some reason or other the Jews have been able with a remarkable vitality to perpetuate a physical type which has, at least in many places, survived to a marked degree. The origin of this type is therefore of particular interest. It is clear that there is a marked resemblance between Jews and Armenians and, though the Armenoid type perhaps predominates, there are clearly other elements in the composition of the Jewish race. Weissenberg suggests that the resemblance of the Jews and the Armenians is due to a mixing during historical times, not in Palestine but in the Caucasus. He suggests that here a blond element was introduced, with the result that there are two types of Jews, the Semitic dark with a fine nose, and an Armenoid with a coarser nose and an appearance of blondness.

The figures which have been published suggest that there are at least two types of Jews, owing, clearly, to the different admixture which has taken place. I have suggested above that the mean cephalic index is about 80 or 81, it is interesting to note that the mean cephalic index of the Greeks is about the same. If, however, the latter are analysed it appears that this mean value is actually illusory, because there are really two types which are welded together more or less imperfectly. The two types seem to be Mediterranean and Armenoid man. It seems not unlikely that a similar mixing has taken place among the Jews and that the resulting index represents a composite figure. It is remarkable that the most brachycephalic Jews (the Grusinian and those from Samarqand) (IV. 20) show the greatest variation[1]; possibly they have the greatest admixture of Armenoid blood from mixing among the peoples with whom they live. Those from Daghestan are also very brachycephalic, but I have not been able to discover their variations. The most long-headed do not appear to be either less or more variable than the others. It is, however, worthy of notice that those who have the least variation of the cephalic index have a cephalic index of about 80 or 81, suggesting that in certain cases the mixed type succeeds in eliminating the extreme variations, a result which needs further confirmation. The nasal index is always so variable and is so liable to be affected by climatic conditions, that the difference between the mean values is probably not of racial significance even in spite of Weissenberg's suggestion.

If we adopt the suggestion that the Jews are a composite race, the differences in the cephalic index at once assume less importance since, in such a race, a further degree of admixture will naturally have a greater effect than such an admixture will have in the case of a purer race. Nor is it by

---

[1] The standard deviations of the cephalic index are, Grusinians (71) 4·2, Samarqand (100) 4·1. A hundred South Russian Jews had as low a figure as 2·48.

any means certain that the cephalic index is the most marked characteristic of the Jewish race. The other features which have been mentioned seem to be almost more persistent in their survival. The characters which they present most frequently certainly suggest a predominance of Armenoid blood, but there is undoubtedly an admixture of Mediterranean blood. That they have mixed, to a certain degree, with other races in various parts of the world is certain, and the mixed nature of their origin would account for many of their variations, while generally, as a type, they seem to be markedly persistent.

The third national type, the " Arabs," now remains to be considered. The association of the Arabic tongue with Islam has made this matter more difficult, especially since many peoples call themselves Arabs, although they may be very different in physical type in the same way that many peoples call themselves Turks, although they had but little Turkish blood in their veins.

The term Semite has often been used in a racial as well as in a linguistic sense, and perhaps even more than in the case of the much-abused term Aryan ; it is sometimes used to mean Jews, sometimes Arabs and sometimes in the much wider sense to signify those who speak Semitic languages. In other cases it is employed in the semi-racial sense to mean the descendants of the Arab conquerors who spread over North Africa in the Year of the Elephant (A.D. 570) and later. I have met men who claimed to be Arabs who were certainly of stocks closely allied to those of Europe, others again who were almost pure negroes ; others were, for the most part, Malays, and some presented to the outward gaze little difference from the Chinese. All of them spoke Semitic languages. A term, therefore, with so wide a connotation cannot be conveniently used for racial distinctions when we are dealing with race from the purely physical aspect.

To-day we have the Jews and the Arabs living side by side in Palestine, and the contact between the Arabs and the inhabitants of Arabia and those of Syria has always been close. For reasons which will appear later, I propose to discuss Mesopotamia before I describe the inhabitants of Arabia, not only because the history of the two countries is closely linked, but also because the problems raised by the ethnology of Arabia can be more easily understood when that of Mesopotamia has been discussed.

In addition to the people who have already been discussed, there are found in Syria, as in Asia Minor, certain religious communities which have preserved the pure Armenoid type, the best known being the Druses and the Maronites of Mount Lebanon.

There are also groups of the Metwali, living in the valley of the Leontes, who have long been inhabitants of Syria. They also seem to have similar characteristics. Such measurements as have been obtained (IV. 15) for them are almost exactly similar to those of the Armenians. Chantre calls attention to the extreme flattening of the occiput, which is characteristic both of this people and also of the Armenoids. He concludes that apart from this brachycephalic, all the other characters of the people are those which are usually associated with dolichocephaly, a statement which seems a little difficult to understand.

To the east of, and rivals of, the Armenians are the Kurds. They are probably a very heterogeneous people, although there are few accurate statistical data. They have been most carefully studied by Chantre (IV. 15). Summing up their general characters, he concludes that they have a narrow face, strong chin, and large stature, but it is difficult to obtain an exact figure, presumably because a good deal of variation occurs. Sixty per cent of them are mesaticephalic, but there are enormous variations, according to the different localities, especially where they have come into contact with different peoples. Those in the neighbourhood of Armenia are brachycephalic, whereas those who have had contact with the Persians or the Arabs are dolichocephalic. In another article he remarks that the Yesidi, who are essentially of Armenoid characteristics, are Kurds, and the Kurds of Constanza appear also to belong to this race. It has been suggested that these people, or at least some of them, are akin to the Nordic race. Chantre, however, describes them as being very dark, with eyes of a deep-brown tint. It seems more probable, then, that they also represent another admixture of the Armenoid and Mediterranean races. It should be noted that they practice certain forms of cranial deformation which clearly makes cranial measurements unreliable.

Until recent years Assyriologists have not taken the same interest in human remains as the Egyptologists. The skeletal material which has reached Europe is therefore scanty. The present expeditions in the field are, however, keenly interested in the matter, and it is probable that by the time these words appear in print considerable material will be available.

The whole racial position, however, of the Sumerians and that historical people whom Assyriologists call Semites[1] has been widely discussed. Dr. Günther, in his recent work on the German people (II. 19), puts forward certain theories which appear to be self-contradictory. He states that in the fifth millennium B.C. the Sumerians " with every probability " appear to have been a people with a Nordic upper stratum and a round-headed, flat-nosed—possibly " Inner Asiatic "—lower stratum, and " it may well be that in this upper stratum we have the earliest of the Nordic migrations." The fall [*untergang*] of the Sumerian world was due to the dying out of the creative Nordic upper stratum, a fanciful suggestion which can hardly be substantiated by any appeal to known facts. Günther further believes that this fall was ushered in by the immigration of Semitic-speaking folk of the Oriental,[2] i.e., Mediterranean race, who formed a further stratum over the Sumerians (see p. 284).

On a later page (loc. cit., p. 454) he states that up to the second millennium B.C. Asia Minor, Mesopotamia, and Armenia were racially a unity, and were peopled by the *Vorderasiatische Rasse*, presumably the Armenoid race, a statement which can be clearly disproved by the discoveries of Woolley at Carchemish and Ur, and Langdon at Kish, which will be discussed in detail later. The Nordic blood he believes to have been introduced in the second millennium, and to have become mixed with Fischer's Oriental race, but this statement ignores again the population of the region to the east (see p. 110).

[1] The Assyriologists appear to mean the people who spoke a " Semitic " language and invaded Mesopotamia from Arabia.
[2] This Oriental race, a description of which will be found in Baur-Fischer-Lenz (II. 17), is the Eastern, or rather Middle Eastern branch of the Mediterranean race; it has not apparently received a name from English anthropologists, nor is Fischer's designation happy, as it is apt to lead to confusion, as Günther points out, with Deniker's *Race Orientale*.

If I understand Günther's position correctly, he appears
to believe that the Sumerians belonged essentially to the
Armenoid race. He has only stated with a query the possibility of inner Asiatic influence, and has nowhere, it would
seem, specifically stated what he considers this influence to
be, but his reference to a flat-nosed people suggests that he
had Yellow man in mind.

Dr. Hall (IV. 3, 174) has put forward the very different
hypothesis that the Sumerians were of Indian origin and
akin to the Dravidian peoples, his theory being based
on the resemblance he sees of the facial features on the
monuments and those of some of the inhabitants of India
to-day. Elliot Smith (II. 17, 151) has suggested that "the
old Babylonian sculptures demonstrate the fact that the
earliest Semites to enter Mesopotamia and Babylonia had
the Armenoid type of nose and the characteristic flowing
beard at the time they intruded into the dominions of the
kings of Sumer and Akkad." He goes on to show that these
Armenoid peoples have left modern representatives, who are
commonly known as Semites, but who have no more claim
to that name than the Egyptians have to the name Arab. In
a later chapter he suggests that "the Egyptians, Arabs, and
Sumerians may have been kinsmen of the Brown race, each
diversely specialized by long residence in its own country."
Subsequently he maintains that the Armenoids of Northern
Syria were able to descend the Euphrates and vanquish the
more cultured Sumerians.

His theories have been attacked by Hall as being self-
contradictory. It seems clear, however, that he wishes to
contrast two types in Mesopotamia, an earlier comer,
Sumerian, whom he believes to have been the true bringers of
culture and to belong to the Brown race, and later Armenoid
and uncultured conquerors, who were the Semites.

Physical anthropology unfortunately cannot speak in terms
of Semites and Sumerians. It is, however, possible to state to
what racial types the early inhabitants of the valley belonged.
It is to be regretted this evidence is at present very scanty.
Till recently the earliest skull which has been recovered from
this area was an early Bronze Age skull from the citadel
in Carchemish, which was brought home by Woolley. It
undoubtedly belongs to the Mediterranean type.

A single skull can tell us little of the ethnology of the country, but it is of value as showing that even at this comparatively remote period Mediterranean man was to be found in the Euphrates valley. The excavations of the joint expedition of the University of Oxford and the Field Museum of Chicago have had more fruitful results (and Woolley has recently brought back a number of skulls which have as yet not been described). A series of ten crania were discovered in sufficiently good condition for removal to Oxford.[1] They were unfortunately much damaged, but their general type was clear. The majority of the crania undoubtedly belonged to the Mediterranean group. They were remarkable for their low cephalic indices, which for the most part were well below seventy. The skull from Carchemish already referred to belongs to the same type, and this may finally turn out to be a local variety, when we have sufficient evidence for a detailed analysis of the cranial characters of these people.

In addition to these long-headed peoples the graves from Kish also yielded the remains of a second broad-headed race of a type which must be described as Armenoid. Both types appear to have existed side by side at the time to which these graves belong, which Langdon tells me probably corresponds to the early Dynastic Period in Egypt. He suggests that the Armenoid people are Sumerians and the long-heads "Semites." The evidence is not sufficient to warrant so categorical a statement. It seems probable, on historical grounds, that the Sumerians were for the most part Armenoid racially. Langdon pointed out that one of the characters of the Sumerians on the monuments was the inclined orbits, a feature which has been shown on page 55 to be an Armenoid character. It is also historically true that the Semitic invaders came from Southern Arabia, and that in all probability they were of the long-headed type. There is, however, the third possibility that the original inhabitants of all Mesopotamia were of this long-headed Proto-Egyptian type. From what we know of the distribution of this type this seems the most probable suggestion. When we speak, then, of Sumerians we are speaking

---

[1] A detailed description of these crania will be found in an appendix to Professor Langdon's account of the excavations. I am indebted to Professor Langdon for permission to quote what I have written in this as yet unpublished report.

rather of a cultural than of a physical unity, although it seems certain from the evidence of the monuments that the predominantly Sumerian type was Armenoid.

In lower Mesopotamia on the shores of the Persian Gulf, in the " hot country," Husing (IV. 28) and others have suggested that there may have been in ancient times the remnants of a population akin to the Negroes, and Husing has gone so far as to call them " Negritos." From their representations in art they appear to have tightly curled hair, though as Husing remarks this may not be due to nature, and short strong beards. Their features are also different from those of their neighbours. Husing suggests that their descendants to-day live in the same region, much intermixed with the offspring of Negro slaves. There is, as far as I am aware, no evidence other than this somewhat shadowy testimony about the actual racial position of these interesting people. In any case, it is difficult very often to decide whether there are Negro characters in skulls which may belong to the Proto-Egyptian race, and secondly, the presence of Negro slaves to-day may have changed the original character of the people. The definitely proved presence of indigenous negroids in Western Asia would be of great interest.

As with most countries the physical type of the inhabitants of Mesopotamia does not seem to have changed essentially since early historical times. Ripley states that the Armenoid type occurs to-day in Mesopotamia " sporadically amongst a few ethnic remnants." I do not feel that this is quite a just interpretation of the evidence which we now possess for this area which has increased since Ripley wrote. It would be true to say that certain rather isolated ethnic groups in Mesopotamia, as in the Middle East, appear to preserve this type in greater purity than is the case with the rest of the population. The dominant type in the population, now as in earlier times, is the Mediterranean race. There is, as far as can be judged, also a very considerable infusion of Armenoid blood. The isolated peoples who are described by Ripley as ethnic remnants are more probably later comers, as we have no evidence to suppose that at any time there was a homogeneous Armenoid population such as Ripley seems to suggest once existed in Mesopotamia. It must be admitted, however, that our evidence for this area is still unfortunately far from being complete and any conclusion advanced must be necessarily tentative.

East of the region of the rivers lies the bridge-land which connects Armenia with the plateau of Iran. This region is of greatest interest ethnologically, as it forms the connecting link, albeit a difficult one, between India and the west. Although it is difficult to fix hard-and-fast ethnological boundaries, I propose in the pages which follow to discuss the inhabitants of the region between Armenia and the Indus on the south-east and north-west, and between the lowlands of Turan and the sea on the north and south.

The whole question of the anthropology of the Arabs has been very clearly discussed by Seligman (IV. 23), who has done much to clear up the difficulties which surround this problem. He divides Arabia into three parts, the northern, central, and southern. The first extends to the edge of the Syrian desert and is for the most part desert, with oases inhabited by nomads. The pasturage is inadequate, but there is a certain amount of feed for the animals at some times of the year. I was informed by an Arab who had spent much of his life in this area that it is possible by carefully arranged travelling to keep the animals alive, but that each of the nomad communities are very jealous of the water rights which they possess, a form of jealousy which probably has considerable effect on the formation of local human strains, especially in a people where cousin-marriage was at any rate at one time the rule.

The central part which includes the Hejaz, the Nejd, and El Hasr is a stony steppe, but includes the fertile area of the holy cities, and there are large stretches of alluvial soil and fertile wadies.

Finally, the south consists of the highlands of the Yemen and Asir and the Hadramut. These surround the southern desert, which is very little inhabited. Our anthropological data are limited practically to the north and the south.

Seligman, after examining the evidence, has come to the conclusion that the north is predominantly long-headed while the south is predominantly brachycephalic. He suggests that there has been Mesopotamian cultural contact, and that the brachycephals from Southern Arabia conform in skull-form and facial characters with the Mesopotamian type. He finds on the evidence of coins that this was the case two thousand years ago. He further discusses the Arab type in North Africa which is beyond our present purpose; it should however be noted that he believes that the brachycephalic element may be due to Arab influence. I am however inclined, as I have shown on page 103, to put this introduction of the round heads at an earlier period, while not denying that the later invasions may have had an important effect.

The recent discoveries in Mesopotamia, which I have been discussing in the preceding pages, throw an important light on Seligman's paper. The round-heads from Kish appear to me to be extremely similar to those which he has figured from Southern Arabia. It seems probable, therefore, that we may consider that there was a kinship between the two countries at a much earlier date than was originally supposed. But unlike the population of Southern Arabia, it would appear as if the long-heads were in the majority in Kish, although our evidence at present is too scanty.

Seligman suggests that the round-headed element in Arabia probably reached that country through Mesopotamia. This seems a very probable suggestion but, as we know that the round-heads were pressing into Egypt and into Northern Africa in early times, there is no reason why it should not have come also from the north, even though the present Northern Arabs show less of this element in their features. At present, however, it is impossible till we have further evidence to make anything more than a very tentative suggestion as to the solution of the problem, and to note that in both the directions whence the round-headed element may have come there is abundant evidence of round-heads, but that the population appears to be predominantly long-headed in Northern Arabia.

The figures which Seligman gives make it clear that these round-heads are for the most part typical Armenoids. The population of Northern Arabia presents less difficulties than does that of the south. The dominant element in the population is essentially of the Brown race, and they were in all probability the aboriginal inhabitants of the whole of Arabia.

Unfortunately we have not at present sufficient evidence to state in any way at all how far the two types have mixed. The problem here in Arabia is, therefore, very similar to the ethnological problem in Asia Minor, and the two same racial stocks are also concerned. It will be abundantly clear that we cannot attach any racial type to the term " Arab." We cannot argue from the invasions of " Semites " from Arabia into Mesopotamia what was the type of the Semites or of the Sumerians, because we have both Armenoid and Mediterranean man in Mesopotamia, and we have both types in Northern and in Southern Arabia, although a different type may be said to be dominant in each area.

B. THE PEOPLES OF THE MIDDLE EAST

The area which forms the subject of this section is one that is ill-defined geographically. Politically it includes two independent states and part of Russia and India. Ethnologically, however, mixed as the population is, it forms a convenient and very interesting unit. I have called it the Middle East, but the limits are beyond what is usually called by that name and does not include all the western part of the Middle East. In this section I propose to discuss the inhabitants of Persia, Baluchistana, and Afghanistan on the south, and what are known at present, under the somewhat fluid conditions of politics in Central Asia, as the Turkoman and Uzbeg Republics. In general terms the area may be defined as the region stretching from the head of the Persian Gulf to the northern extremity of the Caspian, and from the mouth of the Indus to Kashgar, the southern boundary being the sea and the northern the Syr Daria. Between the Caspian and the Aral seas there is no boundary, and the whole region is ill-defined.

If we include the Negroid peoples at the head of the Persian Gulf who have already been described, we have here a true *officina gentium* which numbers among its inhabitants representatives of White, Yellow, and Black races, and which, as recent political activities have shown, is closely connected ethnically with all the great empires of Asia. Although the importance of this country to students of the ethnology of Asia cannot be overestimated, it has not been recently studied carefully as a whole, although among the older anthropological works Ujfalvy's studies especially have attempted to show how this region is related to the neighbouring peoples.

Apart from the Turkoman steppes most of the area is elevated, and rises to great heights in the Pamir plateau. Much of it is desert and much extremely hot, although at certain periods and in some places always the more elevated parts of the region approach tundra conditions. East of the great valley of the twin rivers, and connecting the uplands of Western Asia with those of the central plateau, lies a great plateau region, composed, over much of its area, of mountain ranges which are sometimes irregular and sometimes parallel to one another. The latter are separated from one another by broad intervening plains, while the lower regions of the former consist of valleys—in some places fertile—and of deep ravines. The region is bounded on the north by the steppes of Turkestan and on the south by the Gulf of Oman and the Persian Gulf. On the west there is a sequence first of alluvium, secondly of foothills and forest and a series of marginal oases, whose early history and relation to the people of the valley has been succinctly described by Myres (IV. 1, 90 and 119). The fringing country formed the Land of Elam, and the oases ancient and modern Persia, where is found " the intermont plains and upland valleys, which sustained the old Medes and Persians, the first highlanders to play a part in universal history." Beyond lies the desert, much of which is salt strewn, but which in chalcolithic times must have sustained a population. The northern part, bordering on the steppes, also played a part in early civilization, as we know from the great site at Anau near Askabad (III. 2), although this region lies beyond the borders in Turkestan. To the north-east the country rises to the elevated region of Afghanistan, and so connects with the Hindu Kush and the plateau of the Pamir.

Both Afghanistan and Baluchistan are made up very largely of desert; in the latter region the population is everywhere scarce, and there is little cultivation except in the north-west and on the Sind border. In the former patches of fertile land are found in some of the more favoured valleys, and from the point of view of ethnology the contrast in environmental conditions, which varies with altitude, is of great interest. The desert nature of the country is one that should especially be stressed. There is an undoubted ethnic connection through this inhospitable land between the Near East and India, and apart from the difficult question of Huntingdon's theories, it seems necessary to presume a much drier condition at present than in former times. The boundary between India and the territories on the west is of great interest to our present purpose. The northern part of the boundary is guarded by mountain masses which diminish to the low foothills of Mekran on the coasts of the Arabian Sea. Between the Indus and the foothills there is a strip of territory which varies from as much as 200 miles to practically nothing. This strip is extremely arid, although it is intensely cultivated where there is any water. The vegetation decreases from south to north, and as the hills are approached the landscape is made up of stones and bare rock. In the summer the temperature is very great, in the winter the cold is intense, and Vincent describes the means of subsistence of the tribesmen as " a ragful of grain, a handful of firewood, and water from a stream or contaminated pool."

There is a very ancient road from Koh-i-Malik Siah to Nashki and thence south-east to India. Apart from the Khyber and the Bolan passes there are few other ways through the mountains, and there is a long belt of peaks, 10,000 feet high. Desert, then, and mountains guard the road, and it is difficult to-day to trace the way in which the ancient migrations, which certainly occurred, must have followed.

To the north of Afghanistan lies the home of the Turkomans. The environment in which they live has been carefully described by Javorski (IV. 30). They occupy a big territory between the mountainous region of Persia and Afghanistan and the Oxus, the north-west boundary extending from the Aral to the Caspian Sea. Practically the whole of this region is steppe, nine-tenths of it being plain and the rest mountain and upland. The four rivers of the region are the Amu Daria, the Murgat, the Herirud, and the Atrek, but the last two contain little water and the keynote of this region, like the rest of this whole area, is water. The steppe is made up for the most part of loess and sand with a typical steppe flora. The Duab of Turkestan, between the Amu Daria and the Syr Daria, is made up of steppe of a similar character.

The keystone, as it were, of the whole region is made by

the plateau of the Pamirs, the "roof of the world." This whole area is made up of a series of parallel ridges and valleys. The elevation of the floors of the latter average 11,000 feet and the ridges rise several thousand feet above this. Here in this lofty region is the meeting-place of the different races of Asia.

It seems certain that we have in this whole region representatives of Nordics, or, more probably, Proto-Nordics, among the Turkomans; the bulk of the population is certainly Armenoid or Alpine, while there are abundant traces people who are akin to Mediterranean man. To the east of there is contact with Yellow man.

At present there seems to be little evidence about the early inhabitants of the region. As I shall show later, the undifferentiated character of the Turkomans suggests that they are the remains of an early population, but probably they are more to be connected with the region of the steppes than with this region as a whole. It has been suggested that the early home, and possibly the area of characterization of the Armenoids, was in Turkestan. It seems not unlikely that they may have originated in the region we are considering; indeed, it seems difficult at present to account for their distribution without accepting that suggestion. From this region, possibly at the end of the glacial period, the round-headed races seem to have spread out along the central lines of the Eurasiatic continent. It is, in any case, almost beyond doubt that they originated to the north of the great central massif, and their distribution along it would suggest that their original home was not far to the north. Probably these movements of the round-heads, which resulted in their present distribution, began at an early date, and I am inclined to think that the population of Central Asia was not very unlike what it is at present when the great movements took place in the third millennium B.C., to which Haddon appears to attribute some of the features in the present population of this region. However, such a question must remain purely a matter of conjecture till the spade of the archæologists has given the student of palæo-ethnology more material on which to work.

The ethnology of the region presents particular difficulties, because the races here seem to be very mixed and also to belong to what appear to be the undifferentiated stocks, which in the west are more clearly recognizable. Ujfalvy was inclined to see only two different types, a long- and a short-headed. It seems as if the grouping must be further elaborated.

The long-headed people include various branches of the Mediterranean-Brown race. Some of them are apparently akin to the so-called Pre-Dravidians of India, whose racial affinities are discussed on page 136. Haddon believes that there are traces of these people in Susiana, and Holdich (II. 10) appears to suggest a not dissimilar type in Baluchistan. The exact racial position of these peoples is, however, little known at present. There is, on the other hand, abundant evidence of the presence of people who are closely akin to the present Brown man of Western Asia, and possibly the distinction between the groups is insignificant. Such people are found in the south-west of Persia, especially the Lori in the neighbourhood of Persepolis, and indeed this type may be said to be very general among the Persians.

The Azerbaijani also probably belong to the same group. In all these cases, however, it is extremely likely that there is some alien admixture. It is more than probable that the mixing is due to the presence of Proto-Nordic blood. These latter are characterized by high stature, big-boned build and relative fairness. On the Turkoman steppes we find this type extremely well represented. Javorski (l.c.) found that they were tall in stature, about 169 cms. in the males with a mean cephalic index of 76, although this figure is very variable, the limits being 69 and 82. The head is absolutely long and large, the glabello-occipital length being 193 mm. and the breadth 146 mm.; 45 per cent of the eyes were found to be brown and 14 per cent light grey. It is often extremely difficult in this region to distinguish the two long-headed groups, especially where admixture has taken place, but on the steppes, where the Turkomans seem to have preserved the pure type, the distinction is very clear.

This same type appears to be found also on the highlands to the east. Among the peoples of the Hindu Kush and of Afghanistan there also is found a tall, dolichocephalic type of man. They have been called Indo-Afghan, Indo-Aryans.

and by other names, but it seems that in general terms we may classify them with the Turkomans. It is more than probable that in many, if not most, places they are mixed with other elements, but their main features seem to be unaltered.

Attention should here be drawn to the terminology which is found in the textbooks and which is apt to cause confusion to the student. The Turkomans are usually described as being mainly " Iranian in type." But the term has several different connotations. Ripley clearly defines it as being similar, if not identical, with his Mediterranean type. But Ujfalvy had already used it to mean the round-headed peoples yet to be described. Haddon has returned to the older use of the term, and it is in this sense that it must be used. Even, however, in Ripley's sense it is not entirely satisfactory, as it fails to distinguish clearly between the different types of long-heads.

I have therefore adopted Haddon's term of Proto-Nordic for these steppe peoples and their representatives in other parts of this region, for it is probably here better than else-where that the undifferentiated type from which the Nordic sprang has survived. Many writers, especially in recent years Myres and Peake, have drawn attention to the steppe region which they postulated for the area of characteri-zation of the Nordic race. Here on the Turkoman steppes these conditions are excellently fulfilled. Whether these were the original steppes on which the race began is at present hardly to be discussed, as the archæological evidence is too deficient.

There remains the very important round-headed element in the population. We find here, as is often the case else-where, that the round-headed peoples are more abundant on the uplands than on the plains. In the region of the Hindu Kush and the Pamirs the population is extremely round-headed, especially among such people as the Tajiks. The stature is often fairly high, possibly due in many cases to admixture with Proto-Nordics. The degree of fairness also varies. On the figures given by Ujfalvy there seems to be a definite correlation between the tall statures and the fair-ness of the skin. This would accord well with the suggestion that there is an admixture of Proto-Nordic blood. The most round-headed people are the Tajiks of Ferghana and some of the Galtchas.

The exact relationship of these round-heads to those which we have already studied presents considerable difficulties. The extreme form of the head seems to suggest the presence of Armenoid man. In many other ways, however, the people seem to possess characters which would link them up with the true Alpine race.

The very frequent occurrence of fairness might be attributed to an admixture with Proto-Nordics, but in many cases the people who are comparatively fair present none of the other Proto-Nordic characters. It must, however, be remembered that in Europe at least the Alpine peoples are relatively fair. There is therefore no actual difficulty in supposing that this fairness may not be one of their characteristics even in this Central Asiatic region. It is difficult at present, however, to account for the fact that our evidence seems to point to the presence of both groups of the round-heads. There seems to be two ways out of the difficulty. One possible solution is that we have here a mixture of two different branches of the same race. The other solution, and it is one which the present evidence would rather seem to justify, is that here in the Pamirs we have surviving remnants of the undifferentiated stock from which the two groups both sprang. In other words, we ought, though I should hesitate to do so until we have more evidence on the subject, possibly to describe the Iranian peoples as Proto-Alpine. This round-headed type is that for which the name Iranian should be reserved. Ujfalvy (IV. 31) considers that the Galtchas and the mountain Tajiks are the purest representatives of this type in Central Asia. He draws attention to their three most important characters—their moderate stature, their chestnut hair, and their extreme brachycephaly. They are purer in the mountains than in the plains, and, indeed, the plain Tajiks are very much mixed with Proto-Nordic blood.

I have so far been dealing exclusively with what may be described as the Western element in the population. East of the region we are considering this element, as will be seen, may be described as predominant. Culturally, at least, it has played an important part in the history of all the region, and the matter will be made clearer if the general position of the Turks in Central Asia is now examined. The ethnological evidence has been very carefully summarized by Czaplicka (II. 11). She groups the Iranian Turks as follows into six groups. There are first, the Turkomans who have been already discussed. Secondly, the Sarts in Ferghana and Syr Daria, and sporadically in Turkestan. These she believes to have been a mixture of the original Iranian inhabitants (Tajiks) with their Turanian conquerors the Uzbegs. Thirdly, there are the Taranchi or Ili Tatars, an interesting group who will be described when the inhabitants of Sinkiang are discussed (page 173). The fourth group are the Uzbegs in parts of Syr Daria, Ferghana, and in the Khanates of Khiva and Bokhara. She classes the Kipchah in Ferghana with these peoples. The name is purely a political one and is probably derived from Uzbeg Khan of the Golden Horde (1312-1340). Probably they belong to the same ethnic group as tho Kaizak-Kirghiz. These latter live in the north and east part of the Aral Caspian basin and outside our present area in the Orenburg steppes. They are probably related to the Karakirghiz. Finally, there are the Kara-Kalpak, another Turkic tribe of the same group who live in the region of the Oxus, in Kokand and in the Khanate of Khiva.

It is clear that this grouping, while it cannot be accepted from the physical point of view, throws considerable light on the difficult problem before us. We clearly must reject the " ethnic " grouping which is suggested by the Uzbeg Republic, the Uzbegs being comparatively few in number and representing merely a ruling class. The Sarts are admittedly a mixture. There seems to be little evidence about the remainder. They are, however, probably of the same family as Czaplicka states as the Karakirghiz. These people are better known and will be described on page 197. They are akin to Yellow man. It seems, therefore, that we can safely disregard the term Turk when we are discussing the ethnology of Central Asia. The description of the Central Asiatic type given by Ivanoski seems to be a description of a mixture of Alpine blood with Proto-Nordic which, as we have seen, is widely spread among the Turkic and other peoples of the Middle East.

CHAPTER V

INDIA

IN no part of Asia is it so necessary for the ethnologist to study the geographical features as in India, and there are few parts of Asia where the ethnology and geography have been so carefully studied. I have dealt, therefore, with these problems at what may seem disproportionate length, both because of their intrinsic interest and because of the amount of work which has been done on the subject.

Briefly, India may be described as a vast lozenge, divided longitudinally into two halves. It is over a million and a half square miles in extent. The northern aspect is bounded by the loftiest mountains in the world, and the southern flanked by the sea. In the Himalaya the climate approaches that of the Arctic, the north-western desert has records of fantastically high temperatures, the jungle areas are as humid as almost any country in the world. Between these extremes of heat and cold, dryness and humidity, there are most possible combinations of climate, in places varying considerably according to the season. Temperate conditions are on the whole rare, and for the most part, although much of India lies outside the tropics, the climate is of an extreme type.

Although the political boundaries of India stretch from Mekran on the coast of the Arabian Sea to Yunnan and the Mekong, I propose to limit myself to a narrower area. Ethno-graphically, it is more convenient to treat the north-west frontier of India as running along the line of the Indus, from Gilghit, in the north, to the actual mouth of the river.

The eastern ethnological boundary runs, roughly speaking, along the mountains in a north-easterly direction from Chittagong, along what is the divide between the Brahma-putra and the Irawadi, or, speaking in political terms, the eastern boundary of Assam. I am therefore excluding the north-west frontier province and Burma, but including the rest of India proper.

The area then to which this chapter is devoted extends from the Himalaya on the north to Cape Comorin on the south. It is divided into two parts, the boundary being formed by the Vindhya Mountains. The only practical way into the southern part lies through the northern, but the older geological formations of the south differ both geographically and ethnologically, and deserve separate treatment.

The northern part of India is bounded on its northern aspect by a vast elevation of land surface which radiates, as it were, from the Pamirs and forms a series of mountain ranges connected by high plateaux. The Himalaya, the highest of these ranges, forms the actual northern boundary of India, and has always been one of the most impassable barriers in Asia. This great range cuts off the plains of India from the now barren plateaux of Central Asia. Within the region we are considering, from Srinagar to the valley of the Brahmaputra, a man may hardly pass the barrier ; only by the Chumbi Pass is there any convenient access, along the old road which leads to Lhasa, but even this road is no easy highway. The ways into India are therefore along the north-west frontier and those comparatively easy ranges which form the boundary of Assam. The western elements in the population must have come by the former and the eastern by the latter.

Immediately south of the Himalaya lies the great Indo-Gangetic plain. Here is Hindustan proper, which includes part of the Himalayan system, the great alluvial plains, and the broken central plateau of Malwa and Bundelkhund. The mountain area, which consists of two ranges, not a single chain, communicates in the west directly with the interior of Asia by a series of fertile valleys, Kashmir, Kulu, Dehra Dun, but to the east the mountains are cut off from the lowlands by the unhealthy region of the Terai.

Apart from the broken country which we already alluded to, the plains consist almost entirely of alluvium. The Indus rises north of the Himalaya, but thirteen hundred miles of its length is in India, where it flows in a southerly direction, apt, especially in the old days, to behave as the rivers of

China and to change its course. The Ganges flows almost parallel with the mountains for nearly fifteen hundred miles. It is joined by the Brahmaputra just before it enters the sea. Between them these two rivers form a delta which is 50,000 square miles in area. The two great river systems are separated by the Aravallis, to the west of which mountains there is a strip of desert which was formerly watered by the Hakra, a river which has now vanished.

The climate of the two valleys offers a great contrast. The Indus flows through a hot, dry country. Along the lower reaches cultivated areas are only found comparatively near to the river itself. The population has always a small density in this area, and contrasts strongly with the Ganges valley. Here the climate is humid, the vegetation luxuriant, and the number of persons to the square mile exceedingly numerous. The rainfall then forms one of the most important features which attract the notice of the student of the ethnology of Northern India, and it is possible with Crooke to divide the people into three groups—those who dwell in an area of insufficient rainfall, which passes sometimes into true desert, those who dwell in the area of the deltas, and those who live under the intermediate conditions of the higher valleys. By far the greater number of people live in the humid alluvial region, either in the deltas or in the valleys above the deltas. The occupation of a vast majority is agriculture.

The southern part of India is divided from the north by the deep trench through which the Narbada flows, the Vindhya Mountains thus forming the southern boundary of the Hindustan. The division is, on the whole, marked by a broad belt of hills and forest. To the east the Mahanadi forms a boundary similar to that of the Narbada on the west, but its course is more winding. The peninsula is of an older geological formation and differs thus both in its structure and for the most part in the types of people who inhabit it. There are, however, some curious cases of Himalayan flora, and possibly fauna, in the south. The boundary is by no means so absolute as that which shuts in Hindustan on the north. In the west and the centre the passes are easy and form an easy path for invaders, a fact strikingly demonstrated by the southward extension of the Mahrattas. To the east matters are somewhat different, and Chota Nagpur and the Santal Parganas have formed a place where jungle tribes may and have taken refuge.

Whereas most of the north is alluvial, the Deccan consists of a high-terraced plateau, sloping from west to east, so that, with the exception of the Narbada and the Tapti, at its northerly limit all the important streams flow into the Bay of Bengal. The Western Ghats form a high escarpment on the west, leaving only a small belt of plain between the mountains and the sea. The eastern plain is broader, and on the south-east there are the comparatively broad plains of Madura, Ramnad, and Tinnevelly.

The Ghats themselves are raised above the general level of the plateau, the greatest depression being in the region which is drained by the Kistna. The general surface may be described as a level plain, out of which there rise series of isolated hills. On the western border the surface is diversified by spurs which extend from the Ghats into the plain. This plateau region is bounded on the south by the Nilgiris where, for the most part, the scenery consists of rolling grass covered down, which is broken by patches of dense jungle.

This necessarily brief account does not do justice to the great diversities of natural conditions which affect man in the southern part of India. Although nowhere are the conditions as extreme as in the north, yet the Western Ghats form a blanket which absorbs much of the south-west monsoon, making the rainfall on the coast considerable, and in parts of the plateau very low. The hilly region, however, north of the Godavari has in places a mean annual rainfall of over sixty inches. There are also very considerable differences in vegetation, varying with the rainfall and the basic scenery. The population is nowhere as dense as in the valley of the Ganges nor, speaking generally, as low as the desert area outside the sphere of influence of the Indus. Speaking very generally, the differences between different areas are smoothed out and the southern part of India has a population which may probably be compared to much of China proper, other than the extremely densely, or extremely thinly populated parts of that empire.

The northern boundary has been already discussed. It would have seemed at first sight more logical to have discussed the southern boundaries at the same time, but I have reserved this discussion to the end because this position more clearly brings out the peculiar position of the country. Southern India is a cul-de-sac whose only outlet is the relatively small island of Ceylon, which is ethnologically closely linked up with it. There is no escape for any people who may once pass out of the Indo-Gangetic plains, unless they return by the way in which they came. They must either hold their own against any waves of immigrants which may press upon them, emigrate by sea, or die out. In this way, although there are numerous traces of what may well be called aboriginal populations in the north, such peoples form the dominant feature of the south.

If Peshawar, Gorakhpur, and Nagpur be joined, the triangle so formed on the map will include the principal wheat areas, which extend down the Narbada and the Tapti to Amraoti, and down the Indus to Kanpur. Rice forms the staple food of those who can afford it over most of the south and east country. Its typical home in India is the great valley areas of the Ganges, the Mahanadi and the Godavari. The valley of the Kistna is also a vast rice-growing tract, and Tanjore may be similarly classified. But rice is grown especially in the south wherever it can be grown by means of irrigation, and attempts are made to make it grow, even where the crop often fails. The jungle tribes grow rice where they can, and some of the Mundas are skilful makers of terraces, not unlike those found in Eastern Asia. From the economic point of view it is interesting to note that the west coast is attempting rapidly to substitute commercially valuable crops, such as cocoa-nut, tobacco, spices, pepper, and so on. But the population here is not self-supporting, and imports rice from Burma. Dry grains are grown over much of India, especially where conditions for growing rice are unsatisfactory. The type of grain varies according to the geographical conditions. The natural vegetation needs little comment. It varies from a desert flora to a dense equatorial forest. Although, to a certain extent, man supplements his fare with wild produce, when owing to the failure of his crops he is driven to depend on the jungle, he is then brought to the verge of starvation.

With these geographical features before us it will be clear that man in India is exposed to widely different climatic conditions. In some parts he has been isolated for long periods in regions which can never have been easy to traverse. In others he has been open to continual disturbance and to outside influence. In the former it seems not improbable that the climate has had opportunities to stamp itself upon the bodies of men, in the latter the most potent factors appear to have been the little understood influences of racial admixture. But isolation and contact with outside races are not the only influences which have played an important part in the building of the present races of India.

The influence of geographic environment can be very conveniently studied in India and opens a wide field of research which has been at present but little traversed. The direct influence of climate cannot but strike every student of the peoples of India. There is a great contrast, for instance, between the inhabitants of the great river valleys of the north, the high plateau of the centre and the jungle and hill tracts of the south. But climate has had an indirect as well as a direct effect ; it has, for instance, ensured different types of food supply, and even the jungle peoples only exist on the natural products of their forest homes in time of famine. Most of them, however, probably supplement their stock in this way. On the plateau of the Deccan the basis of the food supply is millet, in the Punjab the most important grains are wheat and barley. The peoples of the humid, warm valley of the Ganges use, as do their kinsmen of Eastern Asia, rice as the staple of their diet.

We shall see in the sequel the very great importance of these direct and indirect influences of climate on the peoples of India. It is of importance to point out here that, as far as we know at present, heredity is a potent factor which is at least equal to, if it does not dominate, all other factors combined. We shall expect to find, therefore, that those races which have been longest under the influence of certain climatic conditions are most in equilibrium with them, and that features which may be justly accounted to be the direct result of certain environmental conditions have become in the course of ages features which may be justifiably called racial. We may, therefore, find two types, for instance Kondhs and Mundas, dwelling side by side, both, it may be, of the same stock, or of very different origin. One may, owing to the time that it has occupied the area, be eminently fitted to the conditions experienced there, whereas the other, a more recent arrival, still preserves many features in common with the parent stock, living possibly under very different conditions.

Although, as far as possible, I have endeavoured to make but small reference in this book to sociological factors in determining ethnographic features, it is hardly possible to do this in India. The caste system with all its complexities is in part at least as interesting to the student of the human frame as it is to the student of human manners. The subject is naturally a very difficult one, but in the main outline the following features of the system seem most important for our present purpose.

In general terms caste may be defined, as Richards (V. 14) has suggested, as the " endogamous group." There are very few exceptions to this rule. In Malabar the relationship of Nambudris with Nair girls is not really marriage, but more probably a relic of an old matrilineal condition combined with overlordship. The Nambudri is a kind of " lord of the manor," and in any case—and this is the important point—his progeny by Nair girls are Nairs. This can hardly be considered as marriage. Concubinage which occurs between a man of higher caste and a woman of lower caste is always considered as such, and the converse is, of course, unknown. There are curious and apparent exceptions to the general rule among the Zemindar class, but these cannot be considered of sufficient force to invalidate the general rule. Tabus, other than marriage, are not to our present purpose, and we may say that at present caste produces, at least in theory, a series of endogamous groups. But the conditions which have been given above show that these groups cannot be considered from the purely physical point of view as absolutely preventing the mixing of different strains.

Where we get such a system, even with exceptions, it might be expected that we should find in India less variation from type than we find elsewhere. This, on the whole, does not hold good, partly owing to the fact that caste is not in itself a very ancient institution in its most rigorous sense, and partly owing to the very nature of the caste system itself which is so vigorous a feature of Indian life that it is continually extending itself.

It would seem at first sight as if caste were essentially a means which divided society horizontally, but its extent is wider, and there are what may be called vertical divisions as well as, for example, the castes among Christian converts. Many different types of castes may be distinguished ; but the classification which follows, essentially that given by Risley, will be found a simple division for practical purposes, although there are difficulties in some cases.

First, there is the tribal type of caste. Tribes, by a natural tendency, become castes. It is possible that the Sudras originally represented the whole mass of the early population. We get good examples to-day in the tribes of Chota Nagpur, the Khonds of Orissa, and the Nagas. The tribes of the North-West Frontier seem to show a tendency to become castes.

The second type may be described as occupational. This form of caste is, perhaps, most familiar to Europeans, and trade castes are so numerous as to need no further enlargement. A third type of caste is of particular interest and shows how fallacious a guide caste may be to the ethnologist. This type may be described as sectarian. Every new reformer in India begins by proclaiming that all men are brothers and that there must be no more caste. His followers thereby out-caste themselves, and in the mass of a population who exists by means of castes very soon not only become a new caste, but soon form new sub-castes among themselves. A series of new castes, which may be described as our fourth class, are formed by the crossing of one caste with another. Risley has suggested as a fifth class the " national castes," of which he gives as an example the Newars, a Mongoloid people who were the ruling race in Nepal till the Gurkha invasion of 1769.

Castes may also be formed by migration where a group moves, and by outcasting itself forms in the new home a different caste from that to which it belonged in the old home. Finally, it has been suggested that certain castes may have arisen from change of custom, as, for instance, the Rajputs and the Jats.

There seems to be no doubt that the original meaning

attached to caste was that of colour. This would suggest that the earliest castes were either of the tribal, the national, or the migratory type. These types, if they never mixed, would tend to have a marked influence on the physical type of their members. Even to-day, as we shall see, there often tends to be a difference in physique between some of the castes. Others, again, have a wide difference of type in their members; the great difference between the Brahmans is very striking, but there is an equally great difference between some of the Jats. In the former case, however, it may be objected that the Brahman community, full of sects, often antagonistic to one another, is too big to be called a caste.

Caste, then, without giving a definite ethnological standard, will at least be of assistance in dividing up the complex races of the vast Indian peninsula.

Deniker's classification is unsatisfactory. He says, " The variety of types found in the country is due to the crossing of two indigenous races, Indo-Afghan and Melano-Indian, or Dravidian, with the admixture here and there of foreign elements, Turkish and Mongol in the north, Indonesian in the east, Arab and Assyroid in the west, and, perhaps, Negritoid, in the centre. The Indo-Afghan race of high stature, with light brown or tanned complexion, long face, wavy or straight hair, prominent and thin nose, dolichocephalic head, predominates in the North-west of India. The Melano-Indian or Dravidian race, also dolichocephalic but of short stature, with dark brown or black complexion, wavy or frizzy hair, is chiefly found in the south. In it two sub-races may be distinguished. A platyrrhinian one, with broad flat nose, rounded face, found in the mountainous regions of Western Bengal, Oudh, and Orissa, also at several points of Rajputana and Gujarat. Then in South India and in the Central Provinces to the south of the rivers Narbuddha and Mahanadi, the other sub-race, leptorrhinian with narrow prominent nose and elongated face, may be noted in some particular groups, especially among the Nairs, the Telugus, and the Tamils." He divides the Melano-Dravidians into Dravidians and Kolarians,[1] a purely linguistic division which need not concern us here.

[1] As the term Kolarian is still to be found in many ethnological textbooks, the following note (for the substance of which I am indebted to Mr. Charles

This classification differs very much from some others which have been suggested, and it is, perhaps, best to defer criticism till other classifications have been examined.

The most general classification of the peoples of India, however, is that of Risley, which was first published in the Report of the Census of 1901 and subsequently in his book on *The Peoples of India*. This classification is so important that it must be given in some detail.

Risley divides the inhabitants of India into the following types. His first type he calls Turko-Iranian, who have practically the exclusive possession of Baluchistan and the North-west Frontier.[1] They have broad heads, the mean indices varying from 80 among the Baloch of the Western Punjab to 85 among the Hazara of Afghanistan. The nose is fine or medium, the average indices running from 67·8 in the Tarim to 80·5 in the Hazara. Some individual indices are very high. " The one feature that strikes one is the portentous length of their noses. . . . There are no signs of that depression at the root of the nose and corresponding flatness of the cheek bones to which the appearance popularly described as Chinese or Mongolian is due. . . . Hazaras are an exception . . . it seems possible that they may partake of both types (Turko-Iranian and Mongolian) and represent the points of contact between the two."

The average stature varies from 162 in the Baloch of Makran to 172 in the Achakzai Pathan of Northern Baluchistan. Risley suggests that this type is the result of a mixture of Turki and Persian, and considers that their most marked features are the long hooked nose and the abundant hair and beard.

The second type Risley has called Indo-Aryan. This type

Henderson) may be of service. The term Kolarian was originally invented by Max Müller. It has now been generally abandoned in favour of the term "Munda" from a conspicuous tribe. These people extend south as far as the Godavari on the east coast and are described by Henderson as "distinctly Mongoloid in appearance." Linguistically they are quite different from the Dravidian aborigines among whom they are found, but Grierson appears to have been misled about the nature of their language. There is some evidence that they are immigrants via Assam and the plain of Bengal from Tibet. Henderson comments on the fact that the division between them and the Dravidians is more than purely linguistic.

[1] The ethnical relationships of these people has already been discussed in the last chapter. It is convenient, however, to consider Risley's theory as a whole here.

predominates in Rajputana, the Punjab, and the Valley of Kashmir, though in parts of this area it is associated with other elements. The head-form is invariably long, the average index varying from 72·4 in the Rajput to 74·4 in the Awan, and presents the greatest contrast with the cephalic index of the Turko-Iranian. In respect to the proportions of the nose there is little difference between the two types. The mean index ranges from 66·9 in the Gujar to 75·2 in the Chuhra, On the other hand, the Indo-Aryans, notwithstanding their greater stature, have noticeably shorter noses than the Turko-Iranians. Their faces are free from any suggestion of flatness. Their stature is the highest recorded in India, that of the Rajput 174·8 to 165·8 in the Arora. "The most important points to observe are the great uniformity of type and the very slight differences between the higher and the lower groups. Socially no gulf can be wider than that which divides the Rajputs of Udaipur from the scavenging Chuhra of the Punjab. Physically they are cast in much the same mould, and the difference in mean height . . . is no greater than might easily be accounted for by the fact that in respect of food occupation and habits of life the Rajput has for many generations enjoyed advantages telling directly on the development of stature."

The Indo-Aryans are described briefly as being tall, fair, but with dark eyes, bearded, long-headed with a narrow prominent nose. They are supposed to have immigrated in bulk through South-east Persia.

The next type is the Scytho-Dravidian, who live in a belt of country on the west of India extending from Gujarat to Coorg. They are represented at one extreme by the Nagar Brahmans of Gujarat, and at the other by the remarkable people who have given their name to the little province of Coorg. The head-form varies from 76·9 in the Deshasth Brahman to 79·7 in the Nagar Brahman, and 79·9 in the Prabhus and Coorgs . . . "the predominance of the broad-headed type is unmistakable." Risley has no comment to make on the proportions of the nose. The indices vary from 72·9 in the Coorg to 81·9 in the Mahar. The mean stature varies from 160 among the Kunbis to 168·7 in the Coorgs.

This group differs from the Turko-Iranians in being shorter, having longer heads, higher noses, flatter faces. Risley associates them with the Sakai, and suggests that they came possibly from China. They occupied the grazing grounds of the Punjab and, finding their way blocked to the west by the Indo-Aryans, turned south and mixed with the Dravidians.

The Aryo-Dravidian or Hindustani type extends from the eastern frontier of the Punjab to the extremity of Bihar, from which point onwards it melts into the Mongolo-Dravidian type of Bengal proper. It occupies the valleys of the Ganges and the Jumna, and runs up into the lower levels of the Himalaya on the north and the slopes of the Central Indian plateau on the south. " The type is essentially a mixed one."

The head is long with a tendency towards medium. " The average index varies from 72·1 in the Kachhi and Koiri of Hindustan to 76·8 in the Dosadh of Bihar and 76·7 in the Babhan, but it throws little light on the problem of their origin.

The nose is the most distinctive feature. The average index runs in an unbroken series from 73 in the Babhan of Hindustan and 73·2 in the Brahman of Bihar to 86 in the Hindustani Chamar and 88·7 in the Musahar of Bihar. " The order thus established corresponds substantially with the scale of social precedence independently ascertained. The height causes a similar conclusion. The range is from 159 to 166, whereas that of the Indo-Aryan is from 165·8 to 174·8."

These people are supposed to have entered India by the Gilgit and Chitral passes, without women, and to be descended from Aryans in the male and Dravidians in the female line. They are long-headed but of short stature, and the bottom of the social scale is essentially platyrrhine, in other words, the lower classes have mixed more with the aboriginal type.

The Mongolo-Dravidian or Bengali type occupies the delta of the Ganges and its affluents from Bihar to Bengal. This type is differentiated from the Indo-Aryan and the Aryo-Dravidian by its broad head. The mean index varies from 79 in the Brahman to 83 in the Rajbansi Magh. The mean proportions of the nose vary from 70·3 in the Brahmans and Kayasths to 84·7 in the Mals of Western Bengal, and 80 in the Kochh.

The stature varies from 167 in the Brahmans of Western Bengal to 159 among the Kochh of the sub-Himalayan region. This group Risley suggests has been formed by an extensive

PLATE IV

TAMIL WOMAN

[face p. 126

mixing of Dravidian and Tibeto-Burman peoples. We have here no theory of an immigration but simply a mixing of aboriginal peoples, but this suggestion of a Tibeto-Burman aboriginal race in Bengal needs proof, which Risley does not supply.

These two aboriginal peoples Risley classifies in this way. He finds the Mongoloid peoples along the Himalaya in an area which grows broader from west to east. The prevalent head-form is broad, but the mean indices show remarkable departures from this type; the Jaintia, for instance, have an index of 72. Risley suggests that possibly these variations are due to the small number of persons on whom observations were made. The nose-form has certain variations, but the higher indices come from those tribes among whom few people were measured. In the larger groups the mean index is 67·2 in the Lepcha to 84·5 in the Chakma, and 86·3 in the Khasia. The Gurings have the tallest stature (169·8) and the Mirs the shortest (156·4).

The face of these peoples is flat, the complexion dark with a yellowish tinge, there is very little beard, and the eyes are often oblique.

Finally, the Dravidians are considered by Risley to be the true aborigines of the great Indian peninsula; they live in the oldest geological formation of India, the medley of ranges, terraced plateaux, and undulating plains which stretches roughly speaking from the Vindhyas to Cape Comorin. On the east and west of the peninsula area the domain of the Dravidian is coterminous with the Ghats,[1] while farther north it reaches on one side to the Aravallis and on the other to the Rajmahal Hills. Where the original characters have been unchanged by contact with the Indo-Aryan or Mongoloid peoples the type is remarkably uniform and distinctive. The head-form is usually medium, with a tendency in the direction of length. In South India the Badagas of the Nilgiri Hills have a cephalic index of 71·7 and the Shanans of Tinnevelly one of 76·6. In the same area the nasal index rises as high as 95·1 in the Paniyans of Malabar. In Chota Nagpur and Western Bengal the range of variation is less well marked.

---

[1] This statement of Risley's is hardly correct, for the east coast fishermen (Jalari caste) extend north into the Orissa Bengal country, *along the coast,* which is a historic highway.

Among the Dravidians of South India the stature varies from 170 among the Shanan of Tinnevelly to 153 among the Pulaiyan of Travancore. The complexion is very dark, the hair black and sometimes curly, the eyes are dark and there is sometimes a depression at the root of the nose. These people Risley considers to be true aborigines, now " modified in some degree by an infiltration of Aryan, Scythian, and Mongoloid elements."

Risley's classifications have met with considerable criticism from various writers, and the subject is of such importance that it seems worth while to give a brief résumé of the main criticisms which have been directed against him. First, it has been suggested that it is difficult to believe that there was a movement of Aryan tribes into the Punjab who retained their physical type in spite of the numerous and almost continual foreign invasions. Crooke has also suggested that Risley has, in dealing with this set of peoples, laid too much stress on the cephalic index, and that the Rajputs, for instance, contain other elements. A similar difficulty occurs with the Jats, a difficulty which Risley himself seems clearly to have been aware of. There is one type which is closest to what has been considered the traditional Aryan invader of India. These men are tall with a fair complexion and dark eyes, plenty of hair on the face, a low head and a narrow nose. Crooke meets the argument put forward by Risley that the Huns and the Scyths are brachycephalic, and could not have given rise to the Rajputs and the Jats, by suggesting that there is a Turki type in Central Asia which is possibly " a modified Mongol " (I am not quite sure exactly what the learned author means by this statement) and, secondly, that there are two types among the Tibetans, one a round-headed, flat-faced, oblique-eyed form, approximating to the pure Mongol from the Steppes (most of the " pure Mongols from the Steppes " have not got oblique eyes, but this, perhaps, does not affect the argument), and the other longer-headed with nearly regular features and a shapely long nose, approximating to the Tatars of Turkestan and the nomads of the great northern plateau. He would then maintain, further, that epigraphical evidence suggests that there is a considerable strain of northern blood among the tribes of the Punjab and Rajputana. Secondly, the Rajputs, Jats, and Gujars are ethnically akin, and their physical position depends upon social status, and he would maintain that the position of the Mahrattas is identical. Finally, Crooke suggests that it is inconsistent with the facts of tribal history to trace a Hun or Scythian element in the population of the Deccan.

Again, some writers of the South Indian School maintain that there is a predominance of the Dravidian element in the present population, and suggest that there is a distinction not of race but merely of cult between the Aryan and their Dasyu predecessors.

A further point of great importance which has been urged against Risley is that Thurston's work shows that the Dravidian group is far from being uniform ; and Risley's extension of the word, so as to include both the hill tribes of Central India and a large part of the menial population of the northern plains, has been objected to on the ground that recent linguistic researches have shown that there is a wide extension of the Mon-Khmer type of language across the Indian continent and that it even at one time extended to Further India and Assam. It has been suggested that this and not the Dravidian element survives in the menial population of the northern plains.

In addition to these criticisms which are due to Crooke, Ramaprased Chanda has suggested in his book on the Indo-Aryan races that the broad-headed elements in both Risley's Scytho-Dravidians and in his Mongolo-Dravidians are akin to "Homo Alpinus" of the type which is found to-day, as has been shown above, in the Pamirs.

It will be seen that most of these criticisms, while attacking Risley in detail, do not on the whole tend to invalidate his general position with the exception of the last, which seems to deny the possibility of a Mongoloid element. There are good reasons, as I shall show later, for preferring Risley's original hypothesis to that of his critic.

It will be seen that on the whole the objections to Risley have been levelled rather at his nomenclature, or at his interpretation of historical facts, than at the actual grouping which he has suggested. In most places, though by no means everywhere, the racial stocks date from before the historic period, and there is no reason to suppose that India is an exception to this general rule. Most of Risley's terms, however, apply

K

to comparatively recent and historic peoples, and probably the main type of the Indian population was settled long before these historic movements took place. That there have been earlier peoples in India there is no doubt, and recently Dr. Hunt has presented to the University Museum in Oxford ancient crania from Secunderabad of a different type apparently from the modern population, but unfortunately they are in too bad a condition to be used as valuable evidence. It is clear, however, that the criticisms which suggest that Risley has not allowed sufficient weight to be attached to the different classes of the Dravidian population are of very great importance. It might further be added that the use of linguistic terms when applied to racial divisions is apt to be misleading, and Risley sometimes comes near to Max Müller's famous dictum of the brachycephalic dictionary.

Unfortunately Risley's figures were not reduced to a condition which would enable them to be used by modern statistical methods, and therefore I have only been able to work out constants in those cases which he describes as " type series " and gives the seriations of the measurements.

TABLE I

STANDARD DEVIATION. CEPHALIC INDEX

(CALCULATED FROM RISLEY'S TYPE SERIES)

Standard Deviation =	Under 3·0	3·0–4·0	Over 4·0
Cephalic Index Over 80	M.	M.T.T.T. T.SD.SD.	T.T.SD.
76–80	M.	MD.D.D.	—
Under 76	MD.D.D.IA. IA.AD.AD.	D.	—

M. = Mongoloid, T. = Turko-Iranian, SD. = Scytho-Dravidian, MD. = Mongolo-Dravidian, D = Dravidian, IA. = Indo-Aryan, AD. = Aryo-Dravidian. Risley's type series include several sub-groups, usually castes, within each "race." Thus, for instance, among Scytho Dravidians he gives as type series Nagar Brahman, Prabhu, and Coorg.

This table shows the relation of the standard deviation of the cephalic index to the numerical value of the mean

cephalic index, calculated from Risley's type series of his
various racial groups. It will be seen that the Turko-Iranians
are all brachycephalic, and tend to have medium or big
standard deviations, whereas the Indo-Aryans are long-
headed and have small standard deviations.

TABLE II

STANDARD DEVIATION OF STATURE

Stature	Under 4·7	4·7–5·4	Over 5·4
Over 166	IA.	T.	IA.T.SD.
161–166	AD.T.D.	MD.D.D.D.AD.	SD.SD.MD.
Under 161	D.M.	M.M.	—

The explanation is the same as Table I. Each letter is the
initial of the group to which the sub-group belongs whose mean
stature and standard deviation of the stature is given in the
table. Altogether twenty such sub-groups are included. It
will be seen that there is no particular relation between the
stature and the standard deviation of the stature.

Table I shows the relationship between the cephalic index
of various groups and the standard deviation of this cephalic
index, Table II shows the relationship between the stature
of the same groups and the standard deviation of the stature.
In the former case the relationship is considerable, in the
latter it appears to be slight. There is no similar relationship
in the case of the nasal index, the range and correlation of
which will be discussed later.

It would appear that on the whole the broader heads are
more variable than the long heads, with the exception of two
Mongoloid groups, Chakma and Lepcha, and to a lesser extent
two of the Turko-Iranian groups. Even in the case of the
exceptions there does seem to be a certain degree of correlation.
It may therefore be reasonably suggested that the long-
headed races are less mixed than the others. Such an interpretation would, however, overlook the possibility of long-
headed invaders who, even though they belonged to a different
group, would if they had a similar cephalic index to the race
with which they mixed, not appreciably affect the standard

deviation of the cephalic index, always provided that the mean cephalic index of both groups was not dissimilar. The introduction of a group with rounder heads would at once tend to increase the variation. On this basis we should expect that those groups which represented either a pure long-headed race or a mixture of two long-headed races would tend to have a low deviation. This we find to be the case in the " Indo-Aryans," in a few of the Dravidians, in some of the Mongoloids, all of whom are said to be of pure race by Risley. In some of the Mongoloids the heads tend to roundness, but the deviation is small, but we have found that the tendency of Yellow man is to possess a round head, so that this fact need cause no surprise.

The groups which show the greatest variation include a Scytho-Dravidian, Nagar Brahman, admitted by Risley to be of mixed race, and two Turko-Iranian groups, Jats and Mir Jats. It is clearly impossible to admit these as unmixed groups. The evidence of the cephalic index, which is less than would be expected in such a race, and the big standard deviation suggest that a mixing has taken place, not improbably a round-headed people and a long-headed.

The groups with a medium variation include, first, some of the Turko-Iranians, and here again we may reasonably expect admixture, especially since, except in certain parts of Anatolia, the Armenoid race to which these people belong is usually very much mixed with other races. Secondly, one of Risley's Mongoloid groups, the Chakma, is included in this division. They have a very high cephalic index, higher than is usual among Yellow man, and it seems possible that they should rather be considered as a mixture of Yellow man with the Armenoid type, a possibility which is not included by Risley in his grouping, but a type of admixture which is extremely common in Asia. Secondly, there are a series of groups which are admitted by Risley to be mixed and, finally, three groups of Dravidians.

It should be noted that none of the Dravidians have a standard deviation over 3·5, and that therefore they all tend to be comparatively unmixed; but, as has been said above, some critics have declared that Risley has not paid enough attention to the possibility of sub-groups among the Dravidians.

If we compare these results with that of stature, the results are of particular interest. Those which show the least variation are, with the exception of one, Aryo-Dravidian (Chamār) (United Provinces), all groups considered by Risley to be unmixed. Those with a great variation are considered by Risley to belong to mixed races, except one Turko-Iranian (Baloch), which we have shown might probably be considered as of mixed race, and one Indo-Aryan (Chuhra).

It has already been suggested that in the latter case the mixing might not cause the cephalic index to vary if two dolichocephalic races mixed. In one case, however, that of the Chamar, an Aryo-Dravidian from the United Provinces, we have a striking indication of a pure type of race with little variation both in stature and in the cephalic index. The other races with big variation in stature are all considered to be mixed by Risley. Of those with little variation in stature one, Chamār (United Provinces), is considered by Risley to be a mixed race, the others are considered to be unmixed. Some of the Dravidian groups, two of the Mongoloid, and one of the Turko-Iranian, show a medium variation.

These results confirm the suggestions made by Risley in many ways; they suggest, however, that more mixing has taken place than Risley seems inclined to suggest, especially among the Dravidians and among the Turko-Iranians. They suggest that on the whole the less variable groups are those which are long-headed, and those which are of short stature, but the evidence from our tables is stronger in the former case than in the latter. This being consistently true it seems reasonable to suppose that the earliest inhabitants who have left traces were short and long-headed, but that their shortness was not so marked a feature as their long-headedness.

As Risley has laid a good deal of stress on the nasal index, it seemed worth while to investigate whether the same held true of this measurement also. There is, however, no relation between the value of the nasal index and its variation. The nasal index is, on the other hand, correlated with certain climatic conditions.

The general nature of this relationship has already been explained. In collecting data for the original paper, correlations were worked out on Indian data, and it was found that here, probably owing to the fact that the nasal indices were all taken in the same way, the correlation was higher than for larger groups collected from various authors. On the suggestion of my friend Professor Fleure, I also tested the relationship between the daily range of temperature and the nasal index. This, as was to be expected, is fairly high. A small range of temperature is associated with a broad nose. Such a correlation is the logical result of Thomson's theory, because the daily range in hot moist climates is less than elsewhere. In India the greatest range of temperature is also correlated with the narrowest noses. This correlation serves to explain some of the exceptions to our general thesis. It will be remembered that I have suggested, following Thomson, that the narrow nose is an adaptation to cold and to dryness. The only way that it was found possible to estimate the cold for purposes of calculation was to take the annual means, obviously only a rough-and-ready method. By taking the daily range into consideration, we can at once explain some of the lower nasal indices which appear in what is a hot climate, if we measure by mean annual temperature, but which, at the same time, if measured by the daily range is obviously exposed at times to a cold temperature.

The data then collected seem to indicate very clearly that in India the nasal index is to a certain extent independent of those characters which we may describe as racial, and is ultimately the result of response to environment. It must be remembered, however, that this response is by no means immediate, and that therefore certain types of noses are associated with certain racial types. It seems not improbable that those peoples which have been longest in India have become most closely stabilized in equilibrium with their environment. We should expect to find, therefore, the broadest noses among the lowest castes, among such people as the pre-Dravidians. This is an interesting comment on Risley's dictum that among all the peoples, except the "Mongoloid," nose is a good indication of social status, the lowest castes having the broadest noses. On the whole also it will be found, though of course there are exceptions to this as to every other dictum about India in general, that the lower castes are darker than the upper; indeed, the very word for caste is merely colour. As it seems probable that colour is also related in some

degree to environment, we should expect to find that among
the aborigines, or at least the tribes who have lived longest in
the hot and moist conditions which are found in so much of
India, that the skin was dark and that the nasal index was
high.   In this way we can explain on simple grounds what
appears at first to be an inexplicable phenomenon.

We are now in a position to enquire into the racial stocks of
India, and to try and link up these stocks with the other
races of Asia.   In the first place, there seems little doubt that
at least two, if not three, of the great stocks of mankind are
represented.   First, the various branches of the stocks which
I have called by the somewhat cumbrous title of races akin
to those of Europe.   These appear to form the greatest proportion of the peoples of India.

Secondly, Yellow man is undoubtedly represented, especially
in the north-east of the peninsula.   How far he has travelled
in relation to the whole sub-continent, from the gateway
through which he entered, is at present uncertain.

There seems no reason, with the evidence before us at
present, to postulate the presence of a Negrito strain.   It
would be of great interest and importance if undoubted
Negrito could be found in India.   Some writers, basing their
opinion very largely on the curly hair of some of the tribes
of Central and Southern India, have maintained that there
is certain evidence of Negrito blood.   The dark colour of some
of the tribes has also been put forward as a piece of evidence
to support this thesis.   Such a theory, however, seems
unnecessary to explain the facts which can be accounted for
on other grounds, it being quite certain that some of the races
of Europe have curly hair.   No people of pure Negrito blood
have been found, as far as I am aware, in India, and until
further archæological work reveals evidence of such a people
it would seem better not to admit their presence in the area.

We are left, then, with two different strains, " White " and
" Yellow " man.   Let us consider them in that order.   I have
given reasons above for suggesting that not only is there
reason for suspecting a mixture in those races which are
admitted by Risley to be mixed, but in some of those which
he suspects of belonging to pure stocks.

I have suggested, also, that the least mixed and earliest of
the populations in India were long-headed and short.   It

seems not improbable that these people belong to a branch of the Brown race, although they must not be confused with later comers of this race. They seem to have been in occupation of Southern India long before the arrival of the mass of the people who speak Dravidian languages, and are classed with them by the great majority of ethnologists. The evidence for their earlier arrival is based on the fact that they are either jungle-dwelling tribes or the menials of the other Dravidian peoples. In addition to their short stature and long heads they have also very broad noses. Among these people we must include the people who are classed in the census as jungle tribes, and also some of the lower castes among the Kanarese and Telugu.

Their skin is always dark and their hair tends to curliness. It is not, however, woolly, so that there is no reason to suggest that they have in them a Negrito strain. It has been suggested that they are possibly akin to the Melanesians, and indeed to the Tasmanians and other primitive peoples. These suggestions are pure speculations, and it seems better to adhere to the theory which I have put forward above that they are a very primitive form of the Brown race. Richards has called them Pre-Dravidian, *not* Proto-Dravidian (the italics are his), and suggests that they are an intermediate race. I should feel more inclined to describe them as the jungle peoples of South India, a descriptive if cumbrous title.

These jungle peoples are in close accord with their geographic environment, and have been in India a long time. It seems not impossible that they may be considered as the true aborigines, a close counterpart of the early non-Neanderthal people of Europe whom they resemble in many ways, but from whom they differ in their striking adaptation to the steaming climate of a tropical jungle.

There is a second class of peoples who inhabit Southern India who are mostly dolichocephalic, although in some cases they have slightly roundish heads. They have narrower noses than the last-named peoples; indeed, Richards has said colloquially but truly, " The jungle tribes begin where the rest leave off." These people include such groups as the Malayalis, the Tamils, and the Telugus. They are also inclined to be short in stature, have very variable skin-colour, and wavy hair. That they differ from the jungle tribes is evident, but there is probably not a difference that can be considered absolutely fundamental. They appear also to be a branch of the Brown race, but they have, no doubt, been in India for a very long time, although there are suggestions in them of mixing with other races, probably both the jungle peoples and a round-headed race, who will be discussed later. Their castes are large and of relatively high social status, which gives the suggestion that they are not the aborigines. It can only be suggested that they represent either invaders from the north, the backwash possibly of people akin to the jungle tribes, or else the refugees from Northern India, driven there by pressure on the arrival or increase of dominant populations in the north of similar stock, but differing from them in many particulars. Most but not all these Dravidian peoples show a fairly wide degree of variation, although the mixing which they have undergone has either been very slight or else is remote in time. If we sum up the evidence I think that we may conclude that the Dravidian peoples are representatives of the Brown race, who have changed to a certain extent in tropical environment, but who with their variable skin-colour and narrower noses suggest that the cradle of their race was not in Southern India, but at least in a semi-tropical or sub-tropical environment.

In addition to these two sub-races there is in India a third group who are dolichocephalic and present certain features in common with the last two groups, but in others are widely separated from them. They are Risley's Indo-Aryan. It is impossible here to discuss the exact meaning of the word Aryan. Modern research has abundantly proved that, whatever philological grounds there may be for supposing an Aryan language, there are none for supposing an Aryan physical type. The linguistic evidence seems to suggest that there were a series of cultural migrations probably through the Kabul Valley, and the habits of the Aryans have been studied through the evidence of the *Rig Veda* and the *Yajur Veda*. It appears to be somewhat difficult to correlate the linguistic and the cultural evidence. They seem to have had a contempt for the broad-nosed Dasyus, and Risley has said that the highest castes to-day are still those with the narrowest noses. That they mixed with the other peoples of India is extremely probable, but how much they mixed is a more difficult problem. The Indo-Aryans are among the people who show the least variation, and are probably therefore the least mixed races. Some, however, of Risley's Aryo-Dravidians are apparently equally unmixed, at least, on the evidence of cephalic index and stature, although we have already seen that in some cases the evidence is difficult to interpret.

The chief characters of these peoples are long-headedness, combined usually with tall stature and narrow noses and often a comparatively fair skin. All these characters serve to distinguish them from the races we have previously been discussing, except the cephalic alone. It is worthy of remark that the stature, the colour and, to a lesser degree, the nasal index, serve also in Europe to distinguish the Nordic from the Mediterranean man.

The problem is not dissimilar to that which faced us in dealing with some of the Steppe peoples in the last chapter. The solution is probably similar. There it was suggested that these tall, long-headed peoples might be described as Proto-Nordics. It seems difficult to link up Risley's Indo-Aryan with any other group of mankind. It is true that there are certain differences between the Indo-Aryans and the peoples of the Steppes, but on the whole these are rather superficial than fundamental. The colour of the skin is, perhaps, the most striking feature. The Rajputs, however, are strikingly fairer than many of their neighbours and, as we have already seen, skin does appear to respond, at least to a greater or lesser degree, to the influence of geographic environment.

The skeletal characters, as far as material is available, seem to point very conclusively to such a suggestion. It is not, however, entirely satisfactory perhaps to describe them as Proto-Nordics. They rather represent another branch of the same strain, of which the nearest kinsmen in Asia are those which we have mentioned, but until the whole question is more fully studied and a greater amount of skeletal material is at our disposal, it is hardly possible exactly to define the relationship of these various groups of tall long-heads.

It seems probable that they entered India comparatively late. Although there is reason to suppose that their blood has been widely dispersed over the country, some of the peoples in the north have retained their physical characters to a very great extent. It is of great interest to note that they have some of the lowest standard deviations of the cephalic index and other measurements of any of Risley's type series. It does not seem possible to interpret this trueness to type other than by saying that they represent an unmixed race. Clearly, also, they cannot be described as being undifferentiated. It is for this reason among others that it seems hazardous to apply the word " Proto-Nordic " to them without some qualification. They appear to be a pure-bred differentiated type which has penetrated into Northern India, probably at some early time, but possibly later than some of the round-heads, although it would appear certainly later than the Dravidian and Pre-Dravidian peoples. Their relationship to the Dravidians is a difficult question, but the distinction between them is clear. The distinction between the two rests on a relative fairness and a relatively narrower nose.

It would seem, then, probable that apart from those peoples with a great variation in the cephalic index, we have at least three long-headed groups in India, though it seems doubtful whether we should be justified in giving them the name of races. There are the jungle and low-caste tribes of the south, whom I have followed Richards in calling Pre-Dravidian. They probably represent the first immigration of members of the Brown race, and have probably every claim to be considered aborigines, though there are suggestions of an even earlier substratum in the population. Secondly, there are the Dravidian peoples, although the term must be used in a narrower sense than Risley gave to it. These are also related to the Brown race and probably represent a second immigration from the west. These two peoples seem to be ultimately derived from the same stock. Thirdly, and widely separated from the other two, we have the " Indo-Aryans." These peoples are probably of the same stock as the Proto-Nordics, but their relationship at present is not clearly defined.

The second great group of the peoples of India have round heads. There can be little doubt that they entered India at a very remote period, although it seems unlikely that they were the aboriginal population. It is possible, of course, that they may have been the first to occupy certain areas, but probably over most of India the people who appear to have been the ancestors of the jungle tribes of to-day were the first comers. Dr. Hunt has found in ancient graves in Haidarabad examples of crania which belonged to this early race. He has been good enough to set his specimens at my disposal, but unfortunately they are too much eroded by time and sun and water to be of great anthropological value.

These groups, as they exist at present, all show evidence of considerable admixture. They are round-headed and of tall or medium stature. It seems not improbable that they belong to the Armenoid branch of the White race. The evidence, such as we have at present, suggests that they originally entered India at an early period, and it is more than probable that their first migration was sufficiently early for them to form a small but integral part of the Dravidian population. Subsequently it would seem as if there were a series of migrations of these peoples. It is otherwise difficult to account for their presence. In any case they have mixed considerably with other types either before they came to India or after or even during their arrival. The fact that they are found in their least mixed state in the north-west suggests that they entered from this direction and indeed, as we have already seen, this type can be found sporadically across the whole continent of Asia from Constantinople to Peking. They were at least a part of the population of Mesopotamia when Kish flourished as a city. It is somewhat remarkable that in most places, excepting certain parts of Anatolia, these people always show considerable variation, suggesting that almost everywhere they were latecomers who mingled to a greater or lesser degree with the aboriginal population. It seems probable that they represent the element in the population of India which has been called Scythian by Risley. Most of these latter groups are very variable in character, as a whole they are the most variable of all groups. They are also intermediate in character between the long-heads and the short-heads and the peoples of tall and short stature. Their general physique seems to correspond with what might be expected of the mixture of two races who were already somewhat mixed. It is natural in a country where we have reason to suspect the presence of both Armenoid and Brown man that we should find in various degrees mixtures of these two peoples.

The final type that we find represented on the continent of India is the Yellow man. The seriations suggest that he is found in some purity. He appears to be less mixed than many of the Dravidians and hardly more mixed than some of the Indo-Aryans. Yellow man represents a definite exception to our dictum that the standard deviation of the cephalic index increases as the mean cephalic index increases. In their case the groups given by Risley as Mongoloid have only a small deviation. Those who are called Mongolo-Dravidian, who tend to have a rather narrower head, are more dolichocephalic. The peoples who are said to be Mongoloid have a small stature, and the Mongolo-Dravidians have a greater stature and an increased standard deviation. It would seem, therefore, as if the branch of Yellow man who penetrated into India were only moderately round-headed and of short stature, and belonged, in fact, to the Parœan branch of that great race. It has already been shown how extremely difficult it often is to distinguish on the basis of cranial measurements alone the difference between some types of Alpine or Armenoid and Yellow man, owing to the difficulty of finding a technique which shall show the exact form of the face, characteristic of Yellow man. It is therefore possible that we may have occasion to revise in detail some of the classes, but on the whole there can be little doubt that the distribution of Yellow man in India is on the general lines laid down by Risley, and that he penetrated India through the eastern borderland. The difficulty of access through these mountainous and forested regions no doubt prevented greater numbers from penetrating. For the most part there is little evidence that Yellow man mixed to any degree with other races before penetrating into India. It is, however, of importance to note that some of the most round-headed of the Mongoloid classes, as defined by Risley, are the most variable, suggesting that as in other parts of Asia there has been an admixture of Yellow and Mongoloid elements. It is interesting to note that Risley says that among these people the nose is no indication of social status. This seems to be a clear indication of what might be gathered from the other evidence that the position of Yellow man in India is very different from that of the other races. The higher indices occur in the smaller groups and, as I have already pointed out, Risley considers that this may be due to the scantiness of the data. In any case, however, they show very wide variations, and often the indices seemed to be singularly at variance with climatic conditions often less easy to explain than the exceptions from other parts of India. Among those which are selected by Risley as typical examples, the Lepchas of Sikkim have the very low index of 70 and the Khasia the high one of 84. It seems possible that these varying indices may not improbably be ultimately correlated with geographic environment. Most of these people live under the widely divergent climatic conditions which prevail in any mountainous area, but there is at present hardly sufficient data to enable one to give a final opinion on the subject. The small stature of this group is also possibly the result of geographic environment, comparing as it does so unfavourably with all the peoples of India, except the jungle dwellers who also are subject to singularly unsatisfactory natural conditions.

It is noticeable that some of the peoples who are considered by Risley to possess other blood than that of Yellow man are less variable than some which he suggests are pure " Mongoloid." The Kochh, for instance, have a standard deviation in the cephalic index which is hardly greater than that of the Andamanese. Owing to the fact that they have a long head, combined with certain characters which Risley considers to be Mongoloid, they have been considered a mixed race. With the possible exception, however, of the Chakma with an unusually round head, all the peoples whom Risley describes as Mongoloid, and partly Mongoloid, show singularly little variation. The actual mean varies considerably. In other words, the variation of the cephalic index within the group is small, but the variation within the Mongoloid class is very considerable. While therefore there is no reason to doubt Risley's general dictum that there are representatives of Yellow man in India, it seems probable that when we have further data to hand we shall be compelled to revise somewhat his classification of these peoples, and for the present it is probably safer to disregard at least some of the classes which he has called Mongolo-Dravidian and to refer to them as being local variants of the type of the Parœcean race.

The exact extent of the Parœcean distribution in India is at present uncertain. It is probably greater than Risley originally suggested. It has already been shown that there is reason to believe that the Munda-speaking peoples are linguistically related to some of the Parœcean peoples. The work of Schmidt (V. 34) has shown a curious linguistic grouping of the Mundas, some of the Tibetan peoples and the Mon-Khmer peoples which is very suggestive. There are further indications, to which I already alluded, that the connection is not merely linguistic, and this point has been emphasized by Schmidt. Working from an entirely different point of view, Morant has come to not dissimilar conclusions. His terminology is somewhat unsatisfactory and obscures the real value of his conclusions. He suggests, using the coefficient of racial likeness, that there is linkage of the Dravidians with Hindus and Hindus with Nepalese. By this he means that the Maravar show a coefficient which relates them with the Bengali type. The latter are called by Risley Mongolo-Dravidian, and it seems from Morant's work that we must admit a further Parœcean strain among the so-called Dravidian tribes of the south. Further detailed studies yet remain to be made. At present the evidence seems to suggest that Parœcean man is more widely distributed in Southern India than had previously been supposed, and that he may, and indeed probably was, of great antiquity in this region. Additional importance is therefore attached to Hunt's work in Haidarabad, and it will be interesting when he obtains more complete skulls to see whether they show any traces of Parœcean characteristics, or whether they are western round-heads, as seems the easier solution at present.

The population of Ceylon bears a close relationship to that of Southern India of which the island is really a disconnected part. The greatest interest to anthropologists has centred round the Veddas. The physical type is more widely scattered than the actual social " nation " which is now very limited in numbers, and appears to be widely spread in the island. It may be described briefly as follows. The stature is very short, with an average height of about 153 cms. (about five feet). The skin is a very dark brown, often approximating to black. The head is usually very small, long, and narrow, and there is often considerable restriction in the frontal area. The hair is coarse and wavy. The brow-ridges are often well-developed in the males, giving them a scowling appearance. There is often a considerable amount of body hair, especially on the chest. The people generally appear to be slightly built, and such of them as I have seen were slender but muscular. The nose is usually very broad. This type is quite distinct from the other peoples of Ceylon. It is in all probability to be connected with the Pre-Dravidian peoples of the mainland, from whom indeed it would be difficult often to distinguish them.

Side by side with these people we find that a large majority of the population of Ceylon are clearly related to the Dravidians of Southern India, with whom they are also related linguistically. There is also another element in the population which Haddon believes is akin to what he describes as the Indo-Afghan, Risley's Indo-Aryan, modified by contact with the Vedda. There appears to be little anthropological data on these people. They are certainly tall, long-headed and, in contrast to their dark-skinned neighbours, very fair. There is also a certain though not very great infusion of Moslem blood which appears in the main to have introduced an Armenoid admixture.

Ceylon is, as it were, the very end of the road in Southern Asia, and it seems that we have here an admixture of most of the races which have at various times poured into India. There can be little doubt that the population is extremely mixed. I was not able to find any ancient trace of Parœcean blood in the population. Morant thinks that there is a cranial linkage between the Veddas and the Maravar. His data on Ceylon is extremely scanty, and in any case such a linkage is to be expected. It can, however, hardly be used as evidence of any Parœcean admixture, even though the Maravar people, on the evidence of forty skulls, are linked with the Bengali on the evidence of apparently under thirty.

Before considering the eastern frontier of India, which presents some special problems, there remain the very

PLATE V

A VEDDA

interesting inhabitants of the Andaman Islands. These people, who have apparently been isolated from the rest of the world for a considerable time, present what is probably one of the few pure races in existence. They belong to the same Negrito type as the pygmy races of the Malay Peninsula, of the Philippine Islands, and of New Guinea. There also seem to be slight traces of these peoples elsewhere on the mainland. The curious fringing distribution is not unremarkable, and it seems more than probable that the Negritos had a much wider distribution. The Andamanese have short woolly hair which is black or sooty in colour, though like that of the Negrillos it is said sometimes to have a reddish tinge. The stature is under five feet, but the body is well proportioned, unlike that of pathological dwarfs. The head is brachycephalic, and the face is broad and rounded. The lips are full but not everted. The jaw is singularly ill-developed and the palate is very small. Only small series of measurements of these peoples have been published, and there are slight differences between the physique of the inhabitants of North and South Andaman. These differences are, however, of small moment. The standard deviations of the cephalic indices of both the males and the females of South Andaman, of whom fifty of each were measured and reported by Risley in the Census, is under 2 in each case. This low figure is very remarkable, and can hardly be accepted without further confirmation. If, however, it proves to be accurate, the very small variation of what is probably one of the purest of human groups is of great interest. As the figures for both the males and the females are almost identical it is probably correct. The corresponding figure for North Andaman is just under 3, a normal figure for a pure stock.

The eastern frontier of India presents certain problems which are very different from those which we have met with previously. In all probability the same racial strains are to be found here as in the rest of India, but there seems to be no evidence of any Negrito blood. The political groupings of the peoples do not coincide with the physical strains, and probably so much mixing has occurred that it is difficult at present to distinguish the different types in any one group, although individuals often recall the various constituent

L

races. In the following analysis I have followed with one or two slight modifications the suggestions made by Haddon (I. 19, 116).

Probably most of the races which we have found in India are here modified with a greater contact with the Parœœan type than elsewhere; indeed, it seems as if this Parœœan type probably penetrated into India by this way. The basal type, and probably the aboriginal, is the Pre-Dravidian, but there is no exact data on this point at present. It is found among many of the more isolated tribes. I am inclined to think that this type spread into Assam from the south, but of this again there seems to be no evidence at present. Attention has already been drawn to the relationship, linguistically, of the Munda-speaking peoples with some of the Mon-Khmer tribes. They have a fringing distribution according to Schmidt (V. 34), of which the epicentre is situated somewhere in the region now under discussion. If we associate a physical type with the linguistic, a hazardous proceeding, but one for which in this case there does seem to be a certain amount of evidence, although the language and the physical type are not always correlated, it would seem necessary to postulate a wide dispersion of these Pre-Dravidian peoples and some early contact or affinity with Parœœan man, although they are for the most part dolichocephalic. The evidence of dark skins and broad noses suggests to me, although I admit that the evidence for this suggestion is at present not entirely conclusive, a continued residence at an undifferentiated period in a hot moist climate.

But there have been other, and probably subsequent, immigrations. There is, especially among the Naga tribes, an element that is certainly akin to the Nesiot. It may probably be most easily distinguished from the Pre-Dravidian element by the lower value of the nasal index. I have already argued that this element probably represents the most eastern extension of strains which are akin to the Brown race. The third strain represented in Assam which is akin to the races of Europe is probably an outlier of the Alpine race, and is possibly a comparatively late arrival in the area, as people of this race contrast very strongly with those so far described as having narrow noses. They are apparently immigrants from the north, probably from the plateau, in the western part of which it has already been seen that they are widely distributed. Finally, there are a series of very different racial elements, some of which have been in Assam for a considerable period. They are all related to the Parœans, but there are certainly two different types. The nose forms the best means of distinguishing between the two. The first is probably closely akin to the Kachin type in Burma, and is characterized by having a broad nose; it will be more fully discussed in the chapter dealing with Burma. The second does not occur in Burma, but is found among the Lepcha in Northern India, and also not infrequently in Bengal. It is possible that this type is due to an early mixture of Parœan with other elements, or it may be a differentiated type of the same stock as the Kachins, possibly effected by long residence in a special environment There have, in addition to these types, been further and more recent immigrations from India which have introduced other types, notably one described by Haddon as dolichocephalic leptorrhine. This great mixture is, perhaps, the natural result of an environment where so many types of men coming from widely different strains have met at various times.

CHAPTER VI

CHINA

THE Chinese Republic extends over an area which probably exceeds 4 million square miles, and has a population within the boundaries of China proper of 400 million. Parts of it have already been discussed, others will form the subject-matter of subsequent chapters; here I propose to discuss Old China proper, that is, the eighteen provinces, and to exclude the three eastern provinces of Manchuria and the New Dominion of Chinese Turkestan, which the Chinese call Sinkiang, and Mongolia and Tibet, over the two latter of which states the Chinese claim a varying amount of authority. Except for a small tongue of land at the north end of the Gulf of Liao Tung, China is bounded on the east by the sea. In the north part this has, on the whole, formed a boundary which does not appear to be traversed very frequently, except, possibly, at an early period. Chinese influence, however, certainly extended from early times eastward through the "Korean gate," and either by sea or land, as we shall see later, Chinese influence both cultural and ethnical reached Japan.

The southern coast has, however, had a different history. Within historic times, and possibly before, Chinese sailors have pushed continually into the islands, and to-day they form an increasing element in the population, most of the immigrants coming from the southern coastal provinces.

The northern boundary of China has always been ill-defined. It may be described in general terms as the Gobi. The actual position of the boundary has varied from time to time; we may probably take the ethnical boundary as being the mountain line, fortified *et arte et natura*, whereon the Great Wall runs. Further to the west, in the Province of Kansu, the desert forms approximately the ethnical and actual boundary.

The west is guarded by mountains and desert, and the

southern boundary, the escarpments from the plateau of Yunnan and Kwangsi, will be found discussed in the chapter dealing with South-eastern Asia.

Parts of the northern boundary are but sparsely inhabited and the regions are hard to cross, but the region north of the great plain of China lies open to migrating peoples. It is certain that through the neck of land between the Ordos bend of the Hwang Ho and the sea, China has at various times received considerable northern influences, Mongol and Tungus. It was hence also that her greatest conquerors came, the Mongols and the Manchus. It is doubtful, however, whether their advent, so late as it was in the racial history, had any very important ethnical influence.

The North-West Frontier is of the greatest interest, because it is along this difficult road that invaders from the west entered China in early times. It is even possible, as some writers have suggested, that it was by this road, north of the Nan-Shan, that the Chinese themselves entered China after having learnt the difficult arts of agriculture in the oases of the Tarim. Too much stress cannot be laid, however, on the broad belt watered by the streams which flow from the Nan-Shan and the Tien-Shan, as this belt forms the most strategic point ethnically in the whole of Eastern Asia, and affords a means of communication between China and Kasgaria and Dzungaria. The actual details of the road must be discussed later in dealing with the ethnology of Chinese Turkestan and Tibet.

The frontier between China and Tibet is probably of no great importance to the student of Chinese ethnology, although there have been ancient roads.

The frontier between Burma and China belongs more properly to the ethnological history of Eastern Asia.

The physiography of this vast area is naturally complicated, but for our present purpose it is convenient to divide China proper into three parts, the basin of the Hwang Ho forming the centre with uplands lying to the north, and to the south the Yangtze basin and the complicated mountainous area south of it.[1]

[1] This division is *ethnological* not physiographic; Roxby has recently suggested (*Geogr. Rev.*, 1925, XV. 4) what he describes as the "provisional natural entities" of China, of which he suggests 15. When more detailed ethnological data are available these should prove of the greatest service.

The northern uplands form a series of escarpments, leading down from the high plateau of Mongolia. Here the
ethnic and the geographical boundaries do not always
coincide. The geological strata underlying these uplands
are horizontal carboniferous rocks, which form, as it were,
a series of steps, on the greatest of which for the most part
the Wall is built. The area is much cut by rivers, and in
places is covered by loess. Owing to its nature, it forms an
area which invites invasion through it on to the plains. To
the north lies the plateau of Mongolia, to the south the
escarpments look down on to the plains, approach to which
can be gained through various defiles. These uplands are
connected geologically with the Shantung group of hills,
which rise like islands out of the plain and some of which
form the peninsula of Shantung.

The plain has long since separated these outlying and
isolated hills from their parent ranges. This plain, which
includes the Hwang Ho and part of the Yangtze Kiang
basins, is undoubtedly the most important feature in Northern
China. It forms a great triangle, the apex being to the
north of Peking, at which city the plain is about 120 miles
broad, and the base is the Yangtze Kiang from Shanghai to
Ichang. It may be described as the delta of the two great
rivers, the Hwang Ho and the Yangtze Kiang, although this
description is not perhaps entirely satisfactory from a geographical point of view. This plain does not, however, form
a single ethnological unit ; the northern part—the basin of the
Yellow River—forms the old home of the Chinese, the southern
part—the Yangtze basin—divided from the north by the
Tsin Ling range differs in many respects. This southern
area formed the old kingdom of the Sungs. It was not,
however, entered by the Chinese until they were driven
south by pressure from the north. Between Hankow and
Ichang this southern part of the plain is actually cut off from
the rest of the plain by the Huai Mountains, which form outliers of the southern uplands in the same way that the Shantung Mountains are outliers of the northern.

The Hwang Ho basin includes the provinces of Kansu,
Shensi, Shansi, Chihli, Honan, and Shantung. Not only does
it differ from the southern part ethnologically, but in climate
and food production it is characteristically different from

the rest of China. Rice is the favourite food of all who can afford it, but it is not grown in any quantity, the chief grains being wheat and millet, and other dry grains. While the characteristic soil is loess, the Hwang Ho brings down enormous quantities of silt, which owing to the erratic habits of rivers are deposited over wide areas. The river bursts its banks at intervals and causes widespread desolation and famine, but in the detritus thus scattered over the land the Chinese, after a short interval, plant and grow rich crops and again establish a large population. The country is, however, dependent on the rainfall for its crops. The mean temperature is moderate, although Northern China is apt to be very hot in the summer and cold in the winter.

The Yangtze valley, on the other hand, is almost sub-tropical. The country is well watered and luxuriant. The river flows for the most part over a hard bottom. The conditions, therefore, make for a different type of life and of manners, and it would appear also a slightly different physical type.

Although the forest country of the southern uplands is very different in appearance from that of the northern part of the Yangtze basin, it is hardly possible to separate the two ethnologically, and the interest from that point of view lies chiefly in the correlation between the physiography and the distribution of physical types.

Briefly, the southern uplands may be described as follows. They may be divided into three folds. Along the north boundary the folds turn from west by north to east by south. In the south the direction of the folds is from west-south-west to east-north-east, becoming in the south more southerly and in the north more northerly. These folds are of the greatest importance in considering the topography of Southern China. In the west there is a series of folds which contrast strongly with the last-named, for whereas these are old, low, and broken up, the southern folds are of more recent formation. Owing to the habit of rivers of eating back into their watershed and at times capturing the supplies of other streams, these folds have resulted in what is a very complicated series of uplands.

They may be conveniently divided into three areas, following the three main folds. In the north there is a series of lofty mountains which still retain, for the most part, their original valley forms. The principal ranges are the Nan-Shan, north of which runs the road to Kashgaria. Secondly, south of the Wei River runs the Tsing-ling Shan, the eastern continuation of which forms the boundary between the rivers. At the eastern end of this range, between it and the Fu-niu Shan, a depression has been formed owing to a fault. This gap is of the greatest importance, as through it runs one of the western roads, that from Siangyan to Sian. The depression which separates the Fu-nui Shan from the Huai Shan is also traversed by a pass, that from Siangyan to Kaifeng.

In the second area it has been shown that the greatest destruction of the old valleys has taken place. The details are not necessary for our present purpose. The most important fact to notice is the deposition of a reddish clayey material, which in places forms an irregular plain. Such soil is very fertile and often supports a big population. The most important areas of this type are the red basin in Eastern Szechuan and part of Eastern Yunnan.

In the third area the folds form a series of valleys which trend from north to south. The rivers run in narrow gorges, although in some cases a certain amount of capturing has taken place.

Much of this southern and mountainous region has formed the homes of aboriginal, or at least non-Chinese tribes, who have been able to survive in the mountains long after the Chinese had occupied the plains. The very complicated nature of the river valleys has made them of little use as highways and prevented the spread of peoples by this usual route. The nature of the plains and of one or two specially favoured areas is such that they have frequently had a surplus population. The general trend of the people has been in a southerly direction. To the west there was little to attract in the high tableland. To the south there was an outlet toward the various river valleys and the coastal plain. The population seems to have followed this possibility of outlet.

In this way the Chinese, or people allied to them, have spread, especially into the coastal plain of what is now French Indo-China and, it would appear, into the valley of the

Ganges. They have also spread and are still spreading into the Dutch Indies.

It is difficult to sum up the movements which have taken place within this wide area. Generally speaking, however, it may be said that in the north geographical conditions have been such as to encourage movements towards the interior of the plain, whereas in the south the movements seem, on the whole, to have been centripetal.

The early history of China is, as I have shown on page 74, entirely unknown. It is impossible to say who were the original inhabitants of much of the area, although certain tribes exist to-day which, as will be seen, have good claim to be considered aborigines. But they, for the most part, have survived only in the mountainous areas, and all trace of early people in the plains has been lost.

The most important research which has been made has been already alluded to. Dr. Andersson has found traces of a culture which is without doubt chalcolithic and clearly connects with Anau. Traces of this culture have been found in Honan and as far east as Fengtien. The exact chronological position of this culture cannot at present be determined. We must presume a migration of culture from the west, probably along the road north of the Nan-Shan, which has already been described. This culture cannot at present be associated with any definite people, as such remains as have been found are considered by Black to be of the same type as the modern Northern Chinese. In any case it would not be reasonable to look for the origins of the Chinese people at so late a date, which in Fengtien may even be after the beginning of the second millennium B.C.

We know that this culture was widely spread in the Tarim basin, and it is possible that the historical grounds which suggested that the origin of the Chinese people was in that region may be rather a reflection of the migration of this culture, which is now known by archæological evidence to have taken place, rather than a real valid suggestion of origin.

At present, however, it is impossible to express any views on the early racial history of the Chinese, from the point of view of somatology. We can, however, say that in China, in chalcolithic times, there lived a people who were of a physique like the Chinese to-day, but who were characterized by a different culture. It has been suggested by another school that we should rather find the origin of the Chinese in the south. On somatological grounds it is equally impossible at present to combat this theory. It is, however, of importance to note that the distribution of the Chinese type is much greater in the south than in the north, and that it is not found in an unmixed state north of the basin of the Yellow river and, indeed, here it seems to be very much mixed with other peoples.

The relationship of these peoples to the Alpine race is also a matter on which we have at present insufficient evidence. It seems probable that there have been at times intrusive elements, of a strain akin to true Alpine and, in the north, Nordic or Proto-Nordic, into China; but here again we have no evidence of a physical nature, and in these questions cultural evidence is likely to prove a somewhat doubtful guide. Summing up, then, the evidence in regard to the early Chinese it must be admitted that at present we have none, and that all our reasoning on the nature of the inhabitants of this great part of Asia must be limited to a discussion of the characters of the modern people.

The flag of the Chinese Republic claims to typify with its five colours the five races of China, the Chinese, the Manchus, the Mongols, the Tibetans, and the Moslems. At first sight the basis of division is unsatisfactory. It forms, however, a very convenient starting-point for a study of the races of China. The Manchus and the Mongols will be described in the chapter (page 177) dealing with the area which formed their home. The Tibetans also form an entirely separate problem. There remain the Moslems, classed on the ground of their religion, and the Chinese proper.

No place has been found on the Chinese flag for the aborigines. They form, however, a very interesting group which has at present been little studied (VI. 1). They are usually classified by the Chinese as follows. There are four divisions, the Man, the T'u, the Miao, and the Yao. These names are not very satisfactory. The Man—the Chinese word is more or less the equivalent of the Greek word barbaros—are said to include the Black Miao, the Meng Chia, the Chung Chia or Ih, and other tribes. The word

T'u means earth or native, practically autochthonous; it is applied in different places to the Chung in Kwangsi and Kweichow, and to other peoples in Kansu and the north-west. The word Miao means plant or shoot, and again practically means autochthonous; it is used of the so-called Flowered races, Black, White, and Red, near Anping, the Ch'ing Kehtu, and others. Yao is a dog name, not neces-sarily a disgrace in Eastern Asia. In Kweichow it is applied to an itinerant race of tinkers; people who are called by this name are also found in Kwangsi and in parts of Kwangtung.

This classification which I have given, because references to it will be found both in Chinese and European writers, is too artificial to be satisfactory, and it is more usual and con-venient to divide the aborigines, at least in Kweichow, Szechuan, and Kwangsi North, into three classes—the Miao, the Lolo, and the Chung-chia. There are also some other tribes who probably belong to one or other of these groups. They include the Limen of South Kweichow, the Beh-gen of Kwangsi and South Kweichow, and the Bin-muh of North-east Kwangsi.

The distribution of these peoples is approximately as follows. There are Black Miao and Chung-chia in Hunan, and there is a mention of aborigines in the annals of the City of Changteh, near Tungting Lake. The real home of the Chung-chia is, however, from Hunan across the southern part of Kweichow and southern Yunnan into Annam and Burma. They are known by various names, of which the most important is T'ai in Burma.

North of these peoples live the Black Miao. They inhabit a belt about 80 miles broad across the south of Kweichow between Anshun and Hingi, from the Hunan border on the south bank of the Yuan river almost to Yunnan. They claim, and there is reason to believe their claim can be substantiated, to have come from Kiangsi.

The two classes of Flowered Miao inhabit a somewhat semicircular tract in West Central Kweichow and North-east Yunnan, but extend even as far as the Kwangsi border. These people who have been detailed above appear to be the only ones who to-day inhabit a definite area.

The general distribution of the aboriginal tribes is, how-ever, much wider. The Black Lolo probably came from

Burma in isolated groups. They are called " Black " because of the darkness of their complexions. In the Chinese pictures, it is interesting to note, they are always associated with horses, an association which occurs in few other tribes. In the third century A.D. they became the ruling class over the Flowered Miao and the White Lolo, or Miao. They may be found in the prefecture of Hingi, and in the districts of Hsin-ts'eng and Chinfeng Chow, and also in the prefecture of Tating where the White Lolo are numerous, and in the west of the prefecture of Anshun. They occur in South-east Yunnan, where they are called Nosu, and in other parts of that province. They are most numerous in an independent state in Szechuan.

These opinions are those expressed by Jamieson, who has collected and arranged the various scattered pieces of information on this very puzzling question. T'ing (VI. 3), of the Chinese geological survey, appears to take a rather different view. He believes that " historically the Lolos, in association with the Ch'iangs, formed an important people in North-west Szechuan, Kokonor, and South Turkestan. In the last place they intermarried with the Iranian people known as Yuchchi. The Iranian element may have found its way into the Lolos through the Ch'iangs."

T'ing's anthropological work in Yunnan seems to have been the most recent and, indeed, one of the few attempts which have been made to secure physical data from these people. He declares that the " Iranians were certainly dolichocephalic," and on the basis of this assumption links up the Lolos with these peoples. There seems, however, to be no doubt that T'ing is using it in the same sense as Ripley. The few measurements which T'ing was able to secure bears out this supposition. He refers to the fact that travellers have noted tall stature, fair skin, and more regular features, which suggest " non-Mongolic " characters. His own measurements, however, suggest that the stature on the whole tends to be short. The most remarkable feature is the extremely small size of the head and the very low cephalic indices. The head tends to be both absolutely and relatively narrow, and absolutely short but relatively long.

Such indications as we have at present, then, suggest that among the aboriginal tribes of Western China we have a type which corresponds to the long-headed populations of Western Asia and to the Mediterranean area, corresponding to Elliot Smith's Brown race. It appears to form a link between the west and the Nesiots, who also possess the same characters. There are some indications that among a number of these aboriginal tribes the main influence was from the west, but suggestions are not lacking that at least some of them came from the south. This is quite possible from the point of view of physique, as we shall see that a sensible proportion of the inhabitants of South-eastern Asia also belong to this type. They are all mixed to a greater or lesser degree with the Parœœan stock, such peoples as, for instance, the Chin-miao of Yinach'ang, Wuting, probably representing an intermediate type.

Their presence in Yunnan is of special importance, as it provides what appears to be an ancient link between the Brown and the Nesiot stocks.

There is a second class of aborigines living more to the east. It is probable that they should rather be considered as non-Chinese, for their present homes have only been occupied by them for a comparatively short time. They include the Hakkas and the Punti.

The Hakkas, whose name means foreigners or new-comers, are found principally in Kwangtung and in Kwangsi, but they occur in small and somewhat scattered groups in Fukien, Kiangsi, Chekiang, and even in the islands of Formosa and Hainan. It seems clear that they originally inhabited Shantung, Shansi, and Anhui. In the third century B.C. they were driven from Shantung, and over six hundred years later they were driven further south into the mountains of South-east Kiangsi and the border of Fukien province. Later they were again driven into the mountains, this time still further south into the Fukienese Mountains and the ranges between Kiangsi and Kwangtung. Finally, in the fourteenth century, they were driven from Fukien and eventually settled in the north of Kwangtung. They spread to the south-west of that province and also into Kwangsi.[1]

[1] The tribes of the mountain regions near Foochow are identified by some with the Hakkas. A recent writer (Woods, in *China Journal of Arts and Science*, 1925, III. 1) calls them San Tak, the name I obtained was Tso Li; they are also known locally and less politely as the Po-tse gen.

At present we have few anthropological data on these peoples. Some of the groups, though they have a culture which differs in many respects from that of the Chinese who surround them, have intermarried so much with the Chinese that the original type has been practically swamped. In other cases it seems probable that the original type can be ascertained. It appears that here also we must link them up with the Brown race, but in a somewhat different manner from most of the western aboriginal tribes. Here we have no link which stretches across Asia, but probably an extension of the Nesiot influence along the periphery of Eastern Asia, the people having reached their present habitat by being driven again to the south.

Among representatives of these peoples in Fukien province I was much struck by the smallness of their stature, which I was inclined to ascribe to the unsatisfactory conditions among which they lived. Their villages were often in comparatively remote parts of the mountains, and they appeared to be suffering from the effects of an inadequate diet, rather like the " misery spots " which Ripley refers to in France. The smallness of stature among the mountaineers was not confined to the non-Chinese, but affected the Chinese hillmen equally, and may probably be considered not a racial character but as the direct result of environment. It is possible that the shortness of stature among some of the Lolos, to which I referred above, may be due to similar causes.

These aborigines and alien tribes are all that is left of the early inhabitants of China. It seems improbable that China was inhabited in palæolithic times. Up to the present, in spite of the large number of implements which have been discovered, there do not seem to be any which can be certainly attributed to any period earlier than the neolithic, although the country has not yet been systematically explored and its prehistoric archæology is not as yet fully known.

There can be little doubt that there was a very advanced neolithic culture in China. Of the inhabitants during the early part of this period we have at present little information (VI. 7). Towards the end of neolithic times we have abundant traces of a culture which without actually possessing, as far as we know at present, any bronze, seems to be undoubtedly reminiscent of bronze technique in many particulars. The pottery is very reminiscent of the Anau wares and probably represents an extension of this or a similar culture to the east. It is, however, of great interest to note that such skeletons as have been excavated so far do not differ from the present inhabitants of the same area.

The evidence suggests, therefore, that we are wrong in associating the term Chinese with any physical type, it is rather linguistic and cultural. But the culture has become so bound up with nationality, and in modern times also with apparently certain physical types, that it is difficult to distinguish them with our present knowledge.

It has been suggested that it is impossible to distinguish physically the Chinese Moslems from their Chinese neighbours. As far as I am aware very little data has been collected on this subject. They may be conveniently grouped into three classes, by their origin and manner of speech, Turki Moslems, Mongol Moslems, and Arab Moslems. The second class need not concern us here. I have had no opportunity of observing the Turki Moslems in Kansu, where they form a considerable and very turbulent part of the population. There are, however, numbers of these Moslems in Peking. They form a very striking contrast to the ordinary Chinese. Although there can be little doubt that they have intermarried very considerably with the Chinese at various times, they preserve their original type in many particulars. They have a better developed pilous system and their beards are usually well developed. Their heads are very round and often flat behind. It seems that in general they represent a cross between the Alpine or Armenoid and Yellow man. A good example of this type can be seen in the frontispiece.

There are in addition to the Turki Moslems, at least in Peking and Tientsin, a number of Arab Moslems. In 1922 they claimed that there were as many as thirty-two thousand families. These people are certainly very commonly endogamous. They proselytize very little, although they do make a few converts. They adhere strictly to the tenets of their religion, a fact which necessitates endogamy, as they cannot enter an ordinary Chinese house where pork forms such an important part in the domestic economy. They also seem to be distinguished chiefly from the Chinese by the greater development of the pilous system. A curious character which these Moslems possess, which shows a racial feature, they are in the habit of cutting the moustache, an operation which is often not necessary and as far as I am aware not practised by the Chinese.

These people claim to have been in China since the Sung Dynasty. They still preserve the Arabic tongue and their old racial characters. They claim to have come from Arabia. How far this claim is correct I am unable to say. In any case they appear also to belong for the most part to the Armenoid race, or more probably a mixture of the Armenoid and the Mediterranean races. They have acquired a few Chinese characteristics, but on the whole differ considerably from them. Some cases occur where there is a fold over the internal canthus of the eye, but this is by no means general. They have an intermediate brownish-yellow colour. They unfortunately would not submit to measurement. On the whole these Arab Moslems have become more absorbed in the general population than have their Turki co-religionists. Both, however, appear, as I have suggested, to show close relationships with the tribes of Central Asia.

There is a further and very interesting element in China which is undoubtedly alien, the Jews of Kaifeng. These have on the whole become absorbed in the Moslem population, and in any case they are hardly sufficiently numerous to warrant them being considered an element in the population.

These various alien elements in the population of China represent a very small and unimportant element. Although the Nesiot type can claim to be of ancient standing they live in the more remote and less accessible regions. The other peoples are for the most part recent intruders. The Chinese themselves remain to be considered. I have already shown that there is at present no direct information as to their origin. The data on them also is extremely scanty, and at present any opinions which are put forward cannot be considered as more than tentative.

Before proceeding to consider the differences between the different groups of Chinese it is important to recall that, as I have suggested above (page 57), the differences between the Chinese and the European types is considered by some authors not to be fundamental. The form of the calvaria is not different but, on the other hand, the face presents certain striking divergencies. The hair, the eyes, and the colour of skin have been considered by most authors, from the seventeenth century onwards, to be distinctive racial characters. The bony framework underlying these structures presents, however, characters which in the opinion of some at least do not serve to differentiate them.

Unfortunately, owing to the social customs of the Chinese, it is extremely difficult to obtain much skeletal material and comparatively little has found its way to this country. Owing also to the difficulties which in the past have attended such work in China, comparatively few measurements have been made. There is therefore hardly an area of equal size, or so great a population, of whom it can be said that somatologically there is so little evidence.

The largest series of Chinese crania which has been published is, as far as I am aware, that described by Morant in the paper to which I have already referred (I. 14). He is not inclined to lay much stress on the difference between the Northern and the Southern Chinese, but his southern material was not well documented and is therefore not entirely conclusive. In regard to the general position he has, by using the coefficient of racial likeness, come to some very interesting conclusions in regard to the relations of the Chinese. He first draws attention to the fact that they represent on the whole a single ethnic unit, although they include a very large number of individuals, a position which would probably be generally conceded. This racial position of the Chinese has long been their peculiar pride, a pride more justified on somatic grounds than the similar claim made by the Hellenes.

Morant believes that the Southern Chinese link up in three directions, other than their linkage with the Northern Chinese. First, they are connected to what he has described as Tibetan A. This type will be more accurately described later; it is called by Sir William Turner the priestly type of Tibet. Secondly, they are linked with the Annamese. The latter people have possibly mixed with other elements, but as will be seen physically they are hardly to be distinguished, except as a local race, from the Southern Chinese.

M

To the north Morant links the Southern Chinese with the Japanese, a theory that is more conveniently discussed in dealing with the Japanese. Finally, the Northern Chinese are linked with the Koreans.

One of the most interesting points which has emerged from the use of the coefficient of racial likeness is the further suggestion that there is an element among the Northern Chinese which shows affinities with the Khams Tibetans—Turner's Warrior Tibetan class. Morant reserves judgment on this point, admitting that a very few Tibetan skulls might have affected the coefficient, but the point is worthy of further consideration when evidence is available.

Morant suggests that the Chinese as a whole belong to the general series of Oriental races, with the exceptions which I have described above. The aberrant Northern Chinese are considered by Morant to differ from the normal Chinese type in the length of the face, the relation of this length to the breadth of the skull, and the length of the palate. To a lesser extent they differ in the bizygomatic breadth, the transverse arc taken through the auricular points and the greatest length of the skull, that is to say, they differ both in facial and calvarial measurements. No suggestion is made as to the possible meaning of these differences, and whereas it would be expected that we should find possibly some relation with the northern tribes, which does not appear to exist, the linkage not only with the normal Tibetan but also with this aberrant type is somewhat unexpected. Possibly both types are more widely spread in Central Asia than the suggestion of Turner, who was originally responsible for differentiating the two types would lead us to believe.

Shirokogoroff has recently published a monograph on the Northern Chinese (VI. 5). He draws somewhat sweeping conclusions from very scanty data, and his methods call for considerable revision in details, as he does not seem to have fully understood the use which can legitimately be made of product moment tables.

He declares that the Chinese are a complex of anthropological types, and suggests that they lived within the limits of West Central China, whence they moved east, north, and south. The movements eastwards resulted in the amalgamation of the Chinese, the Tungus, and the Palæasiatics ;

though he does not appear to define exactly what physical type he means by the last, he clearly defines their culture. He also thinks that the Chinese type is to be observed in the population of Manchuria and Korea.

This interesting hypothesis, though it is supported by much ethnological evidence, is not on the whole supported by the figures which are quoted by Shirokogoroff. Although it is hazardous to base too much evidence on the standard deviations of the cephalic index alone, the author's figures are 3·7 for both the Chinese of Chihli and Shantung. These two provinces have been overrun continuously within historic times, and the standard deviations are surprisingly low, when areas in which similar mixing has taken place are compared. This evidence does not seem then, sufficient to upset the general theory that the Chinese are in general of a remarkably homogeneous physical type. It seems rather more probable that the mixings which have taken place with other peoples have not affected the Chinese type to any very great extent, less than might possibly have been imagined. The tribes with whom he suggests that mixing has taken place are mostly very round-headed, and presumably on Shirokogoroff's hypothesis they have affected an originally long-headed type. Such evidence as we have, however, would rather suggest that if anything the Northern Chinese are slightly more long-headed than most of the Southern Chinese, although this point is by no means fully established.

His data from Shantung and Chihli provinces show that the Chinese are, at least in this region, very tall with a mean stature of nearly 167 cm. This is rather less than Koganei's figure, which was taken on soldiers, and might be expected to be above the average of the general population. It agrees, however, with that of other observers. This great stature is generally considered to be one of the characters of the Northern Chinese.

The current suggestion to account for this stature is a mixture of Mongol blood. This can hardly be the case. The average stature of the Mongols appears to be about 163 cm., although some whom I measured in Inner Mongolia with possibly a slight Chinese admixture were rather taller. The Manchus, Koreans, and Tungus are all shorter, and the

other tribes of Northern Asia are also short. The hypothesis
put forward both by Shirokogoroff and by other observers
seems therefore unsatisfactory. It is, however, of interest
to note that at least among some of the Tibetans a comparable stature occurs. It will be remembered that in one
series of skulls Morant found a resemblance between the
Northern Chinese and one type of Tibetans. He admitted,
however, that further evidence was needed to establish the
point. The further evidence of stature seems to be at least
suggestive. The number of observations which have been
collected is hardly sufficient at present to come to a general
conclusion, but it would seem likely that we have in Northern
China not the mixture of several probably very different
strains, but an underlying strain allied to the Southern
Chinese and a second strain—occurring in Northern China,
and how distributed we do not know at present—linking
up with the Khams Tibetans. We find both these two
strains in Tibet, but not mixed there. In Northern China
it is suggested that they have become sufficiently mixed to
cause a standard deviation of the cephalic index, which
although it is suggestive of mixture, does not imply the very
heterodox population which is suggested by the mixture
of three different strains. It is unfortunate that it is not
possible to identify exactly where Koganei's skulls were
collected, and the source of the rest of Morant's collection
of skulls from China is too doubtful to lay much stress on
the distribution of types.

If we sum up the very deficient data on the Northern
Chinese it would appear that there are two types, one akin
to the Southern Chinese, the other akin to Khams Tibetans.
The evidence on the living suggests the presence of a tall
element in the population; this can only be paralleled among
neighbouring peoples in the Tibetans. On the whole, therefore, it seems not impossible that the evidence of the living
tends to confirm the suggestions made by the use of the coefficient of racial likeness. Such evidence of variation as
we have suggest that, if there is any mixture, such mixing
has reached about the same degree of stability that is
normally to be met with when two strains have been in
contact for a long period.

There can be little doubt that the Southern Chinese

belong to the same ethnic group as the Northerners, but there are, however, certain important differences. Generally the Southerners are of smaller dimensions. The head-length is also smaller, though the head-breadth hardly differs between the two. The slight increase in the cephalic index is probably, therefore, rather the result of a decrease in stature than to any real racial difference, although it may possibly be interpreted in rather a different way. Many authors, Birkner and Morant for instance, would see little difference between the two, a conclusion which seems inevitable if account is taken solely of cranial evidence. Such data as we have, however, suggests that there is a very great difference in stature; the data is admittedly scanty. It seems not improbable that we have in Southern China no trace of the tall element, which undoubtedly occurs in Northern China, and which I have suggested is to be linked up with the Tibetans. This would also account for the difference between Koganei's observations on crania. There does not seem to be any evidence of this aberrant type in the south. But not only is the general stature in the south about 5 cms. shorter than in the north, a difference which seems greater than can be accounted for by chance variations, but also there are other differences on the living. It seems probable that the nose is slightly more platyrrhine. How far this is true is uncertain, because Shirokogoroff's measurements indicate almost an excess of platyrrhiny in the north, but his measurements on other peoples are such that it seems possible that he has not adopted the technique which is in general use. If we accept his figures it is necessary to admit a small area of platyrrhiny in the north which does not agree with other observers. With this proviso it appears that the nasal index increases slightly as we go further south, possibly the result of increasingly hot and moist climates. The colour of the skin also appears to be darker in the south. The difference in skin-colour is essentially a feature which is due to environment and cannot be considered as a racial feature.

The differences between the north and south are not great, but sufficient to allow us to make a distinction between the two groups of Chinese. Their history in recent times has been very different, and the water-shed between the Hwang

Ho and the Yangtze is probably to be considered as the dividing-line between the two sub-groups of the same people.

Up to the present it must be admitted that our evidence is so scanty that any views which are put forward must be considered as extremely tentative. The Chinese represent a single ethnic unit; this unit has probably been sufficiently strong in numbers to be able to maintain its individuality in the face of various invaders. The Tibetan element in the north is probably extremely early, and in our present state of knowledge it is hardly possible to assign a definite place to it.

There is every probability that not only Western culture but also Western physique has affected the population of China in early times, but on this point also it is useless at present to speculate until we have reasonable records, province by province, of the actual physique to-day of the Chinese.

CHAPTER VII

THE FRINGING LANDS OF CHINA

A. CENTRAL ASIA, TIBET, AND CHINESE TURKESTAN

IN the last three chapters I have been describing the
ethnology of the three great parts of Asia which, with
the exception of Japan, are best known to Europe. This
chapter I propose to devote to a study of the people who
inhabit the region which lies at the meeting-point of the
regions already discussed. This can be done the more
briefly because the inhabitants of this area are naturally
related to those who inhabit the peripheral lands. Much
of the region is desert and all of it is sparsely inhabited,
but although comparatively few individuals make up the
groups described in this chapter, the peculiar nature of their
environment has rendered them of particular interest to
ethnologists.

Tibet has an area of 700,000 square miles, but of this
area Little estimates that six-sevenths is uninhabitable.
The high plateau is a frozen stony desert and contrasts
strongly with the lower plateau. The whole country is
about 1600 miles from east to west and about 700 miles
from north to south at its broadest part. It is bounded on
the south by the Himalaya, on the west by the same
mountains and then by the Karakoram Mountains. On
the north it is shut in by the Kunlun, the Akka Tag, and
the Altai Tag, and on the east by numerous ranges. South
Tibet is traversed for 1300 miles by the Tsanpo (the Brahmaputra), and most of the population is situated along this
river, 18 miles north of which lies Lhasa. From a line about
150 miles north of and parallel to the river is the northern
plain, Chang Tang, which extends to the foot of the Kunlun
Mountains. Most of this is at too high an elevation for
permanent human habitation, but the southernmost edge
is peopled by Black tent nomads. As some comparatively

unfamiliar political names have crept into the textbooks, it may be convenient to note that roughly speaking the province of Kham extends from 92 degrees E. to the Chinese border, south of lat. 34 degrees. This province contains the greater part of the population. North-east of Kham province lies Kokonor, which is inhabited partly by Mongols and partly by Tibetans. Amdo, a part of Western Kansu which is inhabited by Tibetans, is included in this area. In a few fertile valleys, especially in the neighbourhood of Lhasa, plentiful crops of wheat, peas and barley are grown, but the main cereal crop is the last-named.

The country may be conveniently divided into four regions. There is, first, the barren and desolate northern plateau where the vegetation is limited to a few stunted bushes. Secondly, especially in Southern Tibet, there are upland pastures, not unlike English moors, where the habitations are nomad tents and small stone-built towns. Thirdly, there are many deep ravines and rocky gorges, on the sides of which villages and monasteries are built. Fourthly, especially in Eastern Kham, rich pasturage and a plentiful vegetation is found in a down-like country. The whole of Tibet is exposed to intense cold and is usually subject to frosts from October to April. These have, of course, a greater effect on the vegetation, because all of the country lies south of 40 degrees and the summer has not therefore the compensating extra light which is such an important factor in high latitudes.

There are three principal roads. The official Chinese road runs over precipitous and rocky ledges from Tachienlu and goes by Batang and Chamdo. There is the easier route which the tea caravans follow, also from Tachienlu, but over rolling downs through Drango, Derge, and Kegudo. Thirdly, there is the northern road from Sining in Kansu, by Lake Kokonor and the Tsaidam and thence across Chang Tang. Tibet is thus extraordinarily shut in by nature from the outside world, with high mountains on the south, deserts on the north, and other mountains on each side. Throughout the historical period the closest culture connection has always been with China, but it has been a far distant dependency of that power. Isolation and hard climatic conditions have therefore combined to make the study of its inhabitants of particular value.

Both in its relation to China and to the West one of the most interesting parts of the central plateau is Chinese Turkestan, called by the Chinese Sinkiang (Hsinkiang), or the New Dominion. This region, which consists of over half a million square miles, is a plateau walled in by high mountains. On the south it is bounded by Kashmir and Tibet, on the west by the Pamirs and Russian Turkestan, on the north by Russian Turkestan, Siberia, and Mongolia. On the east part the boundary is made by the strip of Kansu, which forms a wedge between Tibet and Mongolia and partly by Tibet itself.

On the north it is walled in by the Tien-Shan and on the south by the Altyn Dagh and the Kunlun. It is open to China on the east. It contains a remarkable depression, falling at lowest point, near Lob Nor, to 2000 feet. This is drained by the Tarim, which with the River Cherchen falls into Lob Nor. North of the Tien-Shan the chief rivers are the Ili, which falls into Lake Balkash, and the Yuldur, which falls into Lake Balgrash. The depression of the Tarim basin and Dzungaria, which includes the ways through the mountains between the Tien-Shan and the Altai, form a convenient unit for ethnological discussion and belong ethnologically to the great area which includes China and Mongolia and contrasts with the region to the west, that is the Central Asian desert with its oases of Kashgar and Yarkand east of the Pamirs and the Aral-Caspian region to the west, including Khiva, Bokhara, and Samarqand. As always, however, in studying human geography the boundary is by no means absolute.

The region which we are studying is much of it desolate and "no one passes that way." The coldest inhabited part is Barkul, the hottest Turfan, which the Chinese call Ho-chow, Fire-district. I have discussed the general run of the trade routes, but it may serve to remind the reader that the roads run from Suchow, through the Jade gate of that city to Jili, from Urumchi to Kashgar, and also from Urumchi to Ku-ma-cheeh; there is a camel road to Kwei-wa-cheng; a road from Khotan to Tuen-heng-sien and to Suchow. Great importance attaches to these roads in a land where travel is always difficult, but where there has been great ethnic movement.

Owing to the difference of the geographical conditions and the influences to which the peoples have been exposed, it is convenient to describe the peoples of Tibet and of Chinese Turkestan separately.

Tibetan crania have been carefully studied by Turner and subsequently by Morant (VII. 3). Comparatively few measurements seem to have been made on the living, although a few were included in Risley's ethnographic survey of India. Until recently, of course, few travellers had penetrated into Tibet since the famous journey of the Abbe Huc.

There seems to be a certain amount of difference of opinion among the few authorities which we have. Turner (V. 16) says that there is a dolichocephalic and a "Mongolian" brachycephalic race in Tibet. He associates the former with the warrior or fighting class, drawn for the most part from the province of Kham. The round-headed people Turner believes to constitute the main stock. He suggests that it is from them that a large part of the occupants of the monasteries are recruited. Whether this last statement, which is made reservedly by Turner, is correct remains for further observation. Among the few Tibetan monks whom I examined both classes could be seen, but the long-headed type attracts the attention most, probably because of its unusual nature; it is certainly found in many of the monasteries. The distinction, however, is a useful one and convenient for purposes of nomenclature. I therefore propose to adopt Turner's names and call the long-heads the "Warrior" type and the short-heads the "Priestly" type, since, as will be shown later, Morant has confirmed the existence of two types but has called them A and B, labels which are unfortunately liable to confusion and not easily remembered by those who are not accustomed to think in mathematical symbols.

Rockhill, in his notes on the ethnology of Tibet, believes that with the exception of the north and north-east the population belongs essentially to one type. The purest representatives of this stock may be found among the pastoral tribes or Drupa which, whether found around Kokonor, in east, west, or Central Tibet, offer a uniform type. They are short, brachycephalic, with high cheek-bones, "though not so high as the Mongols"; the noses are usually narrow.

The primitive type is found among the nomads, for the settled people are more mixed and have an increasingly greater Chinese admixture as one goes towards China, and Indian admixture (Nepalese or Kashmiri) as one travels south-west. The reason for this is that the foreign immigrants never bring wives with them. The class whom Morant has called Class A belong to this type. Of the inhabitants of Kham, Rockhill says that there is absolutely nothing Mongol about them, and they are good representatives of the old Tibetan civilization. These are termed by Morant Class B.

Deniker appears to find in the Tibetans two different types, which however are not identical with those of Rockhill. One is "Mongoloid" and the other he connects with the Lolos. The latter type is characterized by a slender figure, straight eye-slits, and long and sometimes wavy hair.

Joyce briefly sums up the characters of the population by saying that the people are in the main Southern Mongolians with a considerable admixture of Indo-European blood.

Morant believes that there are in Tibet at least two distinct races. One of these, that from the southern provinces in the neighbourhood of Sikkim, which he calls Type A, is closely allied to the Southern Chinese, the "Malayans," and the Burmese. The other race, the "Khams Tibetans," show, according to the Coefficient of Racial Likeness method, no marked affinity with any other Oriental race, but resembles most the types called by Tildesley Burmese B and C, that is Karens and hybrid Karens. "The skull is very similar to the Fuegians and the Moriori, and the impression cannot be avoided that we may possibly be dealing with widely scattered fragments of a fundamental primitive human type with a long-headed, broad-faced, rugous and massive cranium."

In a subsequent paper he has enlarged this idea and states that his Tibetan A is intermediate between the Nepalese and the Southern Chinese. On the other hand, "the measurements of Koganei's Northern Chinese which diverge most markedly from the supposed Chinese type are also those which are intermediate between Tibetan B and pure Chinese characters, but the C.R.L. at once disposes of the idea of a relationship between Koganei's Chinese and Tibetan B."

In addition to these two types it is also probable that a

third strain has entered into the population of Tibet, namely the Alpine. So far, however, little definite indications of the presence of this type have been reported and its presence must await confirmation.

There remains then to discuss the relationship of the two types. Haddon (I. 19, 105) suggests that the Warrior class evidently represents an old stock, "affinities to which may be looked for in other marginal areas ; they may, indeed, have been the first inhabitants of Tibet."

In the earlier chapters of this book attention has already been drawn to a tall dolichocephalic race who appear in various parts of Asia and who usually seem to be of considerable antiquity. They have been provisionally called Proto-Nordics. Here again in Tibet this same stock, tall, long-headed, big-boned, and quite distinct from Yellow man, appears. It seems probable that we are justified in relating the two. In Tibet, and as we shall see later in Japan, the stock seems to have survived in a more primitive form than possibly elsewhere, but the general characteristics are not dissimilar. It is probable that there is considerable difference between these various groups which I have classed together under the same name. Such a difference is to be expected when we find isolated units of a primitive stock scattered over a wide area. The evidence seems to point to some sort of a conclusion like this. The hypothesis must, however, be considered as a purely tentative one until further evidence is accumulated in regard to the relationships of these very interesting people.

The other element, Turner's Priestly class, seem in all probability to belong to the Parœcean race. Such a conclusion is accepted by Haddon and agrees with the findings of Morant's coefficient.

In the northern part of Tibet there is no doubt a certain amount of Mongol influence, but the deserts have prevented much admixture. There has been Chinese influence for many generations. This influence has probably done little to change the type of the population which is akin to that of the Chinese.

In the south attention should be drawn to Morant's " cranial linkage " of the Tibetan of the Priestly type and the Nepalese. It would seem as if the westward extension

PLATE VI

A KHAMS TIBETAN

[face p. 172

of the Pareœans into the plateaux and mountainous region had to a certain extent ended in differentiation. Possibly this differentiation may be due to admixture with western strains.

Emphasis in any case should be laid on the fact that if we take the Southern Chinese as typical Pareœans we find that they differ but little from the Northern Chinese, or the inhabitants of the Indo-Chinese area or some of the Tibetans, whereas these various types differ quite considerably from one another.

There is more information in regard to the peoples of Chinese Turkestan. The Chinese themselves admit three classes of inhabitants, very ancient aboriginal races, such as the Hsien-yuen, Chinese and Turkish peoples, and there are both Chinese and Turkish cities.

It has been suggested that in this region the Chinese first developed as a people and that they gradually spread from the Tarim basin, possibly owing to the alteration in oasis conditions which may have driven them from their old homes. The region has been most carefully studied from an anthropological point of view as well as from an archæological point of view by Sir Aurel Stein. Most of his work has, however, been unfortunately devoted to more modern aspects of the problem and the early history is still far from clear. His collection of anthropological data has been reported on by Joyce (VII. 6).

We are concerned with four groups of people in this area. The first are the Taranchi and the Torgot. The second the Kirghiz, the Dolan, the Kelpin, and the Aksu. The third group is composed of desert peoples, the nucleus being composed of Turfan, Khotan, Korla, and Charklik. Finally, there is an interesting group of Chinese, to whom the Loblik are probably related. There are also some intermediate peoples, and Joyce is inclined to class the Polu and the mixed population of Hami with the desert group, to whom he believes that the Niya and Keriya, although mixed with some other element, should also be classed.

The Taranchi or Ili Tatars at present live in Semirechie and in the Transcaspian territory. They migrated from Sinkiang when Kuldja came under Chinese control, they therefore may be considered to belong to their old home from a geographical point of view. Czaplicka believes them to be the descendants of the old Uigur, and to belong more to the western oases than to the eastern part of Sinkiang. They have been variously described. Czaplicka says that they are like the Sarts and are the least "Turkic" of all the Iranian Turks in physical form. Paissel (VII. 8) describes them as being a Turkish folk of mixed "Aryan and Mongolian features." They have a stature that is higher than most of the Mongols (165 cms.), very round heads, the cephalic index being reported to be as high as 87, and narrow noses, with a nasal index of 66. Racially it would seem probable that they should be classed with such people as the round-headed Buriats (see page 180). The evidence appears to suggest that we have among these peoples, as among so many of the Central Asiatic peoples, an ancient mixture of Alpine or Armenoid blood and possibly early branches of Yellow man. It is not unremarkable that we should not find them with a continuous distribution, but that they should be scattered across a very wide area, often in what appears in the present state of our knowledge to be almost ethnological islands, much in the same way that similar isolated round-headed groups are found in Western Asia. There can be little doubt that the Sarts of the uplands belong to the same racial groups as Czaplicka has suggested (see page 114).

Ivanovski has suggested that there is an anthropological type which he calls "Central Asiatic." He describes their features thus. They have dark coloured hair and eyes, light hair and eyes do occur but only in exceptional cases. The stature of the greater number is medium. High stature does occur among some peoples, such as the Kaizak of the Middle Horde, the town Taranchi, and some Sarts. The head is brachycephalic or hyperbrachycephalic. The nose is usually leptorrhine, but broad noses are sometimes found, especially among such peoples as the Kaizak of the Middle Horde. The trunk is usually long.

The presence of blue eyes is of particular interest. I have already called attention to the presence of light eyes in various parts of West Central Asia. Data appear to be lacking in regard to the Ili peoples, but in the Altai region Yadrintseff has drawn attention to the fact that many of the peoples in the region of the Altai who have had no contact with recent colonists have blue eyes, chestnut hair, and non-prominent features, a condition which probably expresses in more accurate language what Paissel meant when he records the presence of " Aryan features " among the Taranchi.

The second sub-group in this area, the Torgots, belong historically to the Mongols and are more conveniently discussed in the section which deals with those widely-spread peoples (see page 180).

The second group, the Kirghiz, Dolan, Kelpin and Aksu, appear to be very distinct from the other peoples in this area, and Joyce suggests that they are a mixture of " Southern Mongolian and Turkish " stock. The Dolan are remarkable for having as many as 65 per cent with a rosy brown colour ; except among the Kirghiz where fair hair is rare, the average amount of fair and medium hair amounts to about 15 per cent. Dark eyes are the rule except among the Kelpin, where 14 per cent had light eyes. All this group are wavy-haired. All these peoples are characterized by a very high cephalic index, the head being both absolutely and relatively short and broad.

The skin-colour of the desert people has often a tinge of yellow in it, due possibly, as Joyce suggests, to contact with Chinese, although possibly this element may be much earlier than recent Chinese intrusion. These people also show a higher percentage of black hair than their neighbours. Their hair is in texture practically always curly, a feature which they share in common with the Pamir people and which isolates them markedly from the Chinese. They have the most deeply pigmented eyes of the region under consideration. Apart from the Korla folk, who have an index of 81, the rest of the desert people are markedly brachycephalic.

The last group includes the Chinese. Of them no less than 65 per cent have a yellow skin, and 75 per cent have black hair, practically all of them have straight hair, and though the majority of them have dark eyes, yet 15 per cent blue eyes are found. Unlike the other peoples we have been describing, they and the Loblik are long-headed, the cephalic index of 20 Chinese being as low as 76.

The general problem raised by these peoples is of great interest. The majority of peoples in the area undoubtedly have a common element. This is described by Joyce as Iranian. It seems better to accept Haddon's use of the term Pamiri. This type is certainly related to Alpine man. Joyce believes that four other elements are represented. The first is a tall, dark, brachycephalic race of White affinities with broad cheek-bones and straighter hair. These he describes as the " Turkish " race. To a large extent, as has been shown, the cultural and physical types do coincide, and the relationship of these Turki people has been discussed in dealing with the area to the west (see page 114). Finally, there seems to be an element which connects these folk with the Tibetans and a very different stock which Joyce describes as Southern Mongolian, i.e. Parœcean. He emphasizes the point that the original inhabitants of the area, including the cities now buried in the sand, were probably of Alpine stock, and that the " Mongolian " type has had very little influence on the population, this being limited to a slight Tibetan influence on the desert peoples and restricted Chinese influence on the east.

These conclusions are of the very greatest importance, especially in relation to the origin of the Chinese. I have already shown that some scholars believe that it is in Chinese Turkestan that the original motherland of the Chinese is to be found, while others put it in West Central China. Haddon places it in Northern Kansu (I. 19, 106) and most authors are, I believe, inclined to consider it axiomatic that they were then at least in close contact with the west. It would seem to follow that either the contact must have been purely cultural, or else all traces of early Chinese influence have been consumed by successive immigrations of Turko-Mongol peoples. There is a further possibility that the Chinese type as we see it to-day must be separated from the culture. That this is by no means an impossibility is shown by the fact already quoted that the chalcolithic culture in China which is non-Chinese is apparently associated with a Chinese physical type. If we accept this solution of the dilemma we are bound to suppose that the early originators of the Chinese culture were mostly of Pamiri type, and that if they had any Yellow blood it was not sufficient to influence the people with whom they came in contact on the west. As they advanced eastwards they would have been absorbed in the Yellow race which has absorbed so many invaders of China. I do not think that there is at present sufficient evidence to support a theory of this type. It appears to be the type of dilemma which faces the enquirer who endeavours to correlate the work of various authors who are approaching the same problem from a different angle.

The other peoples can probably be more simply classified. They seem to consist of different degrees of admixture of peoples who are so far differentiated that they have become sub-groups of the same race, namely, the Alpine and the Armenoid. The Turki race, though it is rather a culture than a race, seems to be an early mixture of western elements and of folk akin to the Yellow race. Probably the mixture is a very early one and had taken place before these peoples were in Chinese Turkestan.

B.   MONGOLIA

Mongolia, which has given its name to a vast number of individuals of the human race, consists of a very extensive area. Speaking generally, it consists of a wide plateau, which in places is waterless. It extends from the Pamirs on the west to the borders of Manchuria on the east, and divides the warm and fertile plain of China from the cold Siberian depression on the north. To the west, except for a narrow strip of country, it has formed a boundary which has prevented all movement from north to south. This whole area has by its conformation played a very important part in the whole ethnological history of Asia, and, indeed, in its political history at certain times.

Mongolia proper is almost as large as China proper. Its northern boundaries are the provinces of Tomsk, Yeneseisk, Irkutsk, and Transbaikalia, the actual boundaries being, for the most part, the Altai and the Zayan Mountains, the latter of which are continued eastwards as the Yablonoi Mountains. The eastern boundary is formed by the Khingan Mountains, which divide it from Manchuria. Along its southern edge it is bounded by the westerly continuation of the Khingan

N

Mountains, and more to the west by the great escarpment on which the Great Wall is built. Further still to the west the southern boundary is formed by that strip of fertile land lying to the north of the Nan-Shan which forms the dividing line between the desert of Taklamakan and Gobi. Physiographically it consists of highlands, which rise gradually from south-west to north-east and are slightly hollowed in the centre. The borders are extremely mountainous and Gobi is divided by the lesser Altai.

The roads through these boundaries are very important for our present purpose. On the west between the Tien-Shan and the Altai there are three depressions, all of which give access to the west. These are, first, the Black Irtish River between Ektag Altai and the Tarbagatai Mountains, the most frequented route which leads past the town of Chuguchah, and thirdly, the road which follows the beds of Lakes Ayar and Ebi, and connects with Lake Balkash. The south-western boundary may be said to coincide with the most strategic roads in Asia; the northern road runs from Barkul along the northern slopes of the Tien-Shan. This is the route for Dzungaria, whence the way to the west lies along one of the roads I have already mentioned. The strategic point to the south-east of Barkul is Hami (Khamil), which is of especial importance in its relation to the Southern Tien-Shan road that leads to Kashgaria. From Hami the road leads to Anshi and along the old desert way into the Jade Gate at Suchow. Of the region by the desert road, which the Chinese kept open for so many hundred years, an old Chinese topographer writes : " For many miles there are no barbarians dwelling, or cattle grazing, nor is there water or grass and, moreover, no one passes that way." It has been suggested by many that the Chinese came into China this way by the swamps of Lob Nor, and the little belt on the slopes of the Nan-Shan which bounds Mongolia. There are also roads through the great Ordos bend, much of which is desert, to the city of Kwei-wa-cheng and to the Kalgan, joining on the way the road that leads to the north, to Urga, to Karakoram, and to Uliassetai, dividing somewhere north of Kalgan in these different directions and sending a further branch to the north-east to Dolon Nor.

Mongolia may be divided into three parts, North-west

Mongolia, Gobi, and Inner Mongolia, or, as it is sometimes divided, into Outer and Inner Mongolia. The great Ordos bend of the Hwang Ho, although it is separated from Mongolia by the river, belongs to it both ethnically and geographically. Much of the country is desert, except in the neighbourhood of the mountains, but Inner Mongolia is better watered and has in recent years, since the fall of the power of the Mings, become in many ways one of the typical wandering grounds of the nomad pastoral Mongols.

The Mongols are regarded by Deniker as a more homogeneous group than the Turks, but he divides them into three groups, the Western Mongols or Kalmucks, the Eastern Mongols, and the Buriats. The extension of these people is far beyond the limits of Mongolia, as the Kalmucks are found as far to the west as the Volga, and the Buriats are at present, for the most part, situated in Siberia, although some of them are to be found in Mongolia.

The racial problem of the Mongols is of the greatest interest but, unfortunately, few skulls have been collected in Western Europe, and the records are not as full as could be wished. Two entirely opposing views have been taken on their racial affinities. Deniker says (I. 9, 379) that "the type of the *Mongolian race* is very strongly marked among most of the Kalmucks and Khalkhas ; it is less distinctly marked among the Buriats." Morant, on the other hand, believes that the Torgots, that is, certain of the nomadic tribes of Western Mongolia, Astrakhan Kalmucks, and the Buriats are intimately related to the Kalmucks and to the Telenghites who are Mongols from the neighbourhood of the Altai. He believes that they occupy an intermediate position between these two extreme and dissimilar types, that is, the Telenghites and the Kalmucks. He finds further that they do not belong to the group which he describes as Oriental and which includes such peoples as the Chinese and the Burmese.

Not only is there this extreme difference of opinion, but also various authors give entirely different measurements for people whom they call by the same name. This being so, it is necessary before discussing the physical characters of these peoples to enquire briefly into the nomenclature in ordinary use. First, the Western Mongols are said by Deniker to call themselves Eleuts and to be known as

Kalmucks by their neighbours. This term has been used very loosely not only by travellers, but also by anthropologists. They are undoubtedly scattered over a very wide area, owing to their warlike and nomadic habits, but there are compact groups of them on the Astrakhan steppes and near Stravropol and also in the territory of the Don Cossack Horde. Ivanovski (J. Anthrop. Soc., Moscow, LXXI, 1893) states that the Western Horde of the Mongols were called Urat by the Manchus and U-lat by the Chinese, which became transliterated into western languages as Eleut. According to the Mongol historians there are four branches, the Dzungar, the Torgot, the Choschot, and the Durbot, each with a colour or banner. Some of the Torgots migrated as far west as the Volga in 1630, when they came under Russian rule, as did many of the Mongols in 1686. There was a great easterly migration in 1771, lasting eight months. They eventually settled in the Ili district. Potanin believes that the Torgots of the Tarbagatai are the direct descendants of the migrants and that the Altai Tatars have been settled in this district for a long time.

Some authors consider that the Telenghites should be considered as Altai Mongols associated with this western group, and they are often called Mongols. Culturally, however, they are Turks and the term Mongol should not be applied to them. Physically, on the other hand, they have undoubtedly absorbed much Mongol blood. The history of these people will show how difficult it is to express clearly the ethnological position of such nomadic habits who have traversed even in recent times such vast areas. A similar account could be given of the other branches, but the Torguts must suffice as an example of their migratory capabilities.

The second important branch of the Mongols, the Buriats, are said to be an offshoot of the Khalkha Mongols. Their centre of dispersion at present is Transbaikalia, and they seem to have absorbed elements of many different physical and cultural groups.

Finally, the third group of Mongols, usually known as the " true " Mongols, the people who claim kinship with Genghiz Khan, belong to Gobi and Inner Mongolia. They also include a number of tribes and banners, of which the best known are the Khalkhas in the north and the Chahkhar in the south.[1]

The majority of these peoples are connected linguistically. They have been bound together in loose but immense organizations and many of them have the same cultural elements. They have also many physical elements in common, but it seems not improbable that they have absorbed, at least in part, a good many other elements.

They are usually but not always distinguished by a high cephalic index, although there appears to be considerable differences even between members of the same group; the Alar Buriats are reported to have an index of 82, the Selanga Buriats of 88, which is closer to Morant's figure for a mixed collection of Buriat skulls of 84, the other measurements being taken on the living. In Inner Mongolia, on the other hand, the indices are closer to those of the Chinese. Generally, however, it seems probable that we may consider the Mongols in the broadest sense to have very broad heads. They are always of medium stature, and on the whole there does not appear to be any great variation in this character, which is usually in the neighbourhood of 163 cms. This is all the more remarkable, because they appear, at least in Southern Mongolia, closely to resemble the Chinese in cephalic index, but not in stature.

The hair-colour appears to be always black and therefore does not serve as any guide to race. The character of the skin is of importance. Reicher states, at second hand, that the skin is yellowish among the Buriats, but he adds that it is lighter on the unexposed parts of the body. Deniker describes it as pale yellow or of a brownish hue. Porotov says that among the Alar Buriats it is not white but brunette. Among the Chahkhar Mongols of Inner Mongolia it is seldom yellow, but brown on the face and whitish, or rather a dull

---

[1] In 1922 the Mongols told me that they were divided as follows : Outer Mongolia, including the four old clans whose rulers claimed to be the descendants of Genghiz Khan, was divided into 57 banners. East and South Mongolia was divided into 49 banners, and the border, under Chinese rule, into 15 banners. Some of them told me that they believed that there were quite recognizable differences between some of the different groups physically although not cultural or linguistically. I have no means of checking their statement. The border country does, of course, present certain differences due to Chinese intermixture, but some of the families have the greatest objection to marrying into families who have Chinese blood in their veins.

brunet, on those parts of the body covered with clothing. It seems probable that although undoubtedly a yellowish tint occurs on the whole, the complexion of the Mongols tends to a brown or a *brunet* rather than yellow.

Among some of the Mongols the Mongolian fold undoubtedly occurs, even in so high a percentage as 25, and among the Buriats Porotov found that the eye aperture was oblique in half the cases which he examined. These observations would suggest that if we accept these characters as being typical of Yellow man, the evidence of which racial group the Mongols belong to is somewhat conflicting.

It seems probable that this disaccord of the evidence is due rather to the difficulty of deciding which tribes who speak Mongol languages do not belong to this physical type, and which of those who are of the physical type do not belong to the Mongol linguistic group ; some of the Tungus tribes, for instance, really belong to the physical group. On the whole the facts adduced by both Deniker and Morant—although they do draw different conclusions—must be construed so that we admit an underlying physical type. This type is not everywhere to be found among Mongol-speaking peoples, but the frequency with which it occurs suggests that at one time there was a comparatively homogeneous stock, extending, perhaps, beyond the limits of Mongolia but centred round that region. This type should probably be called Central Asiatic, rather than Siberian as Morant calls it.

This type differs from all the peoples which we have met with in Southern Asia. The great divide of the desert has prevented them from mixing with the Tibetan stock. I have already argued that though possibly the Northern Chinese may have a certain amount of Mongol blood, a possibility which must be admitted on historical grounds, yet on the whole it has not affected their type. This point is strongly emphasized both by Reicher and Morant, who see very considerable differences between the Mongols, and they were treating for the most part with Northern and Western Mongols and the Chinese.

In dealing with the tribes of Siberia it will be seen that there are clear differences between them and the Mongols. There remain then the people on the west. We have in most the peoples who are vaguely called Turks; here again we have not dissimilar problems, owing to the racial and the cultural boundaries cutting across one another.

The Mongols appear to be a wedge of peoples driven in between the Parœcean man on the south and the Arctic and sub-Arctic tribes on the north. The geographical conditions are such as to render this suggestion not unlikely, for the Mongols may be said to hold the key position which is either the gate of the east or the west. In Turkestan, at Anau, as has been already stated on page 72, we find evidence of an early culture which has its counterpart in the more westerly parts of Asia. That this culture extended also to the east we also know. In China it is not associated with a physical type. It seems, however, not improbable that we, at least to a certain extent, find a physical type which corresponds in its movements to this culture, and that this physical type is the homogeneous stratum underlying the Mongols. It seems also probable from an examination of their physical characters that the Mongols represent a branch of that race which I have described as Alpine with, of course, considerable admixture of other races. It seems not improbable that they are, on the whole, more akin to the Armenoid branch than to any other, but this point has not yet been worked out in detail. There is certainly a large element in the present population of Inner Mongolia which appears from an examination of the living to suggest this branch of the human family.

It is a very remarkable fact that, in spite of differences which are often considerable, we should find such a homogeneity. It must, however, be remembered that within historic times the Mongols have wandered far and that over much of the area the population has always been small. It is also likely that among nomads in a big area there would be less divergence of type than between a settled population of relatively much greater density.

There can be little doubt that the original Armenoid type has been much modified. We may either suggest a new type, or with greater probability suppose that contact with other races has served to modify the original strain. Such a suggestion would serve to show why there is possibly a connection, according to Morant's interesting theory, between the

Buriats and the Koreans, although, no doubt, he would have found a closer connection if he had taken skulls from Inner Mongolia to make his comparison.

We have, however, left the very great and undoubted difficulty that many of the Mongols appear to show features which we are accustomed to call Mongolian, but which would if they were at bottom Armenoid be a misnomer. Several points must, however, be remembered. First, it is by no means certain how far Yellow man is to be divided from the White. It may be that we have among these peoples an intermediate type. It seems on the whole more scientific, however, to suggest that as the Mongols have for long been an intrusive element between the northern and the Pareœan branches of the same type they may represent an intermediate form as the result of mixing. In any case they must be considered as distinct from those whom we usually call Mongolian, a paradox which is merely verbal and not actual. There are certainly among some Mongol tribes traces of a greater degree of admixture with Yellow man, and among those tribes the characters of Yellow man are naturally striking. Among other tribes, however, this mixing is less obvious. The Mongol physical type can be seen in my photograph, which should be compared with that of an average Chinese from Northern China.

I have used the word Mongol all through this discussion for lack of a better term. It must, however, be remembered that the physical type by no means coincides with the cultural and what might be called almost the national type. Nor is the physical type entirely limited to Mongolia or the only type which occurs there. I should rather be inclined to call it the typical form of man who lives in that region at present. The type does not extend to the east to any great extent. It has only passed sporadically, as far as can be judged, beyond the Wall, south of which it is nowhere found as a group. It extends beyond the northern limits of Mongolia into Transbaikalia and the provinces which border the Altai, although there are suggestions that its extension in this direction is recent, as recent, according to Shirokogoroff, as between the first and fourth centuries A.D.

To the west the Mongol physical type in a great many cases becomes indistinguishable from that of the Turks. But this statement must be qualified. There are in the west Mongol tribes who have recently migrated westwards. These on the whole have retained their own characteristics, a fact to be expected, considering that they have only been a short time in their present habitat. In this way we find that the Kalmucks of Astrakhan, recent immigrants to the west, still retain the features which relate them to the Buriats. The Telenghites, on the other hand, who are culturally more closely related to the Turks, present relationships to their neighbours but are further from the Mongol type.

The case is closely paralleled to the Turks who, as we have seen in Asia Minor, on the whole present slight differences which will serve to distinguish them from the mixed Armenoid and Mediterranean population, but more to the east show an Armenoid type, increasingly mixed with other elements till it becomes indistinguishable almost from the Mongol.

Besides the Mongols and their allies there are in Inner Mongolia a large number of Chinese. I have shown elsewhere how, although probably the true ethnic divide may be considered as the escarpment along which the Great Wall runs, yet at various times the advance of the Chinese agriculturist has completely driven back the nomad Mongol. At the beginning of the Ming Dynasty the Chinese sphere ran apparently as far as the edge of Gobi, quite an appreciable distance into Mongolia. They retired later, and are now beginning to regain lost territory. This advance and retreat of the Chinese is particularly instructive in regard to the ethnology of the Mongols, and shows the danger of generalizing too widely. Undoubtedly a good deal of mixing is taking place between the two strains, but, on the whole, at present the Chinese type is making great headway in Inner Mongolia. Side by side then with the Mongol type we have in apparently increasing numbers a population which is in main closely akin to the stock of Northern China, but with a certain, possibly almost negligible, amount of Mongol blood.

There are also other racial elements in Mongolia proper; these are, first, Manchu and other Tungusic elements, who are probably of importance in the east. Their racial affinities will be discussed in the following section. On the north it seems probable that there are northern elements existing as groups, but there seems to be little information on this point. On the south and west the Mongols appear to have invaded other territories and not so much to have been invaded, but here, too, there is an important Chinese element in the population.

If we sum up then the physical characteristics of the inhabitants of Mongolia, we may say that there seems to be an underlying homogeneous element among the people who claim to be Mongols; this is probably, especially on the borders, mixed with other strains, but is essentially different from Yellow or Mongoloid man. Their territory has been invaded by Yellow man, who has at times mixed much with the population, and to-day often exists in groups within Mongol territory, but is always physically and culturally distinct. The Mongols are connected by blood with some branch of Alpine or Armenoid man.

C. MANCHURIA

To the north-east of Mongolia lies the territory which is known to the Chinese as three Eastern Provinces and to Europeans as Manchuria. It now forms part of China proper. Although it can hardly be considered an ethnological province it is convenient to treat it separately, especially since the dynastic name of Manchu is so well known. It is bounded on the north and east by Siberia and Korea, on the south-west by Mongolia, and its southern extremity forms a peninsula which extends into the Yellow Sea. It has an area of something under 400,000 square miles.

Manchuria is traversed from north to south by the Khingan Mountains, which rather than the actual political frontier form the ethnological divide on the north-west, and by the Changpai-Shan on the south-eastern boundary. Spurs from these ranges run towards the centre of the country. This central region in the south is made up of an alluvial plain which occupies most of Fengtien and is of great agricultural value. It is continued northwards in the valley of the Sungari. In the north and centre there are wide marshlands and undulating forest country. There are two main lines of approach. On the north Manchuria lies open to the valley of the Amur and on the south to the Yellow Sea, and a consideration of this fact will serve to explain much of the ethnical history of the land. The political boundary with Siberia is the Amur River, and this boundary has not proved a barrier to ethnic movement. The Chinese frontier is artificial.

Unfortunately little systematic anthropology has been done in this area, and the use of dynastic names has done much to confuse the issue. As is natural from the situation the country has both within recent years and in much earlier times been extensively occupied by immigrants. The Chinese especially have migrated into Manchuria and to-day form one of the most important, if not the most important, element in the population. There has also been considerable Mongol intermixture, a point of considerable interest which will be considered later.

There appears to be considerable difference of opinion in regard to the Manchus themselves. It should be remembered that the name is of recent origin and is not known until the early part of the seventeenth century. The Manchus are generally described as being a Tungusic tribe. This is a linguistic term and cannot be applied to somatological evidence, a confusion which has unfortunately been made by Torii in his otherwise valuable paper on the Manchus. Czaplicka has brilliantly compared the use of the word Manchu in Eastern Asia to the use of the word Bantu in Africa, both terms becoming meaningless when we are dealing with physical characters.

Torii describes the true Manchus, that is the people of the soil who are not immigrant Chinese or other recent settlers, as having a yellow skin, hair absolutely straight and black, beard small, straight and scattered, very little hair on the body, and with two forms of face, one long and the other round. The eyes are always brown. Such few observations as I have been able to make on Manchus confirms this description. I am inclined to believe, however, that occasionally an hazel tinge occurs in the eyes. The observations on the cephalic index are, as usual, the most numerous data available. Here there appears to be considerable difference of opinion. Crania Ethnica give 79, a figure closely corresponding to the cephalic index of the Northern Chinese, and Parjakoff's figure, quoted by Ivanovski, is similar (82 on the living). Other authors have, however, come to different conclusions. Both Ujfalvy and Torii state that the Manchus are extremely brachycephalic, giving indices of 85 and 87 respectively.

It will be seen that there exists here an exact parallel to what is found among the Eastern Mongols. Some of the observations appear to suggest a close relationship with the Northern Chinese, others a very different strain. I think that the skin-colour and the eye-colour, if closely examined, show similar divergences; some of the Manchus are very definitely yellow, others, though no doubt they might be classed as yellow or brown by a superficial observer, incline to brown on the exposed parts of the body and to white on the unexposed parts. The solution which I am inclined to suggest is that we have here again an old mixture of Alpine with Yellow man, not dissimilar to what has occurred in Mongolia. A very large number of Manchus show facial features which belong to the west rather than the east, adding additional weight to this hypothesis. In a small collection of crania, or in a series of measurements made in one area, as, for instance, Torii's were, there is every possibility that such a racial mixture, cutting across national and linguistic boundaries as it does, would be obscured or entirely concealed.

Since the seventeenth century the Manchus, with their military organization of the Bannermen, have been widely scattered over China. For the most part they have become entirely absorbed in the population. Certain exceptions have, however, occurred. It was one of the terms which China forced upon her conquerors that no Chinese woman should ever enter the Imperial harem, and in many families alliance with the Manchus would have been considered a disgrace; there remain, therefore, some Manchus who to-day have probably retained, even in China, their old racial type, but for the most part it is necessary to search in some of the remoter parts of Manchuria for the old Manchu type.

Not only have the Chinese overrun Manchuria, but in recent years Japanese and other immigrants, especially in the railway zone, have contributed largely towards the alteration of the original population.

PLATE VII

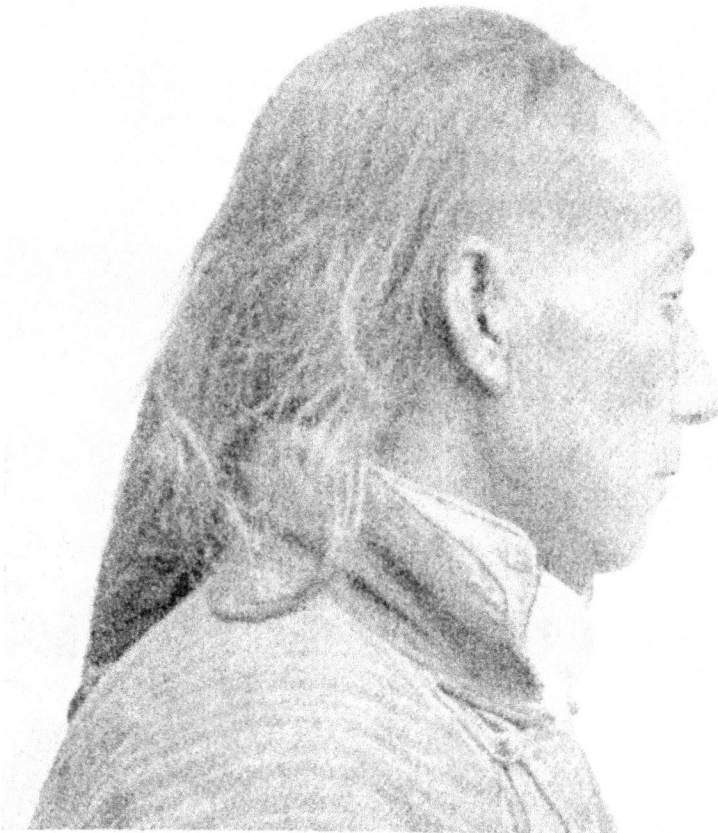

A MANCHU

[*face p. 188*

The examination of the standard deviations of the measurements on Manchus made by Shirokogoroff brings out an extremely interesting point on which sufficient stress does not appear to have been laid. That observer found that the mean value of measurements made on Chinese in Manchuria was not dissimilar to those of the Manchus, but differed from the other Chinese of Northern China. The standard deviations are, however, extremely different. Shirokogoroff does not believe that standard deviations can be used as a measure of racial admixture; his own measurements might, however, be used to confute him. The Chinese standard deviations are very high, as might be expected where there was every reason to expect racial admixture; among the Manchus, however, especially in the cephalic index, the standard deviation is very low. This is all the more remarkable, because most of the neighbouring peoples show high deviations. I am at a loss to account for this small deviation, especially since, as I have shown, other evidence points to a mixing of races. The series would appear to be sufficiently long (82 ♂). It is possible that they may belong to one endogamous group, but in any case the figures deserve a careful investigation, and it is to be hoped that further enquiries will be made in Manchuria and this interesting point considered.

D. KOREA

Korea is the third of the northern peripheral countries of China. It is a country of particular interest, as although it has for the most part been permeated with Chinese culture, it had the misfortune to occupy the middle position between that country and Japan, and the modern connection with Japan, and at an early period intermarriages took place between the Royal houses of the two countries. It was through Korea that the Buddhist missionaries reached Japan. The country consists of a peninsula of high mountain ranges and plateaux. The plain country, nowhere very extensive, is confined to the south and west. It lies immediately contiguous with Manchuria and the Russian Maritime Province, the Tumen and Yalu rivers forming its northern and western boundaries. On the other sides it is surrounded by the sea, but the distance across the Fusan channel is not great.

The term Korea must be considered as national and cultural rather than physical, and although the Japanese scientists have produced monographs of considerable magnitude on the physical characters of the Koreans, their studies have been for the most part intensive and most of the comparisons have been limited to Japanese.

The published figures indicate that the Koreans are very heterogeneous. Both the work of Kubo and Shirokogoroff, each of whom has published figures in statistical form. From the geographical position of Korea it would rather be expected that the Koreans would be a mixed race. We know that within historic times they have been subjected to a series of foreign influences. The Chinese annals give considerable details on this subject and are conveniently summarized by Shirokogoroff. To-day there can be little doubt that all along the western border and in the north Chinese elements form a very appreciable part of the population. In the west the Manchu element is also a dominant feature, to the exclusion, it would almost seem, of the original Korean element. Historically, within recent times, the Mongols have overrun Korea. The mixed type of the population can therefore hardly be doubted and, judging by the statistical constants, it would be unwise to speak of a Korean type. Such a type would only be the mean of a series of elements of wide diversity. The stature alone shows a rather low constant. This is, however, to be expected, as it is approximately about 163 cms., a stature that is found among many of the peoples in this region. Mixing of different peoples with the same stature would not serve to increase the variation. The cephalic index, by itself an uncertain guide but so often pointing the way to racial affinities, is about 83, which is about half-way between the extreme types with a head index of 86 and the more common index which is in the neighbourhood of 81, an additional argument, when combined with the standard deviation, of admixture. It has already been seen that even among the Mongols we get such an admixture of types, the one approximating to the Alpine type of Europe and the other to the type of Northern China. Such a simple explanation is hardly sufficient to explain the general type of the Koreans. Shirokogoroff has suggested that the basic type of the Koreans is that of the Palæasiatics ; he believes such peoples occupied all the coast-line of the Gulf of Chihli, Korea, and practically north of a line connecting Korea with Lake Baikal, at the time which he describes as the first ethnical movement about the fourth millennium B.C. Two millennia later the Palæasiatics were restricted to Korea and the coast-line of the Maritime Province. Our knowledge of the archæology of the whole region is hardly sufficient to justify so definite an arrangement as he suggests, and I can hardly admit such fundamental racial changes in so short a time, if we use the analogy of the west, where we know racial changes have proceeded so slowly, to apply to the east. It seems not improbable, however, that some early type may, as one of the components of the highly complex physical form of the Koreans, include as a basis the aboriginal Palæasiatic type. This is all the more interesting, because we find that they serve as link between the type of Yellow man in the south and those in the north, a fact which suggests that such a type was once widely distributed over Northern Asia, and that the invading wedge of the Mongols and Turki peoples served to separate the two peoples. The best Koreans then, more than any other people, remain as relics of the early population mixed with the later invaders, some of them of Yellow blood and some Alpine. Haddon (*Wanderings of Peoples*, page 337) has drawn attention to the fact already suggested by Bælz, that the Koreans probably played a part in the peopling of Japan. We know, historically, that Korea was a highway through which culture passed to Japan. The physical type may have passed the same way, but it seems not improbable that at the time that Japan was receiving her early inhabitants, other than Ainu, probably the whole of the eastern coast of Asia had a more homogeneous population than at present. It must never be forgotten, however, that there is undoubtedly a great connection between Korea and Japan, and that it is more than probable that the Koreans may justly claim Japan as a daughter country.

CHAPTER VIII

Arctic Asia

SIBERIA occupies a vast area in Northern Asia and forms altogether about a quarter of the whole continent. I propose to include in this term what is usually known as the great Siberian plain, which stretches from Turania and the Urals to the Behring Strait. It forms a triangle; the apex is situated near the mouth of the River Obi and one angle is near the Aral Sea and the other at the Behring Sea. It is bounded on the north by the Arctic Ocean, on the west by the Ural Mountains, and on the south by a series of great mountain ranges, in which the head-waters of the great rivers, the Obi, the Yenesei, and the Lena, are situated. These frontiers make it very difficult of access.

On the south it is separated from China by high mountains and by deserts; on the north the Arctic Ocean forms an impassable barrier and a frozen rampart of the world, less easy to traverse than the flaming ramparts which Lucretius declared to bound the earth. On the east mountains separate it from one of the stormiest seas in the world.

Only on the west is the boundary less severe. Here not only are the mountains far less impenetrable than our maps would suggest, but also the navigable rivers approach comparatively closely to one another. It is along this route, and especially through the steppe land in the southern regions, that migrating peoples have moved, and the wild, conquering hordes of Asia have poured into Europe.

It may be conveniently divided into two parts. The first part is Western Siberia from the Yenesei to the Ural Mountains, and the second Eastern Siberia. The former is generally of tertiary formation, flat, and bounded by mountains on the south. The latter is older geologically. The surface differs considerably as it rises in places into hilly regions, and in the extreme east it is bounded by high mountains.

This broken surface has rendered much of Eastern Siberia difficult of access. In spite, however, of geographical difficulties there is sufficient evidence to warrant the assertion that there has at various times been close communication between the extreme east of this region and the American continent.

Taken as a whole, the region is very large; it is shut off from the south by lofty mountain ranges, but open to climatic influences from the north. It is subject, therefore, to a cold continental climate, some of the greatest ranges of temperature found on the earth's surface being recorded in Siberia; except in certain parts the subsoil remains permanently frozen.

Only parts have a truly Arctic climate, the rest being sub-arctic. The Arctic region includes the Governments of Tobolsk and Yeneseisk, except in the south, the territory of Yakutsk and part of the old Maritime territory which is now included in the Far Eastern Republics. The sub-arctic zone has been divided into various subdivisions; first, the southern part of the Tobolsk and the Yeneseisk Governments and most of Tomsk. Secondly, the region of the Kirghiz steppes in its widest sense, and the south-eastern part of Siberia, including Transbaikalia and the Irkutsk region. Finally, we may consider the coastal area as a separate climatic province.

The Arctic region has a fairly uniform set of conditions. There may be found the greatest extremes of heat and cold of any part in the world. The summer is wetter than the winter, but the climate as a whole is extremely dry. The warm season is extremely short, and even during this period the temperature of the air is low. Light is continuous during the summer, with a corresponding absence of light during the winter, which is the season of extremely cold, dry winds. The coldest places are not on the actual Arctic coast, but in the region of the Middle Yana River. The first of the sub-arctic regions is characterized by a very severe climate which often shows great extremes, although the mean annual temperature at most stations is about freezing. In the Altai Mountains there is in general a severe climate, but some of the valleys which are protected from the north by high mountains have a warmer climate. In the second region

o

the average temperature is about 36° F., that is, distinctly warmer. There is little rain and snow, and in summer rain is very rare. In South-eastern Siberia there are long periods of cold and a rapid transition from cold to warm periods. In contrast to the last region the summer is characterized by frequent rains and the winters are windless with a scarcity of snow. The fourth region is extremely cold, and in Kamchatka very humid.

The Arctic is a land of tundra and tayga, a northern cold forest, in between which there is a marginal forest of dwarf trees and bushes. The southern sub-arctic region includes steppe and Alpine country, often with well-watered fertile valleys.

Although considerable work has been done on the archæology of Siberia, especially in the Yenesei region, we have not at present a great deal of information on the early racial history of that region. Talko-Hryncewicz (VIII. 1, 50) examined a number of early skulls from Oust Kiakhta in Transbaikalia. They were found on the left bank of the Sava River in a tributary of the Selanga. He came to the conclusion that they differed from the modern type of Mongolo-Buriats, and describes them as resembling those from the Kurgans of Southern Russia. As far as can be judged from the descriptions given it would appear that these skulls belong to the type which has already been met with on the Steppes, the Proto-Nordic.

Somewhat similar evidence is brought forward by Goroshchenko (VIII. 5), but his evidence definitely dates from the Bronze Age. The material may be divided into two classes, masks and crania. The former have the disadvantage, which attaches to all works of art, that they cannot pretend to be scientifically accurate ; some, however, seem to have been death-masks and therefore offer valuable evidence. The masks belong to two types, so-called Tagara and Chaatas, and it has been suggested that the latter developed out of the former. The earlier appear to have features which recall the European type of face ("Aryan" is the word used), while the Chaatas masks with broader faces and coarser features are said to recall the Mongolian type. Both, however, belong to the late Bronze Age and do not appear to differ in horizon. It is also more than possible, as Czaplicka

(II. 5) has pointed out, that the difference in form is due rather to varying skill in the makers than to varying racial types in the models.

The skull measurements also indicate a uniform type, although there are, as might be expected, differences in the mean values of the measurements from the two series of Kurgans. The crania from Chaatas are slightly longer and markedly higher than those from Tagara. But there is certainly not sufficient difference to warrant the suggestion of such fundamental racial differences as some authors have been inclined to believe. They show great uniformity with other Bronze Age skulls which are known from the Kurgans of Siberia, and with those from the older Kurgans of the Moscow district. They resemble those which I have already referred to from Transbaikalia. Out of ninety-six skulls forty-two were dolichocephalic. There seems to be every indication from the form of these skulls that not only do they differ from the present inhabitants of the same regions to-day, but that they belong to the Proto-Nordic stock to which the other similar skulls have been referred.

The gap between these ancient peoples and their modern successors has not yet been bridged. There has been continual movement in Asia, and great changes seem to have taken place even in comparatively recent times. The classification of the modern peoples suggested by Deniker contains two groups. The first group includes the tribes of Western Siberia who have some affinities with the Samoyeds and the Eastern Finns. These he calls Yeneiseians or Tubas. The second group is made up of the peoples in the extreme north-east of the continent, whom he calls, following Schrenk (VIII. 17), Palæasiatics. Under the former heading he includes the Samoyeds of Asia and two distinct groups, the Ostyak of the Yenesei and the Tu Po of the Chinese annals, whom he calls the Altaians. The more southerly peoples he groups as Turks and Mongols. The latter he links up physically with certain of the races of Europe, but admits that they are by no means homogeneous; the former he considers to be more homogeneous physically, but he does not appear to express an opinion as to their relationships beyond calling them " Mongoloid," surely a somewhat unsatisfactory adjective when applied to the Mongols.

Czaplicka, in dealing with the ethnology and not the physical anthropology, has suggested a further classification based on that of Deniker. Objecting to the term Palæ-asiatics as being meaningless in the sense in which it is usually employed, she has two main classes, the Palæo-Siberians and the Neo-Siberians. The former includes the following tribes living in the localities which she has been careful to note. It is therefore possible to know fairly exactly the connotation which she applies to the various tribal names.

Under the Palæo-Siberians she includes first the Chukchee living in North-eastern Siberia between the Anadir River and the Arctic Ocean, except in the north-east, and secondly, the Koryak who live south of the Chukchee between the Anadir River and the central part of the peninsula of Kamchatka, except the coast lands between the Gulf of Anadir and Cape Olgontorsky. The third group of peoples are the Kamchadal living in the south part of the peninsula which bears their name. The Ainu and the Gilyak are included by her as Palæo-Siberians, but will be considered in their geographical position. The Eskimo form a sixth group; we are here only concerned with those Eskimo who live on the Asiatic side of the Behring Strait. The Aleut live in the Aleutian Islands and therefore are also beyond our terms of reference. Czaplicka states that the Yukaghir live between the Lower Yana and the Lower Kolyma rivers. They are, however, said by Bogoras (IX. 10) to be practically extinct. The Chuvanzy live on the Upper and Middle Anadir River, and the Ostyak of the Yenesei on the Lower Yenesei between the Lower Tunguska and the Stony Tunguska as far as Turukhansk. Although, as will be seen, some of these tribes differ considerably from one another physically, the classification is undoubtedly a convenient one from which to start on any consideration of the tribes of the Far North.

The Neo-Siberian tribes form a more miscellaneous group. They include first, the Finnic tribes which Czaplicka divides into two groups, first, the Ugrian Ostyak from the northern part of the Tobolsk district to the mouth of the Obi and eastwards as far as the Tomsk district and the Yenesei River, and secondly, the Vogul, also called Maniza or Suomi, between the Middle Obi from Berezov to Tobolsk and the Ural Mountains.

The second group are the Samoyedic tribes who inhabit the Arctic region from the mouth of the Khatanga River to the Ural Mountains, and thence into Europe to Chiskaya Bay.

The third group contains the Turkish tribes, a grouping which has already been shown to be somewhat fallacious from the point of view of physique, but extremely convenient from an ethnological standpoint. They may be divided into two, Turanian and Siberian. The last alone properly concerns us here, but some of the Turanian Turks have at various times occupied this geographical area, and it should be noted that the best known tribe is the Kirghiz, reference to whom has already been made in a previous chapter. In common with so many Central Asiatic tribes the majority of these peoples are characterized by extreme brachycephaly, and seem to have racial affinities which show them to belong to the same group as the brachycephalic elements among the Buriats. One group of these Kirghiz reported on by Ivanovski had a mean cephalic index as high as 89·4. It has been stated that the head-breadth among all these peoples is fairly constant, but that there is considerable variation in the head-length, a point which distinguishes them from the brachycephals who are related to the Pareœan race.

In great contrast to the Kirghiz group are the more Eastern Turks. They include the Yakuts, the Kazan Tatars, the Baskir, the Soyotes and their allies. These peoples seem to have a somewhat shorter stature, especially the Yakuts. But this difference in bodily height is hardly sufficient to distinguish them from the Kirghiz group. The cephalic index, however, is significantly different. It is remarkably uniform and varies between 82 and 83. All observers are unanimous on this point and it seems, therefore, that we may consider it as a reliable figure. The head-length is longer than in the last group, although not to any marked degree, but the head-breadth appears to be nearly 20 mms. shorter.

The racial affinities of these peoples are somewhat obscure. It is clear that in recent times they have become much mixed

THE PEOPLES OF ASIA

with Mongols, but most of them differ physically from the Mongols in many ways. It seems probable that they may be considered for the most part as a mixture of Alpine man with the Palæasiatics, but they probably have the blood of other stocks in their veins also.

It will be seen, therefore, that, as in the case of the Osmanli and the Iranian Turks, it is impossible to speak of a Turkish race, but that the various " Turks " differ in physique according to their geographical surroundings and history, which have combined to amalgamate in one linguistic or cultural group a number of diverse physical elements.

Related to these Turkic tribes, both culturally and often physically, are the Mongolic tribes of Siberia. They are often grouped with the Turks under the name of Turko-Mongols. The only representatives of the Mongol tribes in Siberia—I am, of course, using the word in its strictly cultural sense—are the Khalkhas and Buriats round Lake Baikal. The racial position of these peoples has already been considered in discussing the ethnology of Mongolia (page 180).

Lastly, we have a very important group of peoples who, linguistically, may be described as Tungusic tribes. The Tungus proper are found throughout Eastern Siberia from 60° E. to the Pacific and from the Arctic to the Chinese frontier. There are a number of other Tungusic tribes of varying admixture and degrees of importance. The Manchus have already been described (page 187). There remain the Chapogi between the Lower and the Stony Tunguska, the Goldi on the Lower Amur, the Lamut along the coast of the Sea of Akhotsk, the Manyarg in the Middle Amur region from 126°–160° E., the Oroch on the Lower Amur and the Pacific coast, the Reindeer Tungus (Orochan) on the Olekima River, the Oroke in Saghalien, and the Solon south of the Middle Amur about 120° E.

Considerable data has been collected on the Palæasiatic peoples by the Jesup expedition. Unfortunately their sumptuous volumes do not at present contain more than a short reference to physical anthropology, and we have only a short and valuable paper from the pen of Frau Jochelson-Brodsky (VIII. 3). The figures which she has collected show that the Palæasiatics are by no means a homogeneous group. They present certain features which are shared by the majority; the most conspicuous is short stature. It is possible that this shortness of stature is the result of the extremely hard environment to which they are subjected rather than actually a racial feature. The Chukchee, the Koryak, and the Asiatic Eskimo, and to a lesser degree the Kamchadal, are the only peoples who have not an extremely low or short stature. The cephalic index varies at about 80 ; some of the tribes, Koryak, Kamchadal, and possibly Ostyak, are more dolichocephalic, and some observers suggest that the Gilyak are extremely brachycephalic, the figure quoted by Jochelson-Brodsky being as high as 86. When the other cephalic indices are compared with one another the difference is by no means as great as this. The difference between them is, however, sufficient to be significant and to suggest that there may be local differences.

It has been generally suggested that these peoples are very heterogeneous. On first sight this would seem to be a natural explanation. Such standard deviations, however, as I have been able to calculate from the published figures, suggest that they are at least remarkably pure to type. The standard deviation, for instance, of the cephalic index of the Koryak is under three units, a figure which would elsewhere be considered sufficient evidence for suggesting that the people were remarkably homogeneous. The same figure for the Chukchee is greater, but under three and a half units. It seems probable, therefore, that whatever their origin these people have at least reached a remarkable degree of ethnic unity.

Shirokogoroff (VI. 5) suggests that at the time of what he calls the first ethnic movement, about the fourth millennium B.C., they were in occupation of all the region north and east of Gobi, but that they had been driven out of this region two thousand years later by pressure from Tungusic tribes. In origin they seem probably to contain what may be an early mixture of Proto-Nordic and an early stock akin to Yellow man. The Ainu, who are also classed with the same people, probably have a much lesser mixture of the Yellow stock.[1]

These peoples seem to form the links between the two continents of Asia and America. In many features, especially the exaggerated prominence of the cheek-bones, greater on the whole than is found among many of the representatives

[1] But see page 212, where the racial affinities of the Ainu are discussed.

of Yellow man, they recall the Amerind. The latter, however, often differs from them, especially in stature, and often, though by no means invariably, in head-form. It seems probable that at an early date there was an intrusive movement of peoples from the west, either identical with, or the forerunners of, the modern Turki and Mongol-speaking peoples who separated this branch of Yellow man from the Parecœan stock. I have already suggested that in the Korean population we possibly have traces of this movement, if Shirokogoroff's suggestion should prove to be correct.

An interesting point of detail deserves a short consideration. The American and Greenland Eskimo have attracted considerable attention among anthropologists by reason of certain anatomical features which suggested either a special race or, as others held, specialization to meet the unusual natural conditions to which they are subjected. One of these characters is dolichocephaly. The Asiatic Eskimo appear to differ from the Greenlanders in possessing round heads and generally conforming to the Palæasiatic type. The people have, as far as I am aware, not yet been sufficiently studied to enable a definite pronouncement to be made as to whether we have here a different physical type of racial significance, or whether the Greenlanders are a specialized branch of the Palæasiatics. Here, again, the ethnologist is confronted with two physical types which at least superficially appear very different, but which are known by the same name. It is of interest to note that the Asiatic Eskimo have a character in common of considerable importance, namely, extremely narrow noses due, no doubt, to the conditions under which both live.

The Palæo-Siberian tribes then represent what is probably the oldest surviving stratum on the continent of Northern Asia. They seem to differ to a certain, but not very marked degree from one another. They may represent a very ancient cross between the Proto-Nordic type, or a type akin to this, represented to-day by the Ainu, to a lesser or greater extent, and an early stock akin to Yellow man, whose exact affinities are at present uncertain. If they do represent such a mixture it must be of considerable antiquity, as at least in some measurements the standard deviations are remarkably small.

The Neo-Siberian tribes have recently received a certain amount of attention from anthropologists. Roudenko (VIII. 10, 123) gives their present distribution of the westerly tribes. The Samoyeds are found at present in the north-east of European Russia and in the most northerly part of the basin of the Obi and the Yenesei, the Ostyaks in the Tomsk and Tobolsk governments along the borders of the streams and rivers. The Voguls are found in the basins of the rivers Sasva and Sygva and in the north and north-west districts of Tourensk and Tobolsk (Tobolsk government) and in Perm, The Samoyeds have about 2 per cent blond hair and light eyes. the others a rather lesser percentage than this ; all are about 157 cms. in height. The Samoyedic type is quite distinct from that of the Ostyaks and still more from that of the Voguls. They are well-developed muscularly and very short. Their heads are brachycephalic, the faces are long and broad, with prominent cheek-bones. The forehead is relatively narrow, the nose mesorrhine ; there is a certain amount of alveolar prognathism. The eyes and hair are generally dark.

The Voguls have a longer trunk height than the Samoyeds, but the stature of the two peoples is similar. Their heads approach dolichocephaly. They have smaller faces and less prominent cheek-bones. The forehead is broader and the nose has a tendency to approach the platyrrhine. They seldom have any prognathism or the Mongolian fold, which occurs frequently among the Samoyeds. The hair is sometimes chestnut.

The Ostyaks represent an intermediate type ; they are probably the same race as the Voguls, mixed in places with Samoyed blood.

If the Samoyeds are compared with some of the other Altaian peoples, such as the Koibales, the difference of physical type is at once apparent. The only people which seem to be of the same type are the Uriankhai, who have been examined by Goroshchenko. Both have the same colouring and head-form, the same height index, long face, big bizygomatic width, long trunk and short lower limbs.

The origin and relationship of these interesting peoples is uncertain. They differ on the whole from the Palæo-Siberians, and almost as much, perhaps, from one another. The term

Ostyak, for instance, includes not only Ostyaks of the Obi and those of the Yenesei, but also other groups. Roudenko suggests that there is possibly a relationship between the Samoyeds and the Lapps, and that there may have been a migration westwards from the Altai region, and finally a division of the western and the eastern groups by a migrating people from the south.

There are several features which need special discussion. First, these people, like the northern people, are very short in stature. It would seem that this may be due to environment. Secondly, they usually show features which serve to connect them with some type of Yellow man ; they are usually round-headed, a feature not always associated in such a high degree with Yellow man. They also occasionally show dolichocephaly, and sometimes a certain blondness of colouring. It is more than probable that an important strain in their blood is due to an immigration, such as Roudenko suggests, from the Altai region. Among such peoples as the Voguls there is reason to suggest that the difference in their head-form and colouring may be due to an admixture with a Nordic or Proto-Nordic type. In any case, these Western Asiatic types appear to be the result of considerable racial admixture.

To return to the other Neo-Siberian tribes, the so-called Turks may be more conveniently dealt with in discussing the other peoples of the same cultural affinities, who although not always connected racially are customarily grouped together ; for the sake of clearness I am classing them together.

There remains, then, the Tungusic tribes. The physical characters of the pure Tungusic peoples is thus described by Czaplicka (VIII. 18, 299). She says that they have a stature below the average, although they are not so short as the Samoyed. This description does not entirely agree with the work of other observers who, except in the case of the Tungus of Barguzin who are short, report the Tungus as being about the same height as the Mongols (163 cms.). The head is remarkable for its length, a feature that is commented on by all observers. The head-height, except when influenced by mixture with the Mongols who have a low head, is usually relatively high. The head-breadth is usually also great, so that the Tungus have large heads, a fact that is masked by the cephalic index. The faces are said by Czaplicka to be long and the noses narrow. She concludes by saying that they are nearest to the Southern Chinese and some Japanese types and are unlike the Mongols.

Shirokogoroff appears to take a rather different view. He states (VI. 5, 99) that the fundamental type among the Tungus is found among the Tungus of Barguzin, who are characterized by, first, a very low stature—about 1550—a condition which, as I have observed, does not appear among most Tungus groups ; secondly, a low cephalic index, about 77 (it should here be remarked that most of the cephalic indices reported by Jochelson-Brodsky from various sources, especially the works of Mainoff, put the cephalic index at about 82), and thirdly, low nasal index, 77, a point on which all observers are agreed. He also draws attention to the low frontal index of these peoples. He believes that this type is only " incidental " among the Chinese, and concludes as a final way out of the impasse that the Tungus are, from an anthropological standpoint, not a homogeneous people. We have, in fact, among them the same state of things which has already been met with among the Mongols, and especially the Buriats, namely, the fact that cultural and linguistic classifications cut across racial divisions. The type of the " pure Tungus " will therefore depend on whether a group which has not recently been mixed with Mongols or other tribes is met with by the observer.

Shirokogoroff has collected a great deal of interesting cultural material about the Tungus which serves to throw light on their origins and recent migrations. He suggests that they inhabited in early times a warm country, probably the great plain of China, whence they were pushed by successive migrations to their present habitat. He believes that in the early part of the Christian era they were divided into two groups by the intrusive Yakuts, who are of Turkish origin. Such a theory would negative Czaplicka's suggestion that they are nearest to the Southern Chinese, nor do measurements tend to support her suggestion.

The actual racial position of the Tungus is not made simpler by the suggestion of these migrations. They are clearly extremely mixed and in most cases it is hardly possible to disentangle the threads. If we accept Shirokogoroff's fundamental type as representing the true Tungus it is difficult to find any definite type with which we may associate them. They clearly differ in the size of their heads from the southern aboriginal tribes of China. Their short stature and general form seems to separate them from the Proto-Nordics, unless we are prepared to disregard both hair and stature, an arbitrary proceeding which places too much reliance on the cephalic index. It seems more probable that they represent an early stock of Yellow man, which has become modified both by mixing and also, possibly, by migrations. They would, under these circumstances, be akin to the Palæo-Siberians, with whom they have certainly mixed, and whom it is possible that they have driven out from their old homes.

Such a suggestion can be considered as only tentative and merely a working hypothesis. The Tungus are undoubtedly a people of the greatest importance in the ethnology of Eastern Asia, and it is to be hoped that crania will be obtained which will enable them to be adequately studied.

CHAPTER IX

JAPAN

JAPAN presents a strong contrast to most of the countries with which we have been previously dealing, both as regards its geographical nature and the physique of the people. The Japanese Empire consists of a long string of islands which, if we include the southern extremity of Formosa, and the north end of the Chishima group, extends between 21°–51° N. The largest islands are known to the Japanese as Kiushiu, Shikoku, Honshu, and Hokkaido; the last named is usually marked on foreign maps as Yezo. Japan proper includes an area of about 150,000 square miles, of which the main island, Honshu, forms a very considerable portion, being about equal in area to Great Britain.

The whole country is very much indented and contains a very long coast-line with innumerable small islands and bays. It is extremely mountainous. The northern ranges belong to the system of Saghalien, the southern mountains being outliers of the great Kunlun system. The former are usually low and rounded and the latter higher and more rugged. In between the two the Fuji system forms a bar which runs through transversely. There are many volcanic mountains, and Japan is particularly liable to earthquakes. The rivers are usually short and rapid, and so are on the whole of little service for communications except for short distances. This fact is explained by stating that about three-quarters of Japan are mountainous, and of the remainder 70 per cent is composed of uplands.

Owing to the long belt of islands the temperature of Japan ranges from a tropical to an Arctic climate. In Japan proper, however, this range is much less and the climate, except in the north of Hokkaido, may be considered temperate, the mean annual temperature being 48° at Aomori and 78° at Kagoshima. In more general terms we may say that the

mean annual temperature of the main island varies according
to station from about 50° F. to 60° F. There is little snow
in South-west Japan, but elsewhere there is an annual fall.
In summer the greatest rainfall is on the Pacific coast, the
condition being reversed in winter. Owing to these conditions the flora is abundant and on the whole is that of a
warm climate.

The Japanese islands, although not situated at any great
distance from the coast of the mainland, are sufficiently far
away to be effectually separated, the only point of contact
being Korea. It is probably due to these circumstances that
the Japanese have developed a physique which differentiates
them effectually from their neighbours. It is also worthy of
remark that geographically Japan proper is divided into two
parts, the separation of Hokkaido from the rest being probably of ancient date. Climatic conditions in this island are
also more extreme than in the rest of Japan, the result has
been that although the Japanese have driven out their predecessors from the rest of Japan proper their colonization of
Hokkaido is only recent.

Owing to the work of Japanese scientists we are better
informed on the archæology of Japan than of any other
country in that part of Asia. The earliest graves appear all
to be " neolithic " in character, that is to say there is an
entire absence of metals in the graves, but somewhat remarkable a coarse pottery is usually present.

Some of the most important finds of human remains are
discussed by Hamada (IX. 5). From the site at Ko, in
Kawachi province, seven neolithic skeletons were excavated.
The calvarias much resemble those of the Ainu. The faces,
as compared with the Ainu, are broad and low, the orbits are
low, the nose broad and the palates short and broad. The
facial and palatal length is shorter than in the Ainu and the
faces are more orthognathous. The vertebral column is short
in relation to the limbs, but in comparison with the modern
Japanese the extremities are short in relation to the trunk.
The cervical part of the column is comparatively strong and
large. These characters, Koganei believes, are also characteristic of the skeletons from the shell mounds which have
been ascribed to the Ainu. The femora are pilastered and
the tibiæ markedly platycnemic. Some skulls appear to

approach the Ainu form, but the facial length is less and the maxilla is smaller.

A larger number of skeletons were discovered in Bitchu and Idzumi. All belong to the same type and their characters are of interest. The flatness of the femur and of the humerus in the middle of the shaft are said to be less marked in the neolithic skeletons than in the Ainu. On the other hand, the neolithic bones represent more prominently the characters which distinguish the Ainu from the Japanese. Hamada concludes, therefore, that the Stone Age people seem not properly to have been the ancestors of the present Ainu, but probably in many cases a race intermediate between the Ainu and the Japanese.

Matsumoto (IX. 2, 50) takes a rather different view. He believes that among the Stone Age people at least three types can be distinguished. These he calls, from the sites where they were found, Aoshima, Miyato and Tsukumo. In the first type the adult males are about five feet four inches in height ; they have large heads and are either dolichocephalic or mesocephalic. Skeletons of this type have been found at Aoshima and on Miyato Island. The Miyato type has been discovered at Tsukumo and Ko. These seem, Matsumoto suggests, to have been dwarfs, the adult male stature being two inches less than that of the previous type. They are either brachycephalic or mesocephalic, those from Tsukumo being shorter headed than those from Miyato. Finally, there is a tall type found at Tsukumo and Ko. They have a stature among the adult males of between five feet six and five feet seven ; they vary between meso- and brachy-cephalic. Matsumoto believes that the first two types are represented among the Ainu to-day.

It will be seen that here two views are put forward, using much the same material, which are entirely opposed. The one associates the type of ancient man with the Ainu, the other considers him to belong to a different race. I am unfortunately hampered by the fact that most of Hamada's report is written in Japanese and that only parts are in English and German, and therefore I have found it difficult to be sure of his position. Matsumoto's paper was, he says, written from memory in America, and therefore may not represent his considered opinions.

The first point to be considered is whether the neolithic people really belong to the same physical type as the Ainu or not. The cultural evidence suggests differences. Apart from recent introduction, the Ainu do not appear to have had any knowledge of pottery, their vessels being made of cherry bark. The neolithic people, however, undoubtedly had pottery. This in itself should not be an insuperable difficulty as we only know of the Ainu in Hokkaido, and it is quite possible that the same people in the main island may have been in a much more advanced condition of culture than those on the more northerly island.

It would appear that the principal objection put forward by Hamada to the association of the older remains with those of the Ainu is the form of the tibia and of the femur. Such matters as platymeria and platycnemia, however, can hardly be considered as being definite racial characters. Although their exact origin is at present uncertain it would appear that they are probably due rather to habit of posture and gait than to actual racial distinctions. I have found that in early British bones from sites near Oxford that platymeria and platycnemia were extremely common, apparently in certain classes of the population ; they do not occur in the population to-day, which in many other ways is closely allied to their predecessors. The parallel is not, of course, an entirely good one, as the Ainu do not represent a civilized community, but at least it proves that we may get groups of the same stock which differ in these particulars but which certainly belong to the same race. Even Hamada, on the whole, is inclined to believe that the skulls of both races are very similar. After an examination, necessarily somewhat brief, of the skeletal remains and of the Ainu, in the Anatomical Museum of the University of Kyoto, I succeeded in convincing myself that there was no essential differences between the two types. There are certainly differences of detail, but these are no greater than might be ascribed to the differences in habit of the two peoples. Otherwise they appear to have been the same race. This conclusion agrees well with that of Matsumoto. I am not convinced that the latter's three ancient types can be accepted. It should be noted that the types overlap in the same burial-grounds.

The work of the Biometric School has shown how great,

under certain circumstances, the normal variation can be. We have at present no statistical record of ancient peoples, although Koganei has carefully studied the Ainu. Certainly in many ways type A and type B appear to be variations of one single type, the shorter being more round-headed than the taller. The evidence from Ko is altogether insufficient to warrant any deductions being drawn from it, as only seven skeletons have, as far as I am aware, been excavated. From Tsukumo a larger number have been reported.

It seems better, therefore, until we have further evidence, to suggest at least provisionally that we have in Japan a series of finds of a people in a neolithic stage of culture of unknown date, who are of the same racial stock as the modern Ainu. There is much evidence which suggests that the Ainu were the predecessors of the Japanese over all Japan, as they undoubtedly were in some parts. Whether these neolithic peoples were the direct predecessors or a previous wave of Ainu peoples is at present uncertain.

Matsumoto has put forward the very ingenious theory in regard to the migrations and distributions of these types. He suggests that the Aoshima type was the first to arrive in Japan. They existed in North-eastern Japan as a pure race and as a race mixed with the next type in the Middle Stone Age. The present Ainu of Hokkaido are said to be similar to this mixed race, and the Ainu of the Kurils and Saghalien to the autochthonous pure type.

The next to arrive were the Miyato dwarf type, together with other peoples possibly of similar racial stock. This second type is present in Japan to-day in the north central part of the main island, and kindred stocks also found in South-western Japan.

The Tsukumo type is said to be found in Japan from the Middle Stone Age onwards. To-day it is scattered in every part of Japan, but is found especially in the northern part of Western Japan. The last type to arrive was of a "Mongolian" stock, called the Okayama type, whose significance will be discussed in dealing with the Japanese. The people with whom they mixed were for the most part the later comers, who naturally were to be found in the more accessible regions, and therefore the earliest arrivals have survived and kept their independence to the last.

P

This very ingenious scheme depends on the definite assumption that we can be sure of three physical types; I have shown, however, that at present we have hardly sufficient evidence to warrant such an assumption. It should be noted that on the whole it is independent of the cultural changes, for at least three periods can be recognized in the Stone Age of Japan; the Aoshima type are associated with the early period, but all the other stocks with the Middle Stone Age, except the type which is characterized as Mongolian, is in every respect different. At present, then, we cannot look on it as more than an ingenious theory, which will doubtless be modified or amplified when more evidence is collected.

There remain, then, the modern inhabitants of Japan. They can be divided into the Ainu and the Japanese, who are very different racially even though it is more than probable that there is much Ainu blood in modern Japan. The Ainu are well built and extremely stocky with a short rounded thorax and very thick heavy ribs. The skin-colour is dark, rather than yellow ; they often have olive skins, and this is the usual colour, apparently, on the unexposed parts of the body. The men are extraordinarily hairy all over. The women have thick short black hair on the arms and legs, but none on the body. The hair on the head is more or less straight, but the ends are inclined to curl both in the men and women. The beard in the younger men is wavy, in the older it becomes almost curly. It is of a very different texture from that of the Japanese; the latter have a straight silky type, the Ainu hair is coarse, black, and hard to the touch.

The eyes are not oblique, but like those of the European. In colour they are usually of a clear brown ; among the men I have seen hazel eyes,[1] they probably also occur among the women, but I have not seen them. They usually have a little wisp of lanugo-like hair in the inner corner of the eye.

It has been suggested that the Mongolian fold does not occur. I observed it, however, in one individual. In the remainder I found on the outer aspect of the nose, just anterior to the inner canthus of the eye, a curious little ridge of skin

---

[1] Montandon makes a similar observation. Out of ninety individuals of both sexes, four men had eyes with a greenish or violet tinge, the latter in one individual (IX. 8, 233).

which may be a remnant of a fold, it never stood out from the level of the skin more than an eighth of an inch.

The stature is usually short, about 158 cms. for the men and 148 for the women. The length of the span has been very differently reported by various observers and no reliable figure is therefore available.

The head is usually large and dolichocephalic with an index of about 76, the females having a slightly broader head. In spite of this index, however, the absolute breadth is quite large. The face is broad but not flat. The forehead is high sometimes, but not usually, with the hair quite low. The temporal ridges are usually well developed and the occiput is prominent. The eyebrow region is not overhanging in the sense of forming a big bar, but it presents an appearance of massiveness owing to the depression which usually occurs at the root of the nose.

The nose is straight, but with a curious convexity at the extremity. Although some cases of extremely narrow noses occur this is not usual, and some of the people have extremely broad noses. The statement which has found its way into so many textbooks that they are leptorrhine is due to the report by Koganei, whose figures, without any qualification, are included by Martin in his handbook. Koganei, instead of measuring across the nostrils, measured the nose at the base, getting, of course, a very small measurement. There is as great variation as in most races, but while examining Ainu I was surprised how very leptorrhine some of them were.

The region of the nasion, that is at the root of the nose, is of special note. I have already said that among those which I examined the Mongolian fold occurred only in one case, a woman. They have a slightly lesser width in between the eyes than the Japanese, and in the case of the men a little lanugo in the inner corner of the eye. I failed to see this among the women. At about a centimetre from the inner corner of the eye twenty-seven out of twenty-eight adult women had a ridge of skin, to which I have already referred. This ridge of skin seems to coincide closely in position with the Mongolian fold, and I can only consider it as a kind of vestigial fold. It is about an eighth of an inch high. Those authors who state briefly that the Mongolian fold is absent or extremely small have neglected to stress this rather curious fact, which does not appear unless a careful examination is made.

There is a considerable massing of bone in this region, so that the eyes appear to be very deep set, but often, unless one looks carefully, one is inclined to think that the apertures are perfectly European in shape. The whole build of this part of the skull is peculiar, and as far as I have seen characteristic. When making observations on the Ainu one is struck by the massiveness of the bones. The head is very heavy. The ridges are well developed; frequently, especially among the men, there is a marked ridge which, without being scaphocephaly, suggests that form. This is probably due to the great development of the temporal muscles. The cheekbones are high rather than massive, and the breadth of the face seems to be due to the massiveness of the jaw. The hands are short and broad.

The racial position of the Ainus is a question of great interest. There is every probability that they are very different from all the other Oriental races. Montandon, the most recent writer on the subject who has studied the Ainu on the spot, says of them: "Malgré quelques traits legèrement mongolisés, l'Ainou, mieux que tout essai de reproduction artificielle, est aujourdhui le meilleur portrait, et certainement le descendant le moins evolue, d'un rameau de la souche précaucasique qui, a l'époque palæo-néolithique, habitait les contrées nordiques de l'Euraise " (X. 8).

That the Ainu are of a stock akin to the races of Europe is probable. Anthropologists have in the past been inclined to limit those stocks to those which are actually represented in Europe to-day. It seems manifestly impossible to class the Ainu with any of those. Their long heads might suggest at first a kinship with the long-headed branches of that stock. They are, however, too dark to be called Nordic and of very different anatomical structure to the Mediterranean branch. The members of the latter are slenderly built and small-headed with comparatively slight bones. We have seen that the build of the Ainu is the very antithesis of this.

If the Ainu, then, are of a similar stock to the European races it is necessary to refer them to a separate division to those which at present survive in Europe. There is no inherent difficulty in this; we have already seen that several of the races of Asia, although apparently allied to the races of Europe, will not fit into any cast-iron scheme of classification. The Ainu, however, represent a special case and appear to differ from the other stocks almost more than these differ from one another. Although the other groups differ from the European stocks, yet they do at least to a certain degree correspond to the same general divisions.

The suggestion, then, that they represent a prehistoric stock seems at first sight to be very suggestive. To a high degree, however, there seems to have been specialization among the Ainu. Under these circumstances, then, we can hardly admit them to be the last survivals of prehistoric Europe. Nor does there appear to be among the early races of Europe any that corresponds exactly to the Ainu. It seems, therefore, best to suggest that the Ainu stand to the present races of Europe, not in an avuncular relationship, descendants, closely allied to the prehistoric stocks, but rather as cousins, that is a people, probably descended from the same stock as the races of Europe, but in certain respects less differentiated and in other ways more specialized.

It should be noted that culturally the Ainu are extremely primitive. They are practically in a pre-neolithic, or at the most a transitional stage to a neolithic type of culture. Only the women practice agriculture and their implements were made of shells, the men were primitive hunters. They knew of no pottery, although there is the possibility of this art having been forgotten. Owing to this primitive nature of their culture and their physique they have been associated by some anthropologists with the Australians.

A careful examination of the skeletons of these two groups has convinced me that this association is unsatisfactory. Not only are the crania, on which I believe the opinion was based, extremely different, but the other bones of the skeleton, few of which appear to have come to Europe, are still more differentiated. The Australian skeletons, such as I have seen, are all comparatively slender. I have already called attention to the massiveness of Ainu bones.

There remains, then, the necessity of linking up the Ainu with the other races of the same family. The task is the more difficult, as we have at present but few reports of the

archæology of the vast intervening district. Such reports
as have been made from some of the graves of early date
which have been opened suggest that the early inhabitants
differed in many respects from those which are at present
living in the same districts, and it seems that some of them
may suggest features which we are inclined to associate with
the Ainu. The links are at present far from being complete,
but there is at least a suggestion that the " Proto-Nordic "
race were occupying Northern Asia before the expansion of
Yellow man and the probably subsequent, or possibly almost
simultaneous, expansion of Alpine man.

We must wait, however, till the archæology of Central
Asia is better known before we can say whether this theory
is correct or not. In any case, it seems probable that the
Ainu have good claim to be considered members of this race
and the aborigines of Eastern Asia. They have probably
affected to a greater or lesser degree some of the neighbouring peoples, especially the Japanese, and also probably some
of the tribes of the Amur region, notably the Gilyaks.

The Japanese themselves present in many ways an ethnological problem not less interesting than that of the Ainu.
The older ethnologists, of whom the most distinguished
representative was Baelz, recognized two types. The fine
type, he says, is relatively long-headed, with an elongated
face, straight eyes in the men, more or less oblique and
" Mongoloid " in the women ; a thin, convex or straight nose
is found, especially among the upper classes. The coarse
type with a thick-set body, rounded skull, broad face with
prominent cheek-bones, slightly oblique eyes, flattish nose,
and wide mouth is characteristic of the lower classes. Baelz
(IX. 13) believed these two types to have been the result
of crossings between " Mongol " sub-races, northern and
southern, and " Indonesian," or even " Polynesian " elements,
the influence of the Ainu being shown only in Northern
Nippon. This opinion is followed by Deniker. The exact
meaning of Northern Nippon is uncertain in this context ;
probably Baelz meant Northern Japan, i.e. the island of
Hokkaido.

Deniker suggests that " it might be supposed that the
representatives of the first type were descendants of tribes

who had come by way of Korea and the Tsushima and Iki-shima islands in the south-west of Nippon (in this context obviously the main island) at some period unknown, but at any rate very remote. As to the coarse type, its representatives are perhaps descended from the warriors who invaded about the seventh century B.C. (according to a doubtful chronology) the west coast of the island of Kiu-siu and then Nippon. These invaders, intermixing with the aborigines of unknown stock, founded the kingdom of Yamato, and drove back the Ainus towards the north."

This traditional ethnology, which has found its way into most European textbooks, has been assailed in Japan by Hasebe (IX. 3), Matsumoto (IX. 2), and others, and recently in England by Morant (I. 14). Hasebe has suggested two types, Ishikawa and Okayama, and Matsumoto two more, which he has called Chikuzen and Satsuma types.

The characters of these types may be summarized briefly. The Ishikawa has very short stature, under five feet two inches, a medium cephalic index, with a numerical value of about 78, a straight, short face with feebly-developed jaws. The Okayama has tall stature, relative to the mean stature of Japan, the actual value being over five feet five inches. The head is relatively broad, with a cephalic index of about 82, a deep face and well-developed jaws.

The other two types are variants of these. The Chikuzen is tall with a medium head, and the Satsuma type has short stature and a broad head. Both these two types appear to have short faces.

The distribution of these types is as follows. The first type is found in the north of the middle part and the north-eastern part of the main island. The second type belongs to the coastal districts round the Inland Sea and the neighbourhood of Kyoto and in the west of the middle part of the main island. The third type is found in the northern part of Kiushiu, and the Satsuma type in the southern parts of both Kiushiu and Shikoku.

Matsumoto believes that the first type is an altered survivor of his Miyato type of the Stone Age, and the Chikuzen of the Tsukumo type. The Okayama type, Hasebe has suggested, is the Korean type of the Mongolian stock.

The suggestion apparently of these types is that we have

differentiated early stocks which have been already discussed, and one final type coming from Korea, which survives in Japan and which, or at least kinsmen of which, affected all the other types. How far does our evidence bear out these theories? There is every probability that several types are found in Japan, probably at least three. The division suggested by Baelz is a convenient one and one that is, I think, justified by observation. Baelz suggested that the slenderness of the " fine " type was due to what he considered to be Manchu-Korean influence. I do not feel that the modern Japanese classification lays enough stress on this very interesting element in the population, whatever its origin may have been. It is presumably what Hasebe has called the " Okayama " type. This, however, does not entirely agree with other observations, for the fine type tends to have a long head, whereas the Okayama has a round head. The Koreans are also round-headed and the Okayama type agrees very well with them ; the Manchus have also a round head.

It is impossible, therefore, to accept the Manchu-Korean type of Baelz as corresponding in any way closely to the inhabitants of that area ; yet the slender type does seem really to exist, and possibly, at least to a small extent, corresponds to the Chikuzen type, although the identification is not certain, as such Japanese authorities as I have read do not seem to pay any attention to this classification. That the Satsuma type describes accurately at least a part of the Japanese " coarse " type is probable.

All the types appear to possess certain features in common. The hair is always black. Curly hair may be found occasionally, especially in the northern part of the main island. It is almost certainly due to admixture of Ainu blood. There is a noticeable difference of stature between the sexes. Although the general stature is short, there appears to be considerable variation in the stature, especially of the men. The parts of the body have rather different proportions than among Europeans. The limbs are shorter and the head is larger. In spite of the shortness of the limbs the forearm is relatively long. The cephalic index is variable ; as I have shown, the proportions of the face are variable. The colour of the eyes is practically always a dark brown. There is a

PLATE VIII

A PEASANT WOMAN FROM SOUTH JAPAN

[face p. 216

considerable distance between the eyes, and although the bridge of the nose is normally low, cases of almost aquiline noses occur. The cheek-bones are high, but there appears in this character also to be considerable variation.

The skin-colour is very variable, the men usually being rather darker than the women. Some of the latter seem to be quite fair, and usually in these cases have a rosy spot on the cheeks, some are of a dusky yellow-brown.

In a country like Japan, with so much diversity of geographical feature, variations in racial type might be expected quite apart from the original stocks. This diversity undoubtedly exists, but it does not appear at present that the types have been quite clearly differentiated. There would seem to be short and taller types and mesocephalic and brachycephalic types. The fourfold division which I have detailed above is the logical conclusion from such data. It would, however, appear that this division is somewhat arbitrary, but until we have further evidence it may be the best that has been put forward in periodicals in a Western language.

There remains the question of Japanese origins. The evidence seems too strong to reject the suggestion that the basis of the population is of a stock closely akin to the Ainu. This ancient stock has been very much overlaid with later accretions. The result has been to change the general character of the population, so that it is to-day predominantly of the type of Parœcean man. It cannot but be recognized, however, that the Japanese are a very remarkable people, differing very considerably both in physique and temperament from other Asiatics. It is not beyond the bounds of possibility that they owe this distinction to the blood of the very barbarians whom they profess to despise, and against some of whom they carried out such a long and bloody struggle.

The elements which have provided these later accretions are difficult in the present state of our knowledge to disentangle. I have already suggested that there is probably in Japan an element which is akin to the inhabitants of the opposite mainland, Korea and Manchuria. The association of Japan and Korea is natural, and the Japanese claim to that country which they now hold is based not only on force of arms, but on ancient Japanese tradition. We know that there has been continual cultural migrations by this path and, indeed, the whole basis of Japanese art, which has so delighted the Western world, sprang from Chinese influences which came by this path. When we find, then, that there is a type in Japan which agrees closely with the Korean type, the matter need cause no astonishment. This type appears to have entered Japan in comparatively late times; there is no trace of such a type in the Stone Age, but it appears in Early Metal Age burials. It will probably be possible later to trace the arrival of this type in Japan.

As I have already shown in dealing with the mainland, it seems probable that this type has resulted from the mixture of Yellow man with a strain distantly akin to Alpine man. It is probably to this later mixture that these tribes and peoples have such markedly brachycephalic heads, a characteristic which does not appear to be found among the examples of Yellow man who have no such admixture.

These two strains, however, do not seem sufficient to account for the character of the Japanese, and Baelz suggested that there was an admixture of Malay blood. There can be no doubt that there is in Japan some southern influence. That it can be Malayan, in the sense of the people who now speak Malayan languages, is unlikely. All the people of South-eastern Asia show, as I have pointed out, an admixture of two strains, one essentially extremely long-headed and the other tending towards brachycephaly. If the Japanese were the literal descendants of these peoples it is to be expected that we should find in them traces of Nesiot blood. There does not appear to be any clear indications of such admixture. If we carry the enquiry a stage further back it would seem as though we were nearer the question of Japanese origins. Any traveller in certain parts of Southern China cannot help being struck by the resemblance in physique of some of the people there and of some of the Malayan peoples. I have already suggested that adopting the term Proto-Malayan, we have a convenient term for some of those branches of Yellow man in South-eastern Asia who have become differentiated in the Dutch Indies and elsewhere into a type which contrasts strongly with their Nesiot neighbours.

It seems not impossible that this branch of Yellow man may be also responsible for a great part of the Japanese stock. This would serve to reconcile two theories which appear at first sight to be totally opposed, the first that the Japanese have a strong Malayan strain in them, and the second that the Japanese link up more closely with Southern China than with the Dutch Indies. The first is the more generally accepted theory, the second has been suggested recently by Morant.

This type may possibly be a comparatively undifferentiated form of Yellow man. It is suggested, therefore, tentatively, that the third element in the Japanese people is a type which is akin to the Proto-Malayan, but which is probably best represented to-day among such people as the inhabitants of the hills of South Fukien. It is more than possible that we should say that the Japanese are not the direct descendants of the Southern Chinese, but rather are the descendants of the peoples who are racially akin to them.

This solution of the complicated problem is far from complete, for we do not know at present when the main type of the population was changed, or when (to use Matsumoto's somewhat uncouth adjective) Japan became " Mongolianized." We shall probably have to look for evidence of this sort in the graves at the end of the Stone Age, or possibly as late as the beginning of the Early Metal Age. It would be simpler to suggest that the only elements in the population were Ainu and Korean, but this solution, which appears to be that which principally finds favour among Japanese scientists, still leaves in doubt certain rather puzzling elements in the population.

CHAPTER X

SOUTH-EASTERN ASIA AND INDONESIA

IN this chapter I propose to deal with both the eastern-most of the peripheral countries of Asia and the islands which connect Asia with Australia and Indonesia, and to include for my purposes not only the true peninsula country of Cambodia, Cochin China, Annam and Tonkin, that is what is usually known as French Indo-China, but also Siam and Burma on the west, and Indonesia on the east. Burma forms part of the Indian Empire, both administratively and politically, but it is separated from it both geographically and ethnologically. The western part of the area forms the outermost extension to the south of the countries whose culture is based on Chinese civilization ; the eastern, either culturally or physically, is related both to China and India. In spite, therefore, of diversity of political situation and geographical detail it forms a convenient unit for anthropological purposes.

The area is situated at the foot of the Tibeto-Yunnan plateau and, except for part of Burma, lies within the tropics, but owing to the influence of the monsoons much of it has a comparatively cold winter climate.

Burma is separated from India by the sea and by ranges of hills. It includes an area of over 260,000 square miles. Geographically it has five divisions, Central Burma, Tenasserim, Arakan, the Chin Hills, and the Shan country. Central Burma includes the great delta of the Irrawaddy, hot and moist in climate, and devoted for the most part to rice cultivation. Much of the land is inundated to a great extent, and the habitations are built on such available plots of higher land which can be found. North of this region part of the country is still in the hot moist belt, and all along the rivers are alluvial plains, though there occur in this division arid tracts and large mountainous areas, often covered with luxuriant forests.

South and east of this district lies Tenasserim and Karenni. Within there is a narrow strip of coast land, but the greater part of it consists of rugged mountains covered with dense tropical forests, although it also possesses well-watered alluvial plains. Arakan includes a coastal district with tropical mangrove creeks backed by broken hilly country, usually densely forested.

The Chin Hills consist of an area of considerable elevation, varying from about 5000 to 9000 feet above sea-level. It is covered with dense forests, mostly of pine, and generally temperate in character, remarkable in places for the profusion of the rhododendrons.

Finally, the Shan States form an immense area of over 50,000 square miles. In general form they may be said to consist of a plateau between 3000 and 4000 feet high. Most of this plateau is made up of broken hill country, usually well-wooded and often cut into dense ravines, and divided into two parts by the River Salween. It forms the connecting link between Yunnan and Lower Burma.

From the Shan States, and directly through them, Chinese civilization passed into Siam, which forms the lowlands and the last step down from the great plateau. To-day, Siam is practically restricted to the great valley which debouches at Bankok, and is formed by the Menam and its tributaries. It consists of a gentle slope which is about 150 miles wide and nearly 650 miles long. Siam extends south into the Malay peninsula, and therefore forms a link not only with China but also with Malaysia. The greater part of the country consists of wild and untamed jungle. There is only one road through it, the valley of the Menam, which appears to have formed the path for racial migrations.

To the east of Siam and the Shan States lies the French sphere of influence and actual French possessions. This is also bounded on the north by the high escarpment of Yunnan and the south frontier of the Chinese province of Kwangsi. To the east and south it is bounded by the sea. This area consists in general terms of two deltas, that of the Mekong and of the Red River, and of a narrow coastal strip.

The northern part of the Malay Peninsula is very little known, but surveys have been made of most of the southern part. In general terms the peninsula consists of low-lying

land with mountain ranges in echelon, lying slightly oblique
to the general direction of the land, which is north-north-
west and south-south-east.   There are also isolated hills
apart from the general ranges.   The main range consists of
granite with a cap of sedimentary rocks, the highest of which,
Kerbau, is over 7000 feet high.   A characteristic feature
of the country is the isolated limestone hills, some of which
are as high as 2000 feet.   Owing to the comparative narrowness of the peninsula the rivers are short and, filled by
the abundance of the tropical rains, rush over steep slopes into
the sea.   They bring with them a great deal of sediment which
is deposited on the coast, and this, at least on the southern
side, is mostly muddy.   The rivers are numerous, the three
principal ones being the Perak, the Pahang, and the Kelantan.
These and the numerous other rivers of the peninsula are
of the greatest importance to man.   In a country where so
much of the land is, or was, virgin tropical forest the rivers
form the only road.   They provide the little patches of
ground along their banks which can be rescued from the
jungle and irrigated for the rice crops.

But the jungle itself is the most dominating factor in
man's life, especially of the primitive peoples who are true
jungle dwellers and have not learned like the more civilized
Malays to wander into more open country.   They live in a
climate which, though there are slight variations, has a singular
monotony.   The forest is dark and very damp.   Though the
temperatures are not so excessive as, for instance, in the
neighbourhood of the Persian Gulf, the very slight daily
change makes the annual mean very high.   The forest
presents to the stranger the appearance of a prison, beautiful
but oppressive, one from which to escape.   But the forest
nomad seems to be lost away from the protecting influence
of the great forest trees which seem to run up to an indefinite
height, really not much more than 60 or 70 feet without a
branch.   These people seldom leave the forest, and it would
be hard to find an environment which stamps itself more
on the imagination than that of these forests.   The forests,
however, only extend to a certain height and beyond this
the vegetation becomes temperate, so that one may see the
familiar type of vegetation, violets and scrub oak straggling
down the mountain-side to meet the orchids and the tree

ferns. One of the most characteristic things of this type of scenery and climate is the way in which each day seems to epitomize the annual seasons of our own climate. Just before dawn there is a nip and promise in the air, and I have even heard the song of a bird which sounded quite spring-like at this time. High noon has a silence like midsummer, while the landscape shimmers in the heat. Things become parched and tired, or the rain settles in during the afternoon, and with the cooling of the evening there is almost the feeling that a whole season's changes happened since we heard the spring note of the bird at dawn.

The hand of man has cleared much of this virgin forest. There are now rice fields and plantations, but much of the forest still remains in the peninsula and in the archipelago. At higher altitudes there are in places rolling downs.

The archipelago is a direct but partially submerged continuation of the peninsula. Some of the islands have become separated within comparatively recent times; others are ancient and long isolated fragments of a former continental extension.

Although there has been considerable dispute in matters of detail, both geologists and biologists agree in dividing the East Indies into two parts, an eastern and a western. The western is closely linked up with Asia, of which it may be described as a submerged part. The eastern, at probably a much remoter period, formed part of the continental mass of Australia. Many of the changes which have taken place seem to have occurred since man inhabited the area.

Although the faunal and floral divisions are probably ancient, the division has been accepted by ethnologists as representing a definite means of classifying the physical types of the peoples inhabiting the area. In the western parts the affinities of the peoples are on the whole Asiatic; in the eastern half an entirely different type of peoples predominate, their most noticeable character, the darkness of their skins, having given rise to the term Melanesia, the Islands of the Black Peoples.

It is true that the human and the faunal and floral distributions are not in entire correlation. Celebes, parts of the Moluccas and some of the islands which form a long chain east of Java are Asiatic in affinities, but on the whole

0

the agreement of ethnological and other biological types is greater than the disagreement. It is also of interest to note that religion and social customs on the whole follow the same divisions. The islands, for instance, which have the greatest remains of ancient Hindu temples are those which belong geographically to Asia. Celebes and the other eastern islands have not been shown at present to possess any such ruins.

The Philippines occupy a peculiar position as two series of islands link them up with Borneo, which has Asiatic affinities, a third connects them with Celebes, which belongs to the eastern area, while a fourth binds them with Formosa. Although the geographers and biologists are in some doubt as to their exact affinities, the ethnologist is in a more fortunate position, as everything points to the absence of any Australian racial connection and links them up closely with South-eastern Asia.

From the ethnological point of view it is most convenient to treat the islands in two groups, the Dutch Indies and the Philippine Islands; this division is, however, purely one of convenience, as I have already shown that part of the Dutch Indies belongs to the same ethnological area as the Philippines and part to a different zone. As, however, the Australian zone is outside our present purpose, this apparently cross division is not of practical importance.

There has been considerable discussion as to the best geographical division of the Dutch Indies. For purposes of description I have adopted the following divisions. First, the Greater Sunda (Sœnda) islands which include Sumatra, Java, Borneo, Celebes, and the smaller islands which are scattered around them; secondly, the Lesser Sunda islands, including the long stretch of islands from Bali to Timor; and thirdly, the Moluccas. New Guinea belongs in many respects to this group, but the ethnological problems connected with this great island belong rather to Oceania than to Asia. The group has been known by various names of which the most attractive is that adopted by the Dutch novelist Dekker, who has called them Insulinde. This term has found its way into much scientific literature, especially Dutch and German.

There seems every reason to believe that the western islands have at various times formed part of the continent of Asia and have been connected with one another. It has been stated that as late as the second century there was a connection between Sumatra and Malacca. The eastern islands, at a much remoter date, seem to have formed part of the Australian continent. Thus on the west, at the time when the modern populations were taking shape, the islands were exposed to continental influences; on the east, however, the conditions were very different, and isolation seems to have played an important part in the form and distribution of the stocks which inhabit that area.

Sumatra, which lies directly on the equator, although it has the comparatively small population of about 6,000,000, has an area of over 160,000 square miles. Palæozoic rocks have been found, but the greater part of the island is made up of tertiary deposits. The main physical features is the high Barisan range which runs along the south-west coast. This range includes numerous volcanoes, some of which are still active. North-east of this range there is a wide alluvial plain. On the west coast and in the north-east part of the islands the rivers, although numerous, do not afford any reasonable means of communication. Those of the plain are, however, of greater importance. The largest river is the Djambi, but the Moesi has long been, as it still is, a very important means of communication. The climate of Sumatra is very hot and the relative humidity is great. Owing, however, to the mountainous character of the country numerous temperature enclaves occur above the 3000-foot contour level.

Java is about a quarter the size of Sumatra, but has the very big population of approximately 40,000,000. The most prominent feature of the country is the great mountain ridge, a continuation of a great fold which runs from Burma to the Moluccas. Most of the mountains in the islands are volcanoes and some are still active. Although tertiary formations occur,[1] the greater part of the island is made up of volcanic mud, and although about two-thirds of the whole area is mountainous the island is extraordinarily fertile, and even with the primitive methods which are used in most places produces enough rice to feed the very great population. The vegetation, where it is not controlled by

---

[1] Landenberger, however, admits that there may be earlier strata buried deep under more recent deposits (*Geologie von Niederländisch Indien*, p. 110).

Q

cultivation, is dense and impenetrable. The climate is extremely hot and moist, but here in Java as in Sumatra there are temperate enclaves on the highlands and the gardens are full of roses which never cease to bloom.

Borneo, owing to its position on the equator, has very similar meteorological conditions to Sumatra. It has a rather different and more regular succession of geological strata than the other Dutch Indies and is more continental in general character. The coastal regions, except in the north and north-west parts, are for the most part low and swampy, but the greater part of this enormous island, the third largest in the world, apart from those ranking as continents, is covered with virgin equatorial forests. There are numerous rivers which rise from the central mountainous mass and flow in all directions into the sea. The population has been estimated at something near one and a half millions.

Celebes is comparatively unexplored; it is remarkable for its curious configuration. Four long and mountainous peninsulas radiate from the central mass; the neighbouring island of Halmaheira has a similar shape. The rivers are all short and unnavigable. The geology is still not very well known, but the island appears to be the remains of an isolated continental mass of great antiquity. The northern part has an equatorial climate, but the southern the definite wet and dry seasons which belong to its latitude, and it differs in these respects from many other parts of the archipelago.

The Moluccas, more picturesquely named the Spice Islands, include three clusters of small islands, many of which are volcanic cones. They also have a typical equatorial climate, somewhat modified by their nearness to New Guinea. In flora and in fauna they show a close relationship to the Australian biological area. The Lesser Sunda Islands also belong to this biological area, and on the whole the islands are arid and contrast strongly with their western neighbours. The two last groups, then, belong to a different world from that which we have been studying, and may be considered to lie outside the sphere of Asiatic ethnology. They are peopled to a certain extent, however, by men who are related to those who inhabit that continent and must therefore be noticed at least briefly.

The Philippine Islands are a compact archipelago consisting of a very large number of islands, most of which are separated from one another by narrow channels. Two-thirds of the whole area, which is a little less than that of Great Britain and Ireland combined, is made up by the islands of Luzon and Mindanao. Although these two islands contain large areas of lakes and swampy regions, most of the islands are extremely mountainous, and in most places there is only a narrow belt of rich alluvial soil between the mountains and the sea. The majority of the people, however, live on this narrow coastal strip.

The climate is characterized by considerable humidity, which combined with a hot climate has caused the growth of a luxuriant vegetation. The temperature is extremely equable, and although the precipitation is somewhat variable and very different in different parts of the archipelago, it is generally rather heavy. The climatic conditions are therefore such that even when cultivated by most primitive methods they are capable of sustaining a very dense population, and much of the available land is not at present used for cultivation.

The ethnology of this area falls naturally into three parts following the main geographic divisions: Indo-China, the Malay Peninsula, and the Islands. The ethnological subdivisions also are closely correlated with the geographic subdivisions.

The inhabitants of the south-eastern part of the Asiatic continent have been variously classified. Joyce suggests three divisions: first, the scattered remnants of an early Negrito population; secondly, an Indonesian group including the Mois of the hill country of Annam and the Naga. The third racial type he calls Southern Mongolian, and under this heading he includes the Thai, the Siamese, the Shan, the Tho of Northern Annam, and the Lao of Cambodgia, the Annamese, and the Burmese. He believes the Khmer to be probably a mixture of Malayans and other Indonesians.

Deniker suggests a more elaborate form of classification. He admits two main groups: aborigines and the mixed populations of Indo-China. The first include numerous tribes. The Mois he describes as savage tribes dispersed over the table lands and mountains between the Mekong and the Annamese coast, from the frontier of Yunnan to Cochin China, all of whom are remarkable for their uniformity of physical type. The Kuis Deniker believes include two ethnic groups, one in the south-east of Siam and north-west of Cambodgia and the other in the Shan States. The former are aborigines like the Mois, the latter a branch of the Lolos. The Mons or Talaing are the remnants of a population which formerly occupied the whole of Lower Burma. The Tziam (or Chiam) inhabit the province of Bink Tuan and several other points of South Assam, Cochin China, and Cambodgia. The Karens inhabit the upper valley of the Me Ping and the mountainous districts of Arakan, Pegu and Tenasserim, the country between the Sittong and the Salween, and probably came into Burma at a later date than the Mois. Finally, two peoples he classifies as Indonesians, namely the Nagas and the Selungs.

Among the mixed populations Deniker has four groups: the Cambodgians or Khmers, whom he considers to be a mixture of Malays or Kuis with an intermixture of Hindu, the Annamese, the Burmese and the Thai, whom he apparently considers to be Indonesian. Although he mentions certain physical characters, it would appear that his classification is based partly on the culture and partly on the language of the tribes.

A most careful and succinct account of the peoples of Burma has been given by Sir Herbert White. He states that about two-thirds of the population of Burma are Burmese, who are the predominant element in the population everywhere except in the Shan States, the Kachin, and the Chin Hills and Karenni. The second element in the population includes the Karens of the Karenni. The Shans also form an important element in the population, and among the remainder the most numerous are the Chins, the Kachins, the Talaings, and the Palaungs. There appear always to have been, at least for hundreds of years, a number of Chinese in Burma. At present they are increasing and mix freely with the Burmese.

The history of these peoples is succinctly described by Haddon, who believes that until comparatively recently the inhabitants of Burma were of Nesiot stock, the present

Tibeto-Burman peoples coming from the head-waters of the Yangtze Kiang. "There is no proof," he says, "that the Burmans reached the Irrawaddy Valley before 600 B.C."

Owing to the comparatively inaccessible character of the country we have in this area groups who differ considerably from one another, the various river valleys having formed the areas of characterization of each separate group. It seems also that we should separate Burma from the rest of the country and deal with the whole area as divided into two parts.

There is ample evidence to suggest that at least in some parts of the area the aboriginal population was Negrito; these latter, as we shall see, still survive in the Malay Peninsula. Speaking of Cambodgia, Verneau concludes that this stock forms the substratum of the population, although they have ceased to exist as a group for many years.

The members of the second group which seems to be well represented in the area are akin to the people whom I have called Nesiots. They were the aborigines of much of the area, and where they are found to-day in a comparatively unmixed state are often living in remote and inaccessible regions in the mountains. There is in addition an element which is closely akin to the so-called Dravidian races of Southern India. Although these are apparently akin to the Nesiots, it seems likely that they represent a specialized strain and that they arrived later in the country. Finally, we have a large and important element; the individuals who constitute this have imposed their languages and culture on the people, and ultimately came from China. These last belong to the Parœcean stock.

It is suggested, then, that we have in this area the traces of at least four stocks, on the whole widely divided. We do not know the original home of the Negritos. Their present distribution certainly centres round a point in South-western Asia, but we cannot say whence or when they entered this area, nor do they survive. The Nesiot element has kindred still surviving in Yunnan, and it seems not improbable that they came into the country from the Tibeto-Yunnan plateau. The Negritos have left no trace in Burma, as far as has been reported at present, and it seems that, as far as we know now, the Nesiots may have been some of the earliest inhabitants of the area.

There is every likelihood that there was a migratory movement eastwards from India into this region, and it is possible that it was this Dravidian-like people and not the Nesiots, to whom they are closely akin, who were responsible for the short long-headed part of the Burmese population. The element which Joyce describes as Southern Mongolian, corresponding to Haddon's Tibeto-Burman-speaking people, came into the country from the north. There may, however, have been an earlier invasion of this type of man, as the population seems, in any case, to be very mixed.

Tildesley (X. 9) divides up the Burmese population in the neighbourhood of Moulmein into three groups, one of them being a hybrid. One group she considers to be pure Burman. They are more closely allied to the Malayan, her Malayan group consisting of skulls most of which came from Java, only having the claim to be considered as one group on the basis that their owners probably all spoke languages akin to Malay, and less closely allied to the Chinese, by which is meant Southern Chinese. The second group, which she terms as probably Karen, is more closely allied to the Chinese than to the Malayan, and " as the Chinese are considerably closer to the Caucasian than the Malayan " (i.e. presumably, "as the relationship of the Chinese to the Caucasian is considerably closer than that of the Malayan to the Caucasian ") this section, although quite distinct from the Caucasian, is "closer to that type than the Burman." From the context, I believe her meaning is " closer to the Caucasian than the Burman," but I am not quite sure. By Caucasian, I believe Tildesley means the type of which French and London skulls are more or less typical representatives, but she does not define her exact meaning and this is obscure.

The matter has been more clearly discussed by Morant (I. 14), who has used Tildesley's data but with a wider connotation. He suggests that Burmese " A," to use Tildesley's nomenclature, is physically linked up with the Malayan type, and ultimately with the Southern Chinese. This is a type which we may certainly consider to be a developed type of Pareœan man, and the linkage suggested by Morant, which he expressly says is a linkage of characters, and this he does not want confused with a migration, to be exactly what would be expected if we admit with Haddon the existence of the Proto-Malays. It is possible, however, that there may be an even simpler explanation, although the data has not been fully worked out. The Southern Chinese, although living in a hot country, are not actually dwellers in the tropics, and it seems not impossible that we may find in the pure Burmese type the specialization of the Chinese type due to tropical conditions.

The second type, which Tildesley affirms is more closely allied actually to the Chinese, appears to be differently treated by Morant. He does not include it in his general scheme of Oriental races. He says, however, that what he has termed Tibetan " B," although an aberrant type, and possibly a fundamental human type, is more closely allied to Burmese " B " and " C " than to any other Oriental type. It seems that we have, in Burma at any rate, a second race whose affinities lie with the north and the Yunnan plateau, and this type is allied either to the Southern Chinese or else to the other peoples of the Tibetan plateau. In any case, we are dealing with people who are mostly akin to Yellow man, but who probably have other blood in their veins. The brachycephaly of the Burmese, however, is a distinctive feature which cannot be accounted for solely by a suggestion of Yellow man, for as has been seen the majority of the Chinese appear to be mesocephalic.

The Tibetan plateau and Yunnan, however, contain un-doubted traces of the Alpine race, which exists in some purity in the west in the Tarim basin, and it seems not impossible that where Tildesley found evidence of a " Caucasian " strain she might have suggested " Alpine " man. The Burmese crania are remarkable in several ways, not only are they shorter than the remainder of the Oriental skulls with which they have been compared, but they are also broader. The cephalic index, without giving any certain result, suggests a possible solution to the complex question. The nasal index is as usual not a good indication of racial character ; the nose is platyrrhine in the first two groups of Burmese and consider-ably narrower in the other two groups.

The peripheral region does not seem to have received the attention which it deserves among anthropologists. Verneau and Pannetier (X. 15), in their valuable study of the Cambodgians, have come to the conclusion that there are at least four types in the population. The first and oldest stratum is, they believe, Negrito. To-day this element has ceased to exist as an entity, and can only be found among certain members of the population. It is not improbable that there may be traces of a primitive population, but it is very hazardous, especially when the number of observations is small, to attempt to analyse the elements in any population. The existence of this type must therefore be considered as doubtful until we have further information.

The second element is Nesiot. The remains of this race is found in the graves of the fishing tribes of the Tonle Sap (Bien Ho) and of its tributaries. These primitive tribes are still found in the mountains, where they have sought refuge from the invaders. They have, however, to a certain extent at least, mixed with the later comers, and their influence can be traced.

The third element, called by the authors of the monograph referred to above as " l'element civilisateur," came, it is suggested, either from India or from the islands. They believe that they possess ill-defined characters, the measurements on the heads showing them to be either sub-brachycephalic or mesocephalic. The fourth element in the population is described by the same authors as " Mongolic and Mongoloid."

This is a more elaborate classification than that which had been propounded by Zaborovski (X. 17) earlier. He says, " Les Cambodgians descendent des Tsiams qui eux-mêmes proviennent des Dravidians mêlés aux Mois et aux Indonesians." It is clear that the latter was convinced that there was an element derived from India, whereas the later writers are more inclined to be doubtful on this subject.

Morant has collected the references to the various skulls which have been obtained from this area. He criticizes Zaborovski's statement that the Khmers had the same origin as the Mois, but more mixed with Mongolian peoples, and comes to the conclusion that the Khmers are almost identical with skulls which are acknowledged to be Annamese. He concludes, " We can have little hesitation in stating that the

Khmers are not at all closely related to the aborigines of Annam," i.e. to the Mois.

After testing his stories by the coefficient of racial likeness, he concludes that the Annamese conform to precisely the same cranial type as the Southern Chinese (see page 165), but admits that this deduction is at present based on insufficient evidence. The Annamese occupy a position racially between the Southern Chinese and the Malays. The Siamese bridge the gap between the Malays and the Annamese, being more closely related to the former than to the Chinese.

These statements may seem to be at variance, but it is possible, I think, to combine them and so to form at least a working hypothesis of the population of this somewhat obscure area.

It seems almost certain that we have, apart from problematical Negritos, an underlying Nesiot strain, represented especially by the wilder tribes, who, owing to the isolated position of their present homes, have retained their racial purity not greatly impaired. These are the so-called " aborigines." It is not improbable that they have affected the more civilized population, but we have not at present sufficient evidence to be sure of this point. The Nesiots have been in the country from a remote period, and if the evidence put forward by Verneau is correct, and there is no reason to doubt the archæological evidence, they occupied, even in times not so very long past, an area greater than they do at present.

In discussing the population of Burma, I have drawn attention to the hypothesis put forward by Tildesley that there are two types, the one more closely related to the Malay, and possibly representing the descendants on the mainland of the Proto-Malay type, and the other related to the Southern Chinese type. It seems not improbable that we have, at least in Cambodgia, the same two types which she reports from Burma, the one of the Malay type, and those, if not coming from the islands, as Verneau suggests, at least related to the inhabitants of that area ; the other related to the Southern Chinese, Verneau's " Mongoloid " group.

We have in the Malay Peninsula a comparatively accurate census (X. 25). It reveals several remarkable facts. The total population is over three millions ; of these the aborigines, who are the most interesting for our present purpose, number just over thirty thousand, though it is possible that some of them have been included under Malays. The recent increase has been small; some tribes are dying out, others are rapidly merging themselves in the more settled Malays and losing their jungle habits.

Apart from the increase in Eurasians, who numbered over twelve thousand in 1921, the increase in the other component parts of the population is caused largely by the very great immigration which is taking place, for although the deaths outnumber the births the population continues to increase. The Malays, who number just under half the total population, are recruited from Java and Sumatra and else-where, largely for the rubber industry, but they do show signs of increasing quite apart from immigration. The Chinese form the second largest element in population. They are the trading class, and in the Federated Malay States are almost as numerous as the Malays; altogether in our area they number over a million. The Indians, who number just under half a million, are recruited very largely for labour purposes, and come mainly from the south of India. For the most part they are coolies, but they include a number of small shop-keepers. There are also about thirty thousand other Asiatics, Siamese, Japanese, Singhalese, Arabs and Jews.

The Chinese form a very interesting element in the popula-tion. They certainly visited the country five hundred years ago, and there are Chinese records of Malacca as early as the beginning of the fifteenth century. The earliest Chinese seem to have come from Amoy, and the majority of the im-migrants have always been either Cantonese or Fukienese. The earlier immigrants seem to have married with the Malays, but for the most part Islam has proved a bar to intermarriage, and they have always, wherever possible, returned to China. Recently, however, the Chinese female immigrant has in-creased and many of the Chinese have made their homes outside China, especially since they are secure and have peace, which they much desire as merchants, but which is hard to find in the present disturbed state of China. The Chinese for the most part belong to the type which I have described as Southern Chinese. As far as I am aware no details have been published on the physical characters of this interesting and very important element, not only in the peninsula but also in the islands.

The influence that India has had on Malaya is greater, perhaps, even than that of China : the influence has been both political, religious (for the first missionaries of Mohammedanism came from India), and literary. In Malacca there was a Tamil quarter. The most numerous among the Northern Indian races are the Punjabis, but there are as many as five thousand Bengalis.

The Arabs, though they only number five thousand, are, at least in Singapore, true Arabs, for there has been since the beginning of Islam constant communication between Malaya and the Arab communities, first in India and later in the Hadramut. Religion has in this case, of course, been no bar, and all the old Sayyid families have intermarried with Malay women. Winstedt, however, states that " the Arab cast of countenance is often remarkably preserved," an observation exactly parallel to my own on the Arab Moslems in Peking (see page 159).

Japanese merchants have increased owing to the War, but on the whole their presence is recent and they can hardly be said to have affected the population. It is unfortunate that anthropologists have for the most part interested themselves solely in the Malays and in the aborigines, and there seem to be no physical data on these very interesting and numerous immigrants, who have undoubtedly played a great part in making the population what it is and who to-day collectively represent the majority of the population.

Apart from these immigrant aliens there are three different stocks represented in the Malay Peninsula, Negrito, Sakai, and Malayan, which last includes both Proto-Malays and their advanced kinsfolk.

The Negritos, who in Kedah and Upper Perak are known by their tribal name of Semang, and in Kelantan as Pangan, are reduced to about two thousand individuals. They are small in stature, probably rather over 150 cms., as the measurements reported by different authors vary considerably. They have heads which tend to roundness and frizzy hair. The proportions of the body are of interest, as there is a certain lengthening of the upper arm and a shortening of the leg as compared with Europeans. The nasal index is not apparently so great as in the majority of Negritos. These people present special problems which may be more conveniently discussed in dealing with the ethnology of the Philippine Islands (page 241), where similar groups are found.

The Sakai, who inhabit the mountains from Kula Kangsar to Selangor, represent the second element among the aboriginal tribes of the peninsula. They have mixed considerably with the Negritos in the north and the Proto-Malays in the south. The Senoi and Besisi form part of the same group, but the term Sakai is conveniently used to cover all these peoples. They differ from the Negritos in the colour of their skins; indeed, they are the lightest of the three groups in the peninsula, in their greater stature and in their hair, which is straight or wavy. It has been said that they should be connected linguistically with the Mon-Khmer peoples, and physically with the Veddas. At first sight these two statements seem irreconcilable. Taken in conjunction, however, with comparative evidence the two different statements are of the greatest value in fixing the ethnological position of these peoples. I have already shown that many of the sporadic occurrences of Mon-Khmer languages are to be associated with the Pre-Dravidian type of man.

Intermediate between these peoples and the Proto-Malays, but more closely allied to the latter, are the Besisi. They have Proto-Malay chiefs and physically seem to be closely allied to this stock.

The Proto-Malays and their more civilized cousins form rather less than half the population of the peninsula. There appears to be considerable variation between different localities, probably owing to the intermixing of closely allied stocks. It is possible, however, to distinguish certain common characters which separate them from the peoples just discussed. The hair is always straight and black and tends to be round in section. It is always scanty on the face and body. There are considerable differences in skin-colour, which varies from a dark olive to a light olive, sometimes with a reddish tinge. The eyes are always dark and sometimes are obliquely set. The nose is flat and broad and the cheek-bones are prominent. The chin is square and usually slightly prognathous. The head tends to brachycephaly.

These characters show that the Proto-Malay type is closely connected with the Parœcean, from which indeed it is sometimes difficult to distinguish it. There are, however, quite sufficient differences to justify the division of the type as a sub-variety. It is hardly possible to distinguish the Proto-Malayan type as found in the peninsula from that which is found in the archipelago.

The exact ethnology of these regions, with the exception of the Philippine Islands, has not been sufficiently studied, and considerable doubt yet remains as to exact significance of the various facts which have been reported. Generally speaking, three types are found in the islands, Nesiot, a specialized branch of the Parœcean, and Negrito; but their distribution does not extend equally over the whole area and other stocks have been reported. No Negritos appear to have been reported from Sumatra. The Batin are said to contain traces of a strain akin to the Pre-Dravidians. The Orang Kubu of South Sumatra are believed by Haddon (I. 19. 119) to belong to a very primitive strain; possibly they represent an early type of Parœcean man, as their characteristics on the whole agree with those usually associated with these stocks. Among many of the other stocks of Sumatra the occurrence of curly hair suggests that possibly at one time the Pre-Dravidian element was more widely distrbuted than at present, and that although, except in a few cases, the Pre-Dravidians have ceased to exist as groups yet their blood still runs in the veins of many of the present inhabitants of the island.

The Nesiot strain, which is widely distributed over the island, cannot for the most part be associated with definite tribes but is found, to a greater or lesser extent, among most of the people. The Parœcean element, on the other hand, is found both in a pure and in a mixed state. Among the Battaks, for instance, Volz has noted that two types occur. The Mentawei islanders, on the other hand, seem to be a pure race with but little Nesiot admixture. The nomenclature of the Parœcean strain needs consideration. It has been usual to call them " Malays." The true Malays arose as a people at Menankerbau in Sumatra and crossed over into the Malay Peninsula in the twelfth century. By the end of the thirteenth century they were widely distributed over the archipelago. Like the Mongols they have given their name not

only to the wider extension of their own tribe, but also to the
peoples speaking cognate languages.   The term cannot be
used to connote a physical type without a certain amount of
confusion, as the languages and physical types are by no
means correlated.   It is, however, in general use for the
round-headed peoples inhabiting this region, usually in the
form Malayan.   Haddon has invented the convenient term
" Proto-Malays," to mean the branch of Pareœan man from
whom the various specialized modern " Malay " peoples are
sprung.

The immense population of Java offers a particularly interesting field to the ethnologist, and although the culture
has been very carefully investigated, but little attention
seems to have been devoted to the people.   It has been
stated that the Kalangs in Java proper, that is the centre of
the island, are true Negritos.   It seems very doubtful whether
any pure Negrito people survive in the island, and further
evidence is needed to confirm this statement.   Apart from
these at least four groups of peoples are found in the island.
True Malays are found at Batavia and in the other ports,
the west of the island is occupied by Sundanese, the centre
by Javanese, and the east and Madura by the Madurese.
Although there are marked differences in culture and in
language between these peoples there does not seem to be
any real difference of physique.   I have been informed that
there is a noticeable difference of temperament between the
Javanese and the Sundanese, but such measurements as are
available suggest that there is little if any difference of
physique underlying these variations.   Among some of the
tribes living in the remoter parts of the island, for instance
the Tenggerese, definite Nesiot traits have been observed,
but the people who occupy the greater part of the island are
probably all descended from the Proto-Malays.   They are
extremely round-headed, but this does not serve to distinguish them from the other peoples of this group who live
in South-east Asia, and Morant has recently drawn attention
to their relationship with both the Burmese and the Assamese.
It should, however, be noted that such figures as we have
suggest that the Javanese are a mixed race,[1] and that obser-

[1] Even so small a group as 37 Sundanese had a standard deviation for the
cephalic index of 3·5 [calculated from figures in Garrett (X. 43)].

vations are needed from various parts of the island before any exact opinion can be expressed as to their relationships in detail.

The historical accounts of migrations, although they are of considerable value in suggesting the probable composition of the people, cannot be confirmed by actual reference to physique. These accounts not only show that the Malays had been spreading over the island from early times, but also that at the beginning of the Christian era there was Indian influence, and for a long period this influence appears to have been culturally at least predominant. It has left behind it such magnificent monuments as Borobudur and inscriptions like those at Batutulis, but it is difficult either from measurements or from observations on the people to trace to-day the extent of this influence on the physique of the people.

With the Chinese it is quite otherwise. The Chinese certainly visited Java in early times. They have probably kept up commercial relations with the island for nearly 1300 years. The petty trade of the island is for the most part in their hands. To-day numerous half-breeds are to be found, showing how easily the population absorbs this element. Most of these Chinese who come to the island to-day are natives of the southern seaboard. The distinction in physical types which can be seen side by side in Java serves to emphasize into what widely different groups Parœan man has separated.

In addition to these foreign elements which have probably had an important effect on the physique of the people, the Arabs who have influenced their culture and religion have also left considerable traces in the island. Their numbers are probably insignificant in relation to the total population, but in some towns, especially Djokjakarta, the physical type certainly survives in comparative purity.

If we sum up the racial elements in Java they may be divided into two classes : first, the types which have become thoroughly naturalized in the island ; these include possibly Negritos and certainly Nesiots and the descendants of Proto-Malay immigrants. The second class include comparatively recent immigrants to the islands. They are, first, Malays who are akin to the Proto-Malay element in the island and therefore hardly to be distinguished from them. Next, there have been immigrants from India, but these, except for very recent traders who have immigrated within recent years, do not seem to have left any distinguishing mark on the population. Thirdly, the Chinese element in the population is old-established, and although recent hybrids can easily be distinguished, the ultimate effect of Chinese immigration cannot as yet be stated. The Arab invaders belong individually to a marked type and where they have intermarried have preserved their original type, but they cannot be considered as more than a very negligible element in the total population.

The peoples of Borneo have been carefully studied by Hose and McDougall (X. 47), and by Haddon (X. 46). They are therefore better known than some parts of Indonesia. Here, again, we have no evidence about the aboriginal inhabitants. No trace has been discovered of Negritos, a fact which is all the more remarkable because of the close geographic connection of Borneo with the Philippine Islands. Any Melanesian element seems to be equally absent from Borneo. When geographic factors are taken into consideration this was less to be expected.

The racial history of the island which is suggested by Hose and McDougall accounts in the most satisfactory way that has yet been suggested for the origin of the present peoples. They believe that there are four principal sources for the population. The Klemantans, Kenyans and Punans, these authors suggest, probably inhabited Borneo when it was connected with the mainland. There was a second wave of migration including the present Kayans, Muruts, and Ibans. The Karens are probably the most closely allied to these peoples, who probably represent " an Indonesian stock which had remained and received fresh influx of Mongol blood."

It seems doubtful whether the physique of the people can be quite so simply explained. While it seems probable that the earlier inhabitants were Nesiots, there has been so much mixing at various times that it is extremely doubtful whether the introduction of Proto-Malay influence can be definitely assigned to any particular migration or tribe. Nor can it be definitely stated whether the mixing took place on the mainland or in the islands. It would seem, however, abundantly clear that in the remoter districts the Nesiot blood had maintained itself in comparative purity, for example among the Land Dayak, Murut, and Malay, but that elsewhere and especially on the coast the Proto-Malay and Malay elements had become dominant. This is similar to what has happened in Java. There, however, owing no doubt to the more accessible nature of the country, the Nesiot element has become submerged to a greater extent.

The ethnology of the Philippine Islands possesses many parallels with the rest of Indonesia, except that in this case there are actually surviving Negritos. Modern influences other than European are similar; there are, however, certain differences in detail to which attention should be called. The Arab influence seems to have been more cultural than physical, and probably has had no effect on the racial type of the people. Indian culture has had a wide effect on the islands. Here again, however, it would seem as if the physical effect might be entirely discountenanced. In any case it was by no means so widespread as in Java. No monuments have been found which are comparable to those of Java, nor has there been any deep-rooted survival of Indian customs as in Bali. The effect of culture contact with India is undoubtedly very great and has penetrated even to the remoter parts of the archipelago, but there is no evidence which suggests that any trace of the Indian physical type survives. Chinese traders have visited the Philippines for many centuries. It is more than probable that there may be traces of their blood there. The matter is, however, very difficult to study, because owing to the kinship of the Chinese and the Proto-Malays the exact effects of hybridization are not easy to estimate.

There remain, then, the three basal stocks who form the greater part of the population of the islands. It seems definitely established that at one time the Negritos held the greater part if not all the islands. They were even more widely diffused when Europeans first visited the country than they are at present. Now, however, they form only a small fraction of the population. They live in scattered groups in the forested mountainous regions, four such groups being found in Luzon, and one each in Palasan and Mindanao.

R

In addition to these definitely established Negrito groups there are others, usually called Montesos or " Hill-men," who appear to have some kinship with the Negritos. They are all pygmies, with an average stature of 150 cms. or less, although this figure seems to be exceeded by some of the Hill tribes. They all have round heads and very broad noses. The most remarkable traits are, however, the blackness and woolliness of the hair and the blackness of the skin. There can be no doubt that the Negritos of the Philippines are closely related both to the pygmies of the Andamans and also to certain of the pygmy groups in New Guinea. The general problem connected with these peoples I have already discussed in dealing with the racial problem in Asia (page 65).

It is usual to group the Brown races of the Philippines into two classes, Malayan and Indonesian. This division is probably not entirely satisfactory. According to the ordinary grouping it will be found that all the people loosely grouped together as Nesiot agree in having a very low stature, normally between 151 and 156 cms. mean value. There is, however, a greater variety of nasal index than might be expected. In discussing the ethnology of Southern India a not dissimilar series of facts were noted. Possibly the explanation may be similar. I have already called attention to Haddon's suggestion that there are traces of Pre-Dravidian elements in Sumatra and elsewhere in this area. He has also shown (I. 19, 20) that the main differences between the Pre-Dravidian peoples of Eastern Sumatra and the Toala of Celebes and the true Pre-Dravidians is the greater stature and the more rounded nature of the head. Among such peoples as the Bontok of Luzon and the Ifugao of the same island the mean stature is 155 cms., the cephalic index is 78 and 77 respectively and the mean nasal index 100 and 102. The first two measurements would not serve to distinguish them from the other Nesiot tribes. The nasal index, however, seems to be a clearer guide. It is likely that these tribes have other blood in their veins, but it seems more than possible that they may be considered as true representatives of what is probably one of the most ancient stocks in Southern Asia who have left any living representatives. As we have already seen, there are in Haddon's opinion traces of these peoples surviving in Sumatra and elsewhere. They are of particular interest, because some anthropologists believe that they are connected with the same stock as the Australians and therefore probably occupied all this area at a very remote period.

The true Nesiots of the Philippines are all distinguished by their short stature and relatively long heads, although they are seldom unmixed with other elements, especially Proto-Malay. The nasal indices vary in their mean values from 89 to 93 or 95. They appear to be less platyrrhine therefore than the Pre-Dravidians. The cephalic indices are usually in the neighbourhood of 80, that is they are broader-headed than the Pre-Dravidians and usually slightly more long-headed than the Proto-Malays, but only slightly and hardly significantly so, owing no doubt to the mixture of the two stocks.

Finally, the tribes which are usually classed as Proto-Malays are taller than either the Nesiots or the Negritos. Although in some cases a mean cephalic index as low as 80 is recorded, the majority of these tribes have a mean value as high as 84 or 85, but there appears to be considerable variation. The nasal index, however, serves to distinguish them clearly from their neighbours, the extreme limits of the mean values being between 73 and 85.

It must be remembered that in all these cases we are referring to tribes that probably contain at least two and possibly three elements in their composition. The mean value of any measurements or indices is to a certain extent misleading, as we are often averaging two very different elements. All that can really be said is that the tribes which are classed as Nesiots or Proto-Malays have the characteristics of that stock as a dominant feature, and that probably in most of such tribes we should find individuals of widely different characteristics. These individual differences are, of course, obscured by pooling the measurements on the basis of social groups.

Summarizing them the racial stocks in Indonesia may be grouped into at least four classes. There are, first, the Negritos who have to-day a limited distribution and in this area are only found in the Philippines. The second group, and one that is probably widely scattered but is only found sporadically, consists of the Pre-Dravidians. The third group is related to the races found along the south-western seaboard of Asia, the Nesiots. Finally, the dominant element in the population is the Proto-Malay akin to the Parœan stock. The history and migrations of all these peoples are at present uncertain. There remain other elements, some of which, especially the Chinese, form an important percentage of the total population in many parts. They seem, however, to be recent immigrants for the most part, and in discussing the ethnology of the islands must be grouped as aliens.

CHAPTER XI

SUMMARY AND CONCLUSIONS

I HAVE attempted to sketch in the preceding chapters the physical characters of the chief peoples of Asia. Such a sketch must necessarily be brief if it is to present the facts in broad outline and to avoid the pitfall of superabundant detail. It must also be somewhat in the nature of a stocktaking, showing where we have abundant information and where at present there is a dearth of scientific observations. It will have been seen that, though from the anatomical study of the various peoples there is abundant reason to believe that environment has played an important part in fashioning man's form, yet when the inhabitants of the various areas are described the local groups seem to show relationships which can more readily be correlated with their history and their migrations than with their present environment. We have found marked differences of form among tribes who live under what appears to be exactly similar conditions. On the other hand, if the distribution of a type is plotted on a map, it often seems to retain its constancy in spite of immense divergencies of environment. Yet certain features, as I have tried to show, do seem, as far as can be judged, to be correlated with environment. The material for such study is accumulating, and it becomes almost daily easier to compile the tables on which such a research must be based.

It is clear that such alterations in response to environment, if they do occur, must be in the majority of cases slow in their action. We know little at present of the early racial history of Asia. The more modern history and much of such fragments as we possess of the earlier history make it plain that there have been vast racial movements, the going forward and backward of peoples. Sometimes these movements have, like the invasions of the Huns, been cataclysmic.

Others have been very slow. Not only have there been such migrations, but they have been accompanied by considerable mixings of different stocks. The human races seem for the most part to be capable of producing fertile hybrids, and there is every reason to believe that such hybridization has been taking place in Asia since remote times. There are then many difficulties with which the ethnologist is faced. Among the greatest are the possible effect of environment, the result of migration and the outcome of hybridization. It is difficult to disentangle the effects of these three happenings.

Recent European colonization has not made the matter easier. European hybrids are, however, probably less numerous in proportion to the native races than for instance in Central America. In certain parts, however, they have not been without their effects.

One of the most interesting features of the whole of the racial problems of Asia is concerned with national and psychological factors, but they can hardly be disregarded in considering the physique, because these factors are often considered to be closely correlated with physique. While there has in recent years been considerable immigration or temporary immigrations into Asia by members of European races, there has also been a corresponding immigration of Asiatics out of their own continent. Various efforts have been made to stop such counter migrations. The reason has usually been ultimately economic. The economic factors have, however, a biological background. The peoples of Eastern Asia have been compelled to exist for many generations under conditions which are much harder than those in Europe have been for a long time. The Asiatic can therefore exist under economic conditions which are impossible, or extremely distasteful, to the average European. It has been felt by many nations that the economic competition with Asiatics is unfair to their own nationals and therefore they have, on various grounds, been excluded from certain countries. This policy of exclusion, though often it is called racial, is usually carried out on national and not true racial grounds. It has been seen in the course of the argument that physically there is comparatively little difference between some of the races of Europe and those of Asia, whereas in other races the difference is more profound. On the other hand, I have tried to show that nationality, culture, religion, and language, either together or severally, are often entirely independent of actual physical problems.

Such questions therefore as I have suggested above are quite apart from the study to which ethnology is devoted, though they may frequently borrow data from the ethnologist. Biologically the majority of the races of Asia from the extreme west to the east are closely connected with those of Europe. The distinctions between them are probably not greater than might be said to warrant the term local varieties, although in some cases the differentiation seems to be sufficient to make the use of the word " sub-race " admissible. In Eastern Asia, however, there seems to be very widely spread a group of peoples, conveniently termed Yellow man, who seem to be more remotely connected with the races of Europe. Even here the degree of divergence is to a certain extent a matter of dispute. Finally, in remote parts of South-eastern Asia there are sporadic traces of an entirely different type of man who, all ethnologists are agreed, must be considered as widely differentiated from the other two groups.

In numbers the Negritos are so few as to form an infinitesimal part of the peoples of Asia. Yellow man is very numerous, and probably the greater part of the population of Asia belongs to this race, but the other races are very plentiful and may have slight majority. The smaller varieties of the great stocks are also present in large numbers, although they seem to be divided into certain marked categories. As far as can be judged with evidence that has been collected at present these varieties seem to be dominant in certain well-marked regions, so that in spite of divergencies in detail it is often possible to state in broad outline the physical type which inhabits a certain area. But this can hardly ever be done with the same accuracy as can be attained in plotting the distribution of a language or of a religion. It can never be done with the precise exactitude with which modern nations endeavour to define their political frontiers.

SHORT BIBLIOGRAPHY

THIS bibliography is obviously not exhaustive, but references to further literature will be found in the works cited. A convenient guide to the libraries in which the various publications may be found has been compiled by R. T. Leiper, *Periodicals of Medicine and the Allied Sciences (including anthropology) in British Libraries*, British Medical Association, London, 1923. Unfortunately this does not include references to the Library of the Royal Anthropological Institute. A more complete list will be found in the *World List of Scientific Periodicals*, London (*forthcoming*).

Apart from the usual abbreviations, e.g. Trans. for transactions, etc., the following have been used :—

A.f.A.   *Archiv für Anthropologie*, Braunschweig.

J.R.A.I.   *Journ. Roy. Anthrop. Inst.*, Lond. (no Royal previous to 1907, XXXVII.).

Z.f.E.   *Zeitschrift für Ethnologie*, Berlin.

In some cases it has been found most convenient to repeat a reference; in other cases, where there was no ambiguity, cross references have been given. Students who are hampered by lack of linguistic knowledge or inadequate libraries will frequently find useful résumés of papers in the *Archiv für Anthropologie* (the older numbers of which are especially valuable for Russian literature), in *l'Anthropologie*, and in the *American Journal of Physical Anthropology*.

CHAPTER I

1 Keane, A. H. *Ethnology.* Camb., 1896.
2 Linnæus, C. *Systema naturæ.* Ed. princeps, Lugd. Batav., 1735. [Reprint, Paris, 1830.]
  Linnæus, C. Ed. decima reformata Holmiæ, 1758. [Reprint, Leipsic, 1894.]
3 Blumenbach, J. F. *De generis humani varietate nativa.* Gott., 1775.
  Blumenbach, J. F. Second Ed. Gott., 1781.
4 Duckworth, W. L. H. *Anthropology and Morphology.* Camb., 1904.
5 Huxley, T. H. *Journ. Ethnolog. Soc.* Lond., 1870, N.S., II. 404.
6 Topinard, Paul. *Elements d'Anthropologie générale.* Paris, 1885.
7 Sergi, G. *Specie e varieta Umane.* Turin, 1900.
8 Ripley, W. Z. *Races of Europe.* Lond., 1899.
9 Deniker, J. *The Races of Man.* Lond., 1900.
10 Pearson, K. *The Grammar of Science.* Lond., 1911.
11 Pearson, K. (Editor). *Tables for Biometricians.* Camb., 1923.
12 Yule, G. Udney. *An Introduction to the Study of Statistics.* Lond., 1911.
13 Buxton, L. H. D. *The Anthropology of Cyprus.* J.R.A.I., 1920, L. 194.
14 Morant, G. M. In Biometrika. Camb., 1924, XVII. 1.
15 Thomson, A. [Man's Cranial Form.] J.A.I., 1903, XXXIII. 135.
16 Keith, A. *Human Embryology and Morphology.* Third Ed. Lond., 1913.
17 Keith, A. Huxley Lecture, Nature, 1923, CXII. 257.
18 Thomson, A., and Buxton, L. H. D. *Man's Nasal Index in relation to certain climatic conditions.* J.R.A.I., 1923, LIII. 92.
19 Haddon, A. C. *The Races of Man.* Camb., 1924.
20 Quetelet, A. *Lettres . . . sur la théorie des probabilités.* Brussels, 1846. [Engl. Trans., O. G. Downes, Lond., 1849.]
21 Retzius, A. *Ethnologische Schriften.* Stockholm, 1864.
22 Giuffrida-Ruggeri, V. *Homo sapiens.* Bologna, 1913.
23 Giuffrida-Ruggeri, V. *U l' origine dell' Uomo.* Bologna, 1921.
24 Biasutti, R. *Studi sulla distribuzione dei caratteri e dei typi antropologici.* Mem. Geogr., Firenze, 1912, VI.
25 Dixon, R. B. *The Racial History of Man.* New York, 1923.
26 Keane, A. H. *Man Past and Present.* Camb., 1920.
27 Martin, R. *Lehrbuch der Anthropologie.* [Extensive bibliography.] Jena, 1914.
28 Flower, Sir. W. H. *Cat. Roy. Coll. Surgeons.* Lond., 1879, I. (Man).
29 Quatrefages, J. de. *The Human Species.* Lond., 1879.
30 Quatrefages, J. de, and Hamy, E. T. *Crania ethnica.* Paris.
31 Turner, Sir W. *Sci. Results of " Challenger " Exped.* 1884, XXIV. 10.
32 Brooks, C. E. P. *The Evolution of Climate.* Lond., 1922.
33 Lyde, L. W. Climatic Control of Skin Colour (*Papers on Interracial Problems*, ed. G. Spiller, 1911, 104).
34 Grimble, A. [Effect of Indoor Life on Pigmentation.] J.R.A.I., 1921, LI. 42.
35 Huntingdon, E., and Visher, S. S. *Climatic Changes, their Nature and Causes.* 1923.

36 Mathew, R. *Climate and Evolution.* Ann. New York Acad. Sci., 1915, XXIV.
37 Conklin, E. G. *The Direction of Human Evolution.* Oxford, 1921.
38 Pearl, R. *Modes of Research in Genetics.* New York, 1915.
39 Carr-Saunders, A. M. *The Population Problem.* Oxford, 1922.
40 Keith, A. *The Antiquity of Man.* New Ed. Lond., 1925.

CHAPTER II

(a) HUMAN GEOGRAPHY

It is impossible to give a representative bibliography of the works on the human geography of Asia as they are so numerous. The following contain references to the more specialized books.

1 Keane, A. H. *Stanford's Compendium of Geography and Travel. Asia* (2 vols.). Lond., 1896.
2 *Brit. Mus. Handbook to the Ethnographical Collections.* [T. A. Joyce.] Lond., 1910.
3 Hogarth, D. G. *The Nearer East.* Oxford, 1902.
4 Little, A. *The Farther East.* Oxford, 1902.
5 Czaplicka, M. A. *Aboriginal Siberia.* Oxford, 1914. [Summarizes Russian literature.]
6 Buxton, L. H. D. *The Eastern Road.* Lond., 1924.
7 Richards, L. (S. J.) *Geographie de l'Empire de Chine.* Shanghai, 1905. [Eng. Trans., Kennelly, 1908.]
8 Broomhall, T. H. (Editor). *The Chinese Empire.* Lond., 1907.
9 Richthofen, Freiherr v. *China.* Five vols., Berlin, 1877-1911.
10 Holdich, Sir T., *India.* Oxford, 1902.
11 Czaplicka, M. A. *The Turks of Central Asia.* Oxford, 1918.

(b) ASIATIC RACES

12 Haddon, A. C. *The Wanderings of Peoples.* Camb., 1911.
13 Hrdlicka, A. Amer. Journ. Phys. Anthrop. Washington, 1920, III. 4.
14 Zwaan, K. de. *Die Inseln Nias.* Haag, 1914 (2 vols.).
15 Giuffrida-Ruggeri, V. *Prime linee di un' antropologia sistemica dell' Asia.* Archiv. Antrop. Etnol. Florence, 1917, XLVII., also issued separately, Engl. Trans., Univ. of Calcutta, Anthrop. Papers, 1921, VI.
16 Fleure, H. J. In Eugenics Review. 1922, XIV. 97.
17 Smith, G. Elliot. *The Ancient Egyptians.* London and New York, 1923.
18 Baur-Fischer-Lenz. *Grundriss der menschlichen Erblichkeitslehre and Rassenhygiene.* 1923.
19 Günther, H. F. K. *Rassenkunde des deutschen Volkes.* Munich, 1924.
20 Duckworth, W. L. H. [Note on a skull from Syria.] Studies in Anthropology. Camb., 1911.
21 Haddon, A. C. [The pygmy question] in Wollaston, A. F. R. *Pygmies and Papuans.* Lond., 1912.
22 Martin, R. *Die Inlandstamme der Malayischen Halbinsel.* Jena, 1905.
23 Sullivan, L. R., in Mem. Bishop Mus. Honolulu, 1923, IX. 211.

CHAPTER III

1 Boule, M. *Les hommes fossiles.* Paris, 1921.
2 Pumpelly, R. *Explorations in Turkestan.* Carnegie Inst., Washington, 1904, LXXIII. (2 vols.).
3 Savenkov. Congres internat. d'anthrop. et d'archeol. Moscow, 1892, I.
4 Baye, J. de, and Volkov, Th. l'Anthrop. Paris, 1899, X. 172.
5 Hamada, K., and Hasebe, K. Rep. Archæol. Research, Dept. of Lit., Kyoto Imp. Univ., 1920–1921, IV·V.
6 Teilhard, P. l'Anthrop. 1923, XXXIII. 630.
7 Andersson, J. G. Palæontologica Sinica D. Peking, 1923, I. 1.
8 Andersson, J. G. Bull. Geol. Surv. China. Peking, 1923, V. 1.
9 Buxton, L. H. Dudley. Man, 1925, XXV. 10.
10 Zumoffen, G. L'Anthrop. 1897, VIII. 272.
11 Matsumoto, H. Science Rep. Imp. Univ. Sendai. Japan, 1918, III. 36.
12 Giuffrida-Ruggeri, V. Riv. ital. Sociologia. 1915, XIX.
13 Giuffrida-Ruggeri, V. Riv. ital. Paleont. 1918, XXIV.
14 Giuffrida-Ruggeri, V. A.A.E. 1916, LXV.
15 Keith, Sir A. J.R.A.I. 1915, XLV.
16 Hrdlicka, A. Proc. U.S. Nat. Mus., 1924, LXIII. 12, 1.
17 Hrdlicka, A. Amer. Anthrop. 1912.
18 Hrdlicka, A. Bull. B.A.E. 1907, XXXIII.
19 Hrdlicka, A. *Ibid.* 1912, LII.
20 Hrdlicka, A. *Ibid.* 1918, LXVI.
21 Testut, L. B.S.A.L. 1889, VIII.
22 Sollas, W. J. *Ancient Hunters.* Lond., 1923
23 Bryn, H. Ymer. 1922, 314.
24 Christian, V. Anthropos. 1921–1922, XVI–XVII. 577.
25 Christian, V. Mitth. Anthrop. Ges. Wien, 1924, LIV. 1.

CHAPTER IV

(a) GENERAL

1 Myres, J. L. *The Dawn of History.* Lond., 1911.
2 Luschan, F. v. Huxley Lecture. J.R.A.I., 1911, XLI. 241.
3 Hall, H. R. *Ancient History of the Near East.* Lond., 1913.
4 How, W. W., and Wells, J. *A Commentary on Herodotus.* Oxford, 1912.
5 Boas, F. *Descendants of Immigrants.* New York, 1912.

(b) ASIA MINOR AND SYRIA

6 Myres, J. L. [Dodecannese.] Georgr. Journ., Lond., 1920, LVI. 329 and 406.
7 Luschan, F. v. [Early inhabitants of Lycia.] A.f.A., 1891, XIX. 31.
8 Hasluck, F. W. J.R.A.I., 1921, LI. 310.
9 Peake, H. J. E. J.R.A.I., 1916, XLVI. 154.
10 Buxton, L. H. D. Biometrika. Camb., 1920, XIII. 92.
11 Chantre, E. [Armenians.] Bull. Soc. Anthrop., Lyons, 1896.
12 Weissenburg, J. [Armenians and Jews.] A.f.A., 1915, XIII. 383.
13 Chantre, E. *Recherches Anthropologiques dans le Caucase.* Paris, 1885–1887.

14 Zichy, Count de. *Voyages au Caucase.* Budapest, 1897.
15 Chantre, E. Bull. Soc. Anthrop., Lyons. [Necropolis de Sidon.] 1894. [Metwali, Baktyari, Yesidi.] 1895. [Armenians.] 1896. [Kurds.] 1902.
16 Hogarth, D. G. [Hittites.] J.R.A.I., 1909, XXXIX. 408.
17 Messerschmidt, L. [Hittites.] Smithsonian Rep., 1903, Washington, 1904.

(c) Jews

18 Weissenberg, J. A.f.A., 1895, XXIII. 347. [South Russian.]
19 Weissenberg, J. [Yemen.] Z.f.E., 1909, XLI. 319.
20 Weissenberg, J. [Samarqandi.] Mitth. Anthrop. Ges. Wien., 1913, XLIII. 257.
21 Hauschild, M. W. Z.f.E., 1921, LII-LIII. 518.
22 Salaman, R. N. Journ. Genetics., 1911, I. 273.

(d) Arabia

23 Seligman, C. G. J.R.A.I., 1917, XLVII. 214. [Bibliography.]
24 Bury, G. W. *Arabia Infelix.* Lond., 1915.
25 Christian, V. Anthropos, 1919-1920, XIV.-XV.
26 Pöch, R. *Osten und Orient.* Wien, 1920, III. (i) 729.

(e) Persia and Middle East

27 Danilov, J. [Persians.] A.f.A., 1900, XXVI. 872.
28 Husing, R. [Iran.] Mitth. Anthrop. Ges., Wien, 1916, XLVI. 233.
29 Bogdanof, A. P. [Iranian Colonies in Turkestan.] A.f.A., 1900, XXVI. 800.
30 Javorski, W. [Turkoman.] Mil. Acad. Anthrop. Soc., Petrograd, 1895, II. 145.
31 Ujfalvy, C. E. *Essai d'une carte ethnographique de l'Asie centrale.* Paris, 1896.
32 Troll, J. *Individual Aufnahme central asiatische Eingebornen.* Z.f.E., 1890, XXII. (226).

CHAPTER V

The literature on the ethnography of India is very voluminous. The student will find references to all the more important works in the larger summaries quoted below. The number of studies on the physical proportions of the people is comparatively limited.

(a) General

1 *Imperial Gazetteer of India.* Oxford, 1909 (26 vols.).
2 *Census of India,* 1901 (Anthropometric), Calcutta, 1902–1903.
3 *Census of India,* 1911 (Linguistic), Calcutta, 1912.
4 *The Cambridge History of India.* Camb., 1922, I.
5 Smith, V. A. *The Early History of India.* Third Ed., Oxford, 1914.
6 Macdonell, A. A. *History of Sanskrit Literature.* Lond., 1905.
7 Roberts, S. G. *Historical Geography of India.* Oxford, 1916.
8 Vincent, G. *The Defence of India.* Oxford, 1923.
9 Senart, E. *Les castes dans l'Inde.* Paris, 1896.
10 Lyall, A. C. *Asiatic Studies.* Lond.
11 Bougle, M. C. *Essai sur le regime des castes.* Paris, 1908. [To be used with caution.]

12 Anderson, J. D. *The Peoples of India.* Camb. Univ. Manuals, 1913.
13 Giuffrida-Ruggeri, V. Arch. Antrop. Etnol., Florence, 1917, XLVII.
14 Richards, F. J. Quart. Journ. Mythic. Soc., Madras, 1917, VII. 243.
15 Risley, Sir H. H. *The People of India.* Lond., 1908.
16 Turner, Sir W. [Craniometry.] Trans. Roy. Soc., Edinburgh, 1899,
    XXXIX. 703 ; 1901, XL. 59 ; 1906, XLV. 261 ; 1913, XLIV. 705.

See also Holdich (Ch. 2, ref. 10) and Morant (Ch. 1, ref. 14).

(b) NORTHERN INDIA

17 Tod, J. *Annals and Antiquities of Rajasthan.* Lond., 1829–1832. Re-
    print, Oxford. Ed. W. Crooke. *Annals of Mewar.* Reprinted separately,
    Lond. [N.D.] Ed. C. H. Payne.
18 Enthoven, R. E. *Tribes and Castes of Bombay.* Bombay, 1920–1922.
    [Deals with part of South India also.]
19 Crooke, W. *The Natives of Northern India.* Lond., 1907.
20 Crooke, W. *The Tribes and Castes of N.W. Provinces and Oudh.* Lond.,
    1896.
21 Crooke, W. *The North-Western Provinces of India.* Lond., 1897.
22 Crooke, W. J.A.I., 1898, XXVIII. 220, J.R.A.I., 1910, XL. 39.
23 Dalton, E. T. *Descriptive Ethnology of Bengal.* Calcutta, 1872.
24 Kirkpatrick, W. *An Account of the Kingdom of Nepaul.* 1821.
25 Eickstedt, E. v. [Sikh.] Z.f.E., 1921, LII. 318.
26 Eickstedt, E. v. [Panjabi.] Man in India, 1923, III. 161.
27 Robertson, G. S. *The Kafirs of the Hindu-Kush.* 1896.
28 Charles, R. H. [Panjab craniology.] Journ. Anat. Phys., Lond., 1907,
    XXVII. 1.
29 Holland, Sir T. H. [Kanets.] J.A.I., 1902, XXXII. 96.
30 Risley, Sir H. H. *The Tribes and Castes of Bengal.* 1891.
31 *Ethnographic Survey of India.* Anthropometric data from Bombay,
    Calcutta, 1907. (See note to 18.)

(c) SOUTHERN INDIA

32 Thurston, E. *Castes and Tribes of Southern India.* Madras, 1909 (7 vols.).
33 Thurston, E. Madras Gov. Museum Publs. IV., V.
34 Schmidt, W. A.f.A., 1910, N.F., IX. 90.
35 Holland, Sir T. H. *The Coorgs and Yeruvas.* Journ. As. Soc., Bengal,
    1901, LXX. 59.
36 Hornell, J. [Southern brachycephals.] Mem. As. Soc., Bengal, 1920, VII.
    139.
37 Hornell, J. [Extension of Mediterranean race.] J.R.A.I., 1923, LIII. 302.
38 Hunt, E. H. *Hyderabad Cairn Burials.* J.R.A.I., 1924, LIV. 140.
39 Iyer, Anantha Krishna L. K. *The Cochin Tribes and Castes.* Madras, 1909,
    1912.
40 Lapicque, L. Bull. Mus. d'hist. nat., Paris, 1905, 283.
41 Rivers, W. H. R. *The Todas.* Lond., 1906.
42 Callemand, J. Rev. d'Anthrop, Paris, 1878 (2me S.), I. 607.

(d) CEYLON

42 Parker, H. *Ancient Ceylon.* Lond., 1909.
43 Sarasin, P., and F., Ergeb. Natur. Forschungen auf Ceylon, 1887–1893,
    III. (Veddas).

44 Thomson, A. [Veddas.] J.A.I., 1889, XIX. 125.
45 Seligman, C. G., and Z. B. *The Veddas*. Camb., 1911.
46 Lüthy, A. A.f.A., 1912, N.F., XI. 1.
47 Virchow, R. Z.f.E., XIV. 302 and XVII. 500.
48 Virchow, R. Abh. Königl. Akad., Wiss., 1881.

(*e*) THE ANDAMAN ISLANDS.

49 Brown, A. R. *The Andaman Islanders*. Camb., 1922.
50 Flower, Sir W. H. J.A.I., 1879, IX. 108 ; 1884, XIV. 115.
51 Man, E. H. J.A.I., 1882, XII. 69, 117, 327.

CHAPTER VI

For geography see bibliography to Chapter 2, ref. 7, 8 and 9 ; for archæology
see bibliography to Chapter 4, ref. 6, 7, 8, 9, 11.

1 Jamieson, C. E. *The Aborigines of Western China*. China Journ. of Arts
   and Science, 1923, I. 376.
2 Legendre. Bull. Mem. Soc. d'anthrop., Paris, 1910 (6me Series), I. 77,
   158 (Lolo).
3 Ting, C. K. (should read V. K.). *Native Tribes of Yunnan*. China Medical
   Journ., March, 1921. [Reprinted in Proc. Anatom. and Anthrop. Soc.
   of China, 1920–1921, Peking, 1921.]
4 Birkner, F. A.f.A., 1906, IV. 1.
5 Shirokogoroff, S. M. *Anthropology of Northern China*. Roy. Asiat. Soc.
   (North China Branch, extra vol. III), Shanghai, 1923.
6 Koganei, Y. Mitth. Med. Fak., Tokio, 1903, IV. 1 ; Intern. centralblatt
   f. Anthrop., 1902, VII. 130.
7 Black, D. [*Early Chinese.*] Paleontologica Sinica (forthcoming).
8 Hagen, B. Anthropologischer Atlas, Ostasiatischer und Melanesischer
   Völker, Wiesbaden, 1898.
9 Henry, A. [Lolo.] J.A.I., 1903, XXXIII.
10 Reicher, M. Zeit. f. Anthrop. u. Morphologie, 1912–1913, XV. 421.
11 Haberer, K. A. *Schädeln and Skeletteile aus Peking*. Jena, 1902.
12 Rose, A., and Brown, J. C. [Lissu] Mem. As. Soc. Bengal, 1910, III. 249.
See also Morant (I, 14).

CHAPTER VII

(*a*) TIBET

1 Rockhill, W. W. Rep. Nat. Mus., 1893 ; Washington, 1895, 673.
2 Delisle, F. Bull. Soc. d'Anthrop., Paris, 1908 (5e Series), IX. 473.
3 Morant, G. M. [Craniometry.] Biometrika, Camb., 1923, XIV. 196.
4 Grenard, F. Le Turkestan et le Tibet. *Mission scientifique dans la haute
   Asie*. J. L. Ducreuil du Rhins, Paris, 1890–1895.
5 Bell, C. *Tibet Past and Present*. Oxford, 1924.
See also Turner (V. 16) [1906 and 1913] and Joyce (II. 2).

(*b*) SINKIANG

6 Joyce, T. A. J.R.A.I., 1903, XXXIII. 305 ; 1912, XLII. 450.
7 Stein, Sir Aurel. *Serindia*. Oxford, 1921, III. 1351.
8 Paissel, V. E. [Taranchi.] A.f.A., 1900, XXVI. 174.

See also Czaplicka (II. 11) and Broomhall (II. 8).

(c) MONGOLIA

9 Ivanovski, A. A. [Mongol Torguts.] A.f.A., 1896, XXIV. 1; 1900, XXVI. 852. This summarizes paper in Anthrop. Soc., Moscow, 1893, LXXI.
10 Porotov, M. T. (Alar Buriats.] A.f.A., 1896, XXVI. 159.
11 Shrendrikovski, J. J. [Selanga Buriats.] A.f.A., 1900, XXVI. 152.
12 Fridolin, J. A.f.A., 1901, XXVII. 304.
13 Torii, R., and Torii, K. Journ. Coll. Sci. Tokyo Imp. Univ., 1914, XXXVI. 44.
14 Deniker, J. Rev. d'Anthropologie. 1884, XIII. 297.
15 Howarth, Sir H. H. *History of the Mongols.* Lond., 1876.
16 Carruthers, D. *Unknown Mongolia.* Lond., 1913.
17 Buxton, L. H. D. [Inner Mongolia.] Geo. Journ., Lond., 1913, LXI.

(d) MANCHURIA

18 Torii, R. Journ. Coll. Sci., Tokyo Imp. Univ., 1914, XXXVI.

See also Shirokogoroff. (VI. 5).

(e) KOREA

19 Koganei, Y. Z.f.E., 1906, XXXVIII. 513.
20 Koganei, Y. Mitth. Med. Fak. Imp. Jap. Univ., Tokio, 1, 226.
21 Virchow, R. Z.f.E., 1899, XXXI. 751.
22 Kubo. *Beitrage zur physischen Anthropologie der Koreaner.* Tokio, 1913.
23 Chantre, E., and Bourdaret, E. Bull. Soc. d'Anthrop. de Lyons, 1902, XXI;

CHAPTER VIII

(a) SIBERIA (General)

1 Talko-Hryncewicz, J. D. [Early inhabitants.] L'Anthrop., 1896, VII. 80.
2 Merhart, G. von. [Archæology of Yenesei.] Amer. Anthrop., 1923, XXV. 21.
3 Goroshchenko. Bull. Krasn. S.E. Sib. Sect. I.R.G.S., 1905, I.
4 Goroshchenko. [Soyotes.] Russ. Anthrop. Journ., 1901, II. 2.
5 Goroshchenko and Ivanovski, A. A. [Yenesei.] Russ. Anthrop. Journ., 1907, i. and ii.
6 Ivanovski, A. A. *Anthropological Composition of the Population of Russia.* 1904.
7 Ujfalvy, C. E. *Expédition scientifique en Russie, Sibérie et dans le Turkestan.* Paris, 1878.
8 Jochelson-Brodsky, Frau D. [North Siberian peoples.] A.f.A., 1906, N.F.V., 1. See also Czaplicka (II. 5).

(b) WESTERN SIBERIA

9 Czaplicka, M.A. Art. *Ostyak* and *Samoyed.* Hastings Encyclop. Religion and Ethics.
10 Roudenko, S. [Samoyed, Ostyak and Vogul.] Bull. Soc. d'Anthrop., Paris, 1914 (Série VI.), V. 123.
11 Crahmer, W. [Samoyeds.] Z.f.E., 1912, XLIV. 105.
12 Montefiore, J. [Samoyeds.] J.A.I., 1894, XXIV. 400.
13 Charusin, A. [Kirghiz.] Imp. Soc. Friends of Nat. Sci. Anthrop. and Ethnol., Moscow, 1889, LXIII. 1.

(c) EASTERN SIBERIA

14 *Jesup North Pacific Expedition.* Various authors. [A mine of information on all these northern tribes.]

15 Bogoras, W. Amer. Anthrop., 1901, III. 80.

16 Iden-Zeller, O. [Chukchee.] Z.f.E., 1911, XLIII. 840.

17 Schrenck, L. von. *Reisen in Amur·Lande.* III. St. Petersburg, 1891.

18 Czaplicka, M. A. [Tungus.] Scottish Geo. Mag., Edinburgh, 1917, 299.

19 Seeland. [Gilyaks.] A.f.A., 1900, XXVI. 790.

See also Shirokogoroff (VI. 5).

CHAPTER IX

(a) ARCHÆOLOGY

1 Koganei, Y. Globus, 1903, LXXXIV. 101.

2 Matsumoto, H. Amer. Anthrop., 1921, XXIII. 50.

3 Hasebe, K. Jap. Anthrop. Journ. Tokyo, 1918, XXXII.; 1920, XXXIV.

4 Monro, N. G. *Prehistoric Japan.* Yokohama, 1911.

5 Various authors in the Journal of Research, Imp. Jap. Univ. Kyoto (Department of Literature). This publication is devoted to the study of prehistoric Japan.

(b) AINU

6 Koganei, Y. Mitth. Med. Fak. Imp. Jap. Univ., Tokyo, 1893, II. 1.

7 Koganei, Y. A.f.A., XXVI.

8 Montandon, G. Archiv. suisses d'anthrop. gen., 1921, IV. 233.

9 Donitz, W. Mitth. Deutsch. Ges. Natur u. Volkerkunde Ostasiens, 1874, VI.

10 Scheube, B. *Ibid.,* 1882, XXVI.

11 Lefevre, A., et Collignon, R. Rev. d'anthrop., Paris, 1889, XVIII (Sér. 3, IV. 129) (hair and eye colour).

12 Batchelor, Rev. J. *The Ainu.* Lond., 1901.

(c) JAPANESE

13 Baelz, E. Mitth. Deutch. Ges. Natur u. Volkerkunde Ostasiens, Tokyo, 1881, III. 330 ; 1885, IV. 35 ; 1900, VII. 227.

14 Baelz, E. Sitz. Anthrop. Ges., Wien, 1911–1912 [133], Riu Kiu.

15 Brinkley, F. Smithsonian Rep., 1903, MDXXXVII. 793.

See also Morant (I. 14).

16 Chamberlain, B. *Things Japanese.* Lond., 1891.

17 Toldt, E. A.f.A., 1903, XXVIII. 143.

18 Adachi, B. Zeit. f. Morph. u. Anthrop., Stuttgart [Orbit and general], 1904, VII. 379 [Foot]. Mitt. Med. Fak., Tokyo, 1905, VI. 307 [Hand], *id.,* 340 [Foot]. Journ. Anthrop. Soc., Tokyo, 1904, XX. 21, and numerous other papers on the anthropology of the Japanese referred to in the above.

19 Shimada, K. [Central nervous system.] Acta scholæ Med. Univ., Kioto, IV., 1921, 319 (in German).

(d) RYUKYU

20 Baelz, E. Sitz. Anthrop. Ges., Wien, 1911–1912 (1912) [133].

(e) FORMOSA

21 Turner, Sir William. Proc. Roy. Soc., Edinburgh, 1907, XLV.
22 *Report on Control of Aborigines.* Gov. of Formosa Bureau of Aboriginal Affairs, Taihoku, Formosa, 1911.

CHAPTER X

(a) BURMA

1 Logan, J. R. *The Ethnology of Eastern Asia.* Journ. Indian Archipelago, IV. 478.
2 McMahon, A. R. *The Karens of the Golden Chersonnese.* Lond., 1876.
3 Milne, Mrs. L. *The Home of an Eastern Clan.* [Palaungs of the Shan States.] Oxford, 1924.
4 *Anthropometric Data* (Burman). Ethnographic Surv. India, Calcutta, 1906.
5. Lowis, C. C. *Ethnographic Survey of India* (Burma). No. 4, Calcutta, 1919.
6 Scott, J. G. *Burma, A handbook, etc.* 1906.
7 White, Sir H. T. *Burma.* (Provincial Geographies of India.) Camb., 1923.
8 Temple, Sir R. C. D. Journ. Roy. Soc. Arts, Lond., 1910, LVIII. 695.
9 Tildesley, M. A. [Craniometry.] Biometrika. Camb., 1921, XIII. 695.
10 Turner, Sir W. Trans. Roy. Soc., Edinburgh, 1913, XLIX. 719.

In addition to the " Imperial Gazetteer of India " the following gazetteers of Burma have been published

11 Scott, Sir G. *Upper Burma.*
12 Carey, Sir B. S., and Tuck, H. N. *Chin Hills.*
13 Hertz, W. A. *Myitkyina District.*

(b) SIAM AND INDO-CHINA

14 Graham, A. W. *Siam* (Handbook). 1912.
15 Verneau, R., and Pannetier, G. [Cambodgia]. L'Anthrop., Paris, 1921, XXXI. 279.
16 Deniker, J., and Bonifacy, A. L. M. Bull. et Mem. Soc. Anthrop., Paris, 1907, 5e Série, VIII. 106.
17 Zaborowski, S. *Ibid.*, 1897, 4e Série, VIII. 44, and 1900, 5e Série, I. 327.
18 Roux, P. [Tonkin.] *Ibid.*, 1905, 5e Série, VI. 155 and 324.
19 Maurel, E. *Ibid.* 1889, 2e Série, IV. 459.
20 Verneau, R. L'Anthrop., Paris, 1909, XX. 545.
21 Abadie, M. *Les races de Haut Tonkin de Phong-Tho à Lang Son.* Paris, 1924.

(c) THE MALAY PENINSULA

22 Martin, R. *Die Inlandstamme der Malayischen Halbinsel.* Jena, 1905. [The standard textbook and a mine of information.]
23 Annandale, N., and Robinson, H. C. *Fasciculi Malayenses.* Lond., 1903.
24 Skeat, W. W., and Blagden, C. O. *Pagan Races of the Malay Peninsula.* Lond., 1903.
25 Winstedt, R. O. *Malaya.* Lond., 1923.
26 Morgan, J. *L'age de pierre polie dans la presqu'île Malaise.* L'Homme, II. 494.
27 Swettenham, Sir F. *The Real Malay.* Lond., 1900.

28 Swettenham, Sir F. *British Malaya.* Lond., 1906.
29 Turner, Sir W. Trans. Roy. Soc., Edinburgh, 1907, XLV.
30 Evans, I. H. N. *Religion, Folklore and Custom in North Borneo and the Malay.* Camb., 1923.
31 Skeat, W. W. *Malay Magic.* Lond., 1900.
32 Schmidt, W. A.f.A., 1906, N.F., V. 59.

(d) THE MALAY ARCHIPELAGO

33 Giuffrida-Ruggeri, V. Archiv. Anthrop. Etnol., 1916, XLVI. 125.
34 Hagen, B. *Anth. Studien aus Insulinde.* Ver. Kon. Akad. Wiss., Amsterdam, 1890, XXVIII.
35 Hamy, E. T. *Les races malaiques et americaines.* L'Anthrop., 1896, VII.
36 Hamy, E. T. [Alfourous de Gilolo.] Bull. Soc. Geogr., Paris, 1877, 6, XIII. 491.
37 Meyer, A. B. The Negritos. Dresden, 1899.
38 Quatrefages, J. L. de. *The Pygmies.* Lond., 1895. [*Les Pygmées*, Paris, 1887.]
39 Turner, Sir W. Trans. Roy. Soc., Edinburgh, 1907, XLV. 781.

(e) SUMATRA

40 Hagen, B. Veroffen. Stadt. Volker-Mus. Frankfurt a. M., 1908, II.
41 Volz, W. A.f.A., 1900, XXVI. 719 ; 1908, XXXV. 89.
42 Volz, W. *Nord-Sumatra.* (Two vols.) Berlin, 1909 and 1912.

(f) JAVA

43 Garrett, T. R. H. J.R.A.I., 1912, XLII. 53.
44 Stratz, C. H. [Javanese Women.] A.f.A., 1899, XXV. 233.
See also Hagen (Ch. VI., ref. 8).

(g) BORNEO

45 Haddon, A. C. Archiv. Anthop. Etnol., Florence, 1901, XXXI. 341.
46 Haddon, A. C. Appendix to 47.
47 Hose, C., and McDougall, W. *The Pagan Tribes of Borneo.* Lond., 1912.
48 Kohlbrugge, J. H. Mitth. Niederl. Reichmus, f. Volk., II. 5.

(h) CELEBES

49 Sarasin, F. *Mat. Naturgesch. der Insel Celebes.* Wiesbaden, 1906, V., Pt. 2

(i) PHILIPPINE ISLANDS

50 Beyer, H. O. *The Population of the Philippine Islands in* 1916. Manila, 1917.
51 Folkmar, D. *Album of Philippine Types.* Manila, 1904.
52 Meyer, A. B. *The Negritos.* Dresden, 1899.
53 Reed, W. A. *Negritos of Zambales.* Etno. Surv., Manila, 1905, II. 1.
54 Sullivan, L. R. *Racial types in the Philippine Islands.* Anthropolog. papers, Amer. Mus. of Nat. Hist., New York, 1918, XXIII. 1. [Reference to all the literature.]
55 Bean, R. B. *Racial Anatomy of the Philippine Islanders.* Philadelphia, 1910 [an unconventional work].

INDEX OF TRIBAL, RACIAL, AND NATIONAL NAMES

Achakzai Pathan, 124
Aeta, 45
Afghan, 45
Ainu, 43, 44, 69, 77, 78, 199, 200, 206, 208, 257
  Czaplicka's classification, 196
  physical characters, 210 ff.
Aksu, 173, 175
Aleut, 196
Alfourou, 259
Alpine race, 6, 44, 49, 53 ff., 80, 113, 146, 154, 172, 174, 176, 183, 198, 231
Altaian race, 47, 195, 201
Altaicus, Homo, 47
Amerinds, 62, 82, 200
Andamanese, 5, 45, 142, 255
  physical characters, 145
Annamese, 161, 232, 233
Armenians, 95 ff., 100, 252, 253
Armenoid race, 53, 55 ff., 80, 88, 90, 91, 96, 98, 100, 103, 104, 110, 113, 132, 140, 144, 160, 174, 177, 183 ff.
Armeno-Pamirensis, Homo, 46
Arabs, 2, 43, 99, 159
  in China, 159
  in Java, 239
  in Malaya, 235
  physical characters, 105 ff.
Arora, 125
Aryans, 99, 129, 137, 174
Aryo-Dravidians, 126, 130 ff.
Assyroid race, 43
Australian aborigines, 4, 5, 22, 34, 213
Awan, 125

Babhan, 126
Badajas, 127
Baktyari, 253
Balti, 45
Baluchi, 46, 124
Bashilanges, 20
Baskir, 197
Battaks, 237
Batin, 237
Beh-gen, 155
Bektasch, 91
Bengali, 126, 144
Besisi, 236
Bin-muh, 155

Bontok, 242
Botocudos, 20
Brahui, 46
Brown race, 30, 42 ff., 52, 66, 70, 79, 102, 111, 136 ff., 141, 157, 158
Buriats, 47, 56, 57, 174, 179, 197, 198, 203
  physical characters, 180 ff.
  Alar, 181, 256
  Selanga, 181, 256
Burmese, 171, 179, 228, 231, 237
Bushmen, 5

Cambodgians, 232
Cantonese, 234
Carians, 1
Caucasians, 3, 230
Chahkhar, 181
Chakmas, 127, 131, 132, 142
Chamar, 126, 133
Chapogi, 198
Ch'iangs, 156
Chiam, 228
Chinese, 6, 20, 22, 46, 56 ff., 64, 65, 154, 175
  aboriginal tribes, 154 ff.
  ancient, 153
  hybrids with Mongols, 181
  in Java, 239
  in Malaya, 234
  in Mongolia, 185
  migrations, 153
  northern, 164
  physical characters, 160 ff.
  southern, 164, 233
Chins, 228
Ch'ing Kehtu, 155
Chin-miao, 157
Choschot, 180
Chuhra, 125
Chukchee, 47, 196, 199, 257
Chung-chia, 154
Chuvanzy, 196
Cinghalese, 144
Coorgs, 125, 130, 254
Coreans. See Koreans
Cro-Magnon race, 80

Dardi, 45
Dasyu, 129, 137

Dehwar, 46
Deshasth Brahman, 125
Dinaric, 53, 55, 80
Dissentis type, 20, 57
Dolan, 173, 175
Don Cossacks, 180
Dosadh, 126
Dravidians, 4, 43, 52, 102, 123, 127, 129 ff., 143, 144, 229, 254
Drupa, 170
Druses, 100
Durbot, 180
Dzungar, 180

Eleuts, 179, 180
Eskimo, 20, 43, 82
  American, 82, 200
  Asiatic, 82, 196, 199
Ethiopic, 3
European races. *See* Alpine, Mediterranean, Nordic, etc.

Finns, 195, 196
" Flowered races," 155
Fuegians, 171
Fukienese, 234

Galtchas, 113
Georgianus,Homo, 46
Gilyaks, 214, 257
Goldi, 198
Greeks, 90, 91
Grussini, 46, 98
Gujar, 125, 128
Gurings, 127
Gurkhas, 122

Hakkas, 157
" Han type," 61, 63, 64
Hazara, 47, 124
Hindus, 143
Hittites, 53, 253
Hsien-yuen, 173
Huns, 128, 129

Ibans, 240
Ifugao, 242
Ih, 154
Ili-Tatars, 114, 173
Imeri, 46
Indo-Afghans, 43, 111, 123, 144
Indo-Afghanus, Homo, 45
Indo-Aryans, 45, 111, 124, 130 ff., 144
Indo-Chinese, 43
Indo-Iranus, Homo, 46
Indonesians, 43, 44, 227, 242. *See also under* Nesiot
Iranians, 45, 46, 112, 113, 156
Irano-Mediterraneus, Homo, 45

Jaintia, 127
Jalari, 127

Japanese, 206 ff., 257
  in Malaya, 235
  origin of, 217
  physical characters, 214 ff.
Jats, 122, 132
Javanese, 238
Jews, 96 ff., 160, 252, 253

Kachhi, 126
Kachins, 147, 228
Kaizak, 174
Kaizak-Kirghiz, 114
Kalang, 238
Kalmuck, 56, 57, 179
Kamchadal, 196, 199
Kanarese, 20, 136
Kanets, 254
Kara-Kalpak, 114
Kara-Kirghiz, 114
Karens, 171, 228, 230, 240, 258
Kashmiri, 45, 171
Kayans, 240
Kayasths, 126
Kazan Tatars, 197
Kelantan, 235
Kelpin, 173, 175
Kenyans, 240
Khalkha, 179 ff., 198
Khasia, 127, 142
Khmer, 227, 232
Kipchak, 114
Kirghiz, 173, 175, 197, 256
Klemantan, 240
Kochh, 126, 142
Koibales, 201
Koiri, 126
Kolarians, 123
Kondhs, 120
Koreans, 43, 163, 200, 216, 256
  physical characters, 190
Koryak, 199
Kuis, 228
Kunbis, 125
Kurds, 93, 100, 253

Lamut, 198
Land Dayak, 241
Lao, 227
Lapps, 202
Lepcha, 46, 127, 131, 142, 147
Limen, 155
Lissu, 255
Loblik, 173, 175
Lolo, 155, 156, 171, 228, 255
Lori, 111
Lycians, 91, 94

Madurese, 238
Magyars, 43
Mahar, 125
Mahrattas, 129
Malayalis, 136

Malays, 65, 67, 68, 171, 218, 233 ff., 242, 258
history, 237. *See also under* Proto-Malays
Mals, 126
Man, 154
Manchu, 43, 47, 149, 154, 163, 180, 185, 198, 216, 256
physical characters, 187 ff.
Man-tse, 44
Maniza, 196
Manyarg, 198
Maravar, 143
Maronites, 100
Medes, 108
Mediterranean race, 5, 6, 30, 46, 49, 50, 58, 77, 79, 88, 90, 98, 111, 138, 157, 160, 185, 212
Melanesians, 45, 136
Melano-Indians, 123
Meng-chia, 154, 155
Metwali, 100, 253
Miao, 154, 155
Mingreli, 46
Mir Jats, 132
Mirs, 127
Mois, 227, 228, 232
Mongolians, 43, 176, 232
Mongolo-Dravidians, 126, 130 ff., 141
Mongoloid race, 44, 56, 57, 130, 142
Mongols, 43, 47, 56, 57, 64, 149, 154, 159, 163, 168, 170, 174, 175, 179 ff., 195, 202, 256
distribution, 184
history, 180, 183
physical characters, 181, 186
Mon-Khmer, 129, 143, 146, 236
Mons, 228
Montesos, 242
Moriori, 171

Naga, 146, 227, 228
Nagar Brahman, 130
Nair, 121
Nambudris, 121
Nearcticus, Homo, 47
Negrillos, 67, 145
Negritos, 43, 45, 49, 65 ff., 104, 136, 145, 227, 229, 232, 233, 238, 241, 242, 247, 259
physical characters, 145, 235 ff., 242
Negroes, 4, 5, 58, 67 ff., 83, 88, 104
Oceanic, 68
Nepalese, 143, 171
Neo-Siberians, 196, 202
Nesiots, 52, 65, 67, 146, 157, 158, 160, 218, 229, 233, 237, 240, 242, 243
Newars, 122
Nilotic Negroes, 22

Nordic race, 6, 22, 49, 50, 53, 69, 77, 78, 90, 93, 100, 101, 138, 212. *See also under* Proto-Nordic
Nosu, 156

Orang Kubu, 237
Oriental race, 52, 101
Oroch, 198
Orochan, 198
Oroke, 198
Ostyak, 196, 199, 201, 202, 256

Palæarcticus, Homo, 46
Palæasiatics, 63, 162, 191, 195, 198, 200
Palæo-Siberians, 196, 200, 201, 204
Palaungs, 228, 258
Pamiri, 45 n., 46, 176
Pangan, 235
Paniyans, 127
Papuans, 45
Pareœans, 63, 141, 143, 146, 157, 172, 176, 184, 200, 229, 237, 239
Patagonians, 22
Persians, 45, 108, 111
Polynesians, 5
Po-tse, 157
Prabhus, 125, 130
Pre-Dravidians, 111, 136, 139, 146, 236, 242, 243
Pre-Nordics, 50, 77
Proto-Dravidians, 136
Proto-Egyptians, 50, 53, 88, 103, 104
Proto-Ethiopians, 80
Proto-Malays, 44, 65, 218, 231, 233, 235 ff., 240 ff.
Protomorphus, Homo, 46
Proto-Nordics, 44, 50, 51, 78, 110 ff., 112, 138, 139, 154, 172, 194, 199 ff., 214
Pulaiyan, 128
Punans, 240
Punjabi, 45, 235
Punti, 157
Pygmies. *See* Negrillos *and* Negritos

Qirghiz, Qara-Qirghiz, etc. *See under* Kara-Kirghiz, Kirghiz

Rajbansi Magh, 126
Rajput, 45, 122, 125, 128, 138
Russians, 39

Sakai, 126, 235, 236
Samarqandi, 98, 253
Samoyeds, 195, 197, 201, 202, 256
San-Tak, 157
Sarts, 174
Scyths, 128, 129, 140
Scytho-Dravidians, 125, 130 ff.
Selung, 228
Semang, 45, 235

Semites, 99
Senoi, 236
Shanans, 127, 128
Shan, 227
Shia, 93
Siamese, 227, 233
Sikh, 45
Sinicus, Homo, 46
Solon, 198
Soyotes, 197, 256
Spaniards, 20
Sundanese, 238
Sumerians, 44, 89, 92, 101 ff.
" Sung type," 63, 64
Suomi, 196
Svani, 46

Tadchadsky, 91
T'ai, 155
Tajiks, 112 ff.
Talaing, 228
Tamils, 136, 235
Taranchi, 47, 114, 173 ff., 255
Tasmanian aborigines, 22, 45, 136
Tatars, Altaian, 180
  Ili, 114, 173
  Kazan, 197
Telenghites, 179, 180
Telugus, 136
Tenggerese, 238
Thai, 227
Tho, 227
Tibetans, 43, 46, 128, 143, 154, 162, 164, 168, 170 ff.
Tibeto-Burmans, 127, 230
Tibetanus, Homo, 46
Toala, 242
Todas, 254
Torgot, 47, 173, 179, 180, 256
Tse-Li, 157
T'u, 154

Tubas, 195
Tungus, 47, 149, 162, 163, 185, 187, 198, 257
  physical characters, 202
  racial movements, 199
Tupo, 195
Turko-Finns, 43
Turko-Iranians, 124, 130 ff.
Turko-Mongols, 176, 198
Turkomans, 43, 77, 109, 110, 112, 253
Turks, 43, 44, 91 n., 95, 99, 114, 128, 159, 173, 176, 177, 180, 195
  Eastern, 197
  Iranian, 174, 198
  Osmanli, 198
  Siberian, 197
  Turanian, 197
  relation to Mongols, 185
Tziam, 228

Ugrian, 43, 44
U-lat, 180
Urat, 180
Uriankhai, 201
Uzbegs, 114

Veddas, 23, 143, 144, 236, 255
Vogul, 196, 201, 256

" White races," 42 ff., 49, 58

Yakut, 197, 203
Yao, 154
" Yellow races," 48, 56, 58 ff., 66, 70, 80 ff., 135, 141, 142, 199
  divisions of, 62
Yeneseians, 195
Yeruvas, 254
Yesidi, 100, 253
Yueh-chi, 156
Yukaghir, 196

GENERAL INDEX

Abadie, M., 258
Acheulean period, 72
Adachi, B., 257
Afghanistan, 37, 47, 107, 108 ff.
Akhotsk, Sea of, 198
Akka Tag, 167
Aleutian Islands, 32, 37, 196
Altai Mountains, 36, 40, 44, 167, 169, 174, 177, 193
Altyn Dagh, 169
Amdo, 168
America, early man in, 81, 82
Amoy, 234
Amur, River, 39, 187, 198
Anadir, River, 196
Anatolia, 35, 37, 85 ff.
Anau, 72, 74, 153, 159, 183
Andaman Islands, 37, 43, 145, 242, 255
Anderson, J. D., 254
Andersson, J. G., 153, 252
Anghelu Rhu, 92
Angora, 86
Anhui, 157
Annam, 155
Annandale, N., 258
Anping, 155
Anshi, 178
Anshun, 155, 156
Antelias, 75
Aomori, 205
Aoshima, 207, 210
Arabia, 37, 85, 99, 105 ff., 253
Arabian desert, 41
Arakan, 220
Aral-Caspian basin, 114
Aral Sea, 41, 192
Archæology, 71 ff., 153, 194, 206, 252, 256, 257
Arctic Ocean, 35, 40
    region, climatic conditions in, 40, 193
Aristotle, 1, 2
Armenia, 35, 37, 105
Asia, Arctic, 192 ff.
    Central, 36, 167 ff.
    climate of, 39
    early man in, 71 ff.
    Minor, 72, 80, 94, 252
    racial geography of, 32

Asia, Arctic, South-eastern, 220 ff.
    Western, 84 ff.
Assam, 46, 47, 129, 146, 258
Astrakhan, 180
Aurignacian, 72
Australia, 33
Averages, significance of, 8 ff.
Ayar, Lake, 178

Bab-el-Mandeb, Straits of, 34
Baelz, E., 191, 214, 216, 257
Baikal, Lake, 198
Balgrash, Lake, 169
Bali, 241
Balkash, Lake, 41, 169, 178
Baltic Sea, 50
Baluchistan, 37, 107, 108, 111
Bankok, 221
Banners, Manchu, 188
    Mongol, 181 n.
Barguzin, 202
Barkul, 169, 178
Batang, 168
Batchelor, Rev. J., 257
Baur, 251
Baye, J. de, 252
Bean, R. B., 259
Behring Strait, 32, 82, 192
Bell, Sir Charles, 255
Berezov, 197
Bernier, F., 2
Beyer, H. O., 259
Biasutti, R., 250
Bihar, 126
Biometry, 7 ff., 208
Birkner, F., 165, 255
Bitchu, 207
Black, Davidson, 60, 75, 153, 255
Blagden, C. O., 258
Blumenbach, J. F., 3, 250
Boas, 96, 97, 252
Bogdanof, A. P., 253
Bogoras, W., 257
Bokhara, 114, 169
Borneo, 67, 224, 226, 240 ff., 259
Bougle, M. C., 252
Boule, M., 71, 76 ff., 252
Bourdaret, E., 256
Brinkley, F., 257
Broca, P., 18

265

Bronze Age, 80, 91, 194
Brooks, C. E. P., 250
Broomhall, T. H., 251
Brown, A. R., 255
Brown, J. C., 255
Bryn, H., 252
Budapest, 57
Burma, 47, 147, 149, 155, 220, 233, 258
Bury, G. W., 253

Callemand, J., 254
Cambodgia, 227 ff., 258
Carchemish, 101, 103
Carey, Sir B. S., 258
Carr-Saunders, A. M., 251
Carruthers, D., 256
Caspian Sea, 41
Caste, 12., 134
Caucasus, 252
Celebes, 223, 224, 226, 259
Ceylon, 51, 61, 67, 143, 144, 254
Chaatas masks, 194–5
Chalcolithic Period in China, 74, 75, 153
Chamberlain, B., 257
Chamdo, 168
Chancelade cranium, 82
Chang Tang, 167
Changteh, 155
Chanpai-Shan, 186
Chantre, E., 100, 252, 253, 256
Charklik, 173
Charles, R. H., 254
Charusin, 256
Chekiang, 157
Chellean period, 72
Cherchen, River, 169
Chihli, 150, 163
Chikuzen, 215
China, 148 ff., 251, 255
    aboriginal tribes in, 152, 154 ff.
    ancient remains in, 73
    Chalcolithic Period in, 74
    ethnological divisions, 149
    Neanderthal man in, 75
    Neolithic Period in, 74
    prehistory, 252
    southern, 151
    (See also under names of provinces.)
Chikuzen, 216
Chinfeng Chow, 156
Chin Hills, 220, 221, 258
Christian, V., 252, 253
Chiskaya Bay, 197
Climate, Asiatic, 39
    India, 117
Climatic conditions, effect of, 21, 22
Coefficient of correlation, 10
    racial likeness, 11, 12
    variation, 9
Collignon, R., 23, 257

Communications, Western Asia, 88 ff.
    Afghanistan, 109
    China, 148, 149, 178
    Northern India, 116
Conklin, E. G., 251
Contingency, theory of, 10
Coorg, 125
Correlation, theory of, 10
Crahmer, W., 256
Cranial base, 19
Crooke, W., 128, 129, 254
Cyprus, 11, 29, 56, 95, 250
    prehistory, 91, 92
Czaplicka, M. A., 114, 174, 187, 194, 196, 202, 203, 251, 256, 257

Daghestan, 98
Dalton, E. T., 254
Danilov, J., 253
Darwin, C., 3
Deccan, 4, 118, 129
Delisle, F., 255
Deniker, J., 6, 20, 43, 52, 55, 97, 123, 179, 182, 195, 196, 227, 228, 250, 256, 258
Deserts, effect on man, 41
    in Western Asia, 86
Dixon, R. B., 250
Djokjakarta, 239
Dolichocephaly, 19
Dolon Nor, 178
Donitz, W., 257
Duab of Turkestan, 109
Dubois, J., 71
Duckworth, W. L. H., 3, 4, 56, 250, 251
Dynastic Period, in Egypt, 80
Dzungaria, 149, 169, 178

East Indian Archipelago, 37, 223 ff.
East Indies, ethnology of, 224 ff.
Easter Island, 33
Ebi, Lake, 178
Economics in relation to ethnology, 246
Egypt, 53, 79, 80, 88
Eikstedt, 254
Ektag Altai Mountains, 178
Elam, 108
Elburz Mountains, 85, 89
Elephas primigenius, 73, 75
Enthoven, R. E., 254
Environment, effects on man, 16, 17, 25 ff.
Erzeroum, 86
Ethnic movements in Far East, 191
Euphrates, River, 38, 103
European colonization, effect of, 246
Evans, I. H. N., 259
Evolution, progressive, 17
Eye colour, 25 ff.
    form, 61

Face, architecture of the, 58
Fauna, in relation to man, 76
Fengtien, 74, 153, 186
Ferghana, 113, 114
Fischer, 52, 101, 251
Fleure, H. J., 50, 77, 134, 251
Flower, Sir W., 250, 255
Folkmar, D., 259
Foochow, 157
Food, effect of, 23
Forests, temperate, 40
    tropical, 42
Formosa, 37, 157, 205, 258
Fossil man, 252
Fridolin, J., 256
Fujiyama, 205
Fukien, 24, 157, 219
Fu-nui Shan, 152

Galton, Sir F., 7
Ganges, River, 38, 116, 117
Garrett, T. H. R., 238, 259
Geography, racial, 32, 120
Germ-plasm, 16
Ghats, Western, 39, 118
Ghenghis Khan, 56, 180
Gilbert Islands, 26
Giuffrida-Ruggeri, V., 45 ff., 50, 76,
    79, 250, 251, 252, 254, 259
Gobi, 36, 41, 148, 178 ff., 185, 199
Goroshchenko, 194, 256
Graham, A. W., 258
Great Lakes, 39
Grenard, F., 255
Grimble, A., 26, 251
Günther, H. F. K., 101, 251

Haberer, K. A., 255
Haddon, A. C., 14, 44 ff., 62, 65,
    110 ff., 144, 147, 172, 191, 228,
    230, 237, 240, 242, 250, 251, 259
Hagen, B., 255, 259
Hainan, 157
Hair, 25 ff., 49, 60
Hall, H. R., 102, 252
Hamada, 206 ff., 252
Hami, 169, 178
Hamy, E. T., 250, 259
Hankow, 150
Hasebe, K., 215, 252, 257
Hasluck, F. W., 92, 252
Hauschild, M. W., 253
Head-form, factors contributing to,
    19
Henry, A., 255
Heritable characters, 16
Herodotus, 1
Hertz, W. A., 258
Himalaya, 116, 126, 167
Hindu Kush, 45, 111
Hingi, 155, 156
Ho-chow, 169

Hogarth, D. G., 251, 253
Hokkaido, 37, 205, 206
Holdich, Sir T., 111, 251
Holland, Sir T. H., 254
Homer, 1, 2
Honan, 150, 153
Honshu, 205
Hornell, J., 254
Hose, C., 240, 259
How, W. W., 252
Howarth, Sir H. H., 256
Hrdlicka, A., 44, 81, 251, 252
Hsin-ts'eng, 156
Huai, Mountains, 150, 152
Hunan, 155
Hungary, 55
Hunt, E. H., 130, 140, 254
Huntingdon, E., 109, 251
Husing, R., 104, 253
Huxley, T. H., 3, 34, 250
Hwang Ho, 36, 38, 149, 150
    palæolithic stations near, 73
Hybrids, human, 16

Iden-Zeller, O., 257
Idzumi, 207
Ikishima Islands, 215
Ili, River, 169, 174, 180
Immigrants, Jewish, into America, 96
Index, cephalic, 20, 27, 48, 130, 141
    nasal, 21, 28, 49, 66, 133, 134
India, 52, 61, 67, 115 ff., 253 ff.
    food materials in, 119
    influence on Malaya, 235
    jungle tribes, 136
    negritos in, 145
    palæoliths in, 72
    racial stocks, 135 ff.
Indian Ocean, 34, 35
Indo-China, 43, 152, 258
    ancient remains in, 74
Indo-Gangetic plain, 116
Indonesia, 220 ff., 240, 243, 259
Indus, 116, 117
Inland Sea (Japan), 215
" Insulinde," 37, 224
Irak, 85
Iran, 35, 37, 88, 105, 253
Iranian Asia, inhabitants, 90
Irkutsk, 72, 177, 193
Irrawaddy, River, 220
Irtish, River, 40, 178
Ishikawa, 215
Ivanovski, A. A., 114, 174, 180, 188
    256
Iyer, A. K., 254

Jamieson, C. E., 156, 255
Japan, 35, 37, 148
    archæology, 206 ff., 257
    climate, 205
    kitchen-middens, 73

Japan, migrations into, 209
  modern inhabitants, 210
  palæoethnology, 206
  racial geography, 205 ff.
Java, 67, 71, 223, 225, 238, 259
Javorski, W., 109, 111, 253
Jaw, form of, 58
Jesup expedition, 62, 198, 257
Jili, 169
Jochelson-Brodsky, D., 198, 203, 256
Joyce, T. A., 43, 68, 171, 173, 175,
  176, 227, 230, 251, 255
Jungle, influence on man, 222

Kabul, 137
Kagoshima, 205
Kaifeng, 152, 160
Kalgan, 178
Kamchatka, 37, 196
Kansu, 148, 150, 168, 176
  palæolithic stations in, 73, 74
Karakoram, 178
  mountains, 167
Karenni, 221
Kashan, 86
Kashgar, 169
Kashgaria, 149, 152
Kashmir, 125
Kawachi, 206
Keane, 2, 250, 251
Keith, Sir A., 16, 19, 72, 250, 251, 252
Keriya, 173
Kerman, 86
Kham, 164, 168, 170
Khatanga, River, 197
Khingan Mountains, 36, 40, 177, 186
Khiva, 114, 169
Khorassan, 89
Khotan, 169, 173
Kiangsi, 155, 157
King Yang, 73
Kirghiz Steppes, 193
Kirkpatrick, W., 254
Kish, 56, 92, 101
Kitchen-middens, 73
Kiushiu, 205, 215
Ko, 73, 206, 207
Koganei, Y., 163, 164, 171, 206, 209,
  211, 255, 256, 257
Kohlbrugge, J. H., 259
Kokonor, 156, 168, 170
Kolyma, 196
Konia, 86
Korea, 163, 189 ff., 205, 215, 256
  relation to Japan, 191
" Korean Gate," 148
Korla, 175
Krasnoyarsk, 72
Kublai Khan, 56
Kubo, T., 190, 256
Kuldja, 173
Ku-ma-cheeh, 169

Kun Lun, 35, 36, 167, 169, 205
Kurdistan, 37, 86
Kurgans, 194, 195
Kuril Islands, 209
Kwangsi, 149, 155, 157
Kwantung, 155, 157
Kweichow, 155
Kwei-wa-cheng, 169, 178
Kyoto, 208, 215

Landenberger, E., 225
Langdon, S., 101, 103
Language, as a test of race, 1
Lapicque, L., 254
Lapithos, 56
Lartet, E., 72
Lebanon, Mount, 100
Lefevre, A., 257
Legendre, 255
Leiper, R. T., 249
Lena, River, 39, 192
Lenz, 251
Leontes, River, 100
Leucoderm, 45
Lhasa, 167
Linnæus, 2, 250
Little, A., 167, 251
Lob Nor, 169, 178
Locality, effect of, 23
Loess, ancient remains in, 73
Logan, J. R., 258
Loochow, see Ryu Kyu
Lowis, C. C., 258
Luschan, F. v., 90 ff, 252
Luthy, A., 255
Luzon, 242
Lyall, A. C., 253
Lycia, 91, 252
Lyde, L. W., 251

Macdonell, A. A., 253
Madagascar, 35, 68
Madras, 72
Magdalenian period, 72
Mainoff, 203
Malabar, 121
Malacca, 235
Malaria, 24
Malar bones, 58
Malay Archipelago, 259. (See also
  under names of islands.)
  aborigines, 235 ff.
  Peninsula, 43, 45, 66, 145, 221,
  233 ff., 258
Malta, 34, 92
Man, E. H., 255
Manchuria, 148, 163, 177, 186 ff., 256
Mandible, 58
Marco Polo, 56
Martin, R., 66, 68, 211, 250, 251, 258
Masseter muscles, 58
Mathew, R., 75, 251

Matsumoto, H., 75, 207, 209, 252, 257
Maurel, E., 258
McDougall, W., 240, 259
McMahon, A. R., 258
Mean, significance of, 8
Measures of dispersion, 8, 9
Mediterranean Sea, 34, 35, 41, 87, 90
Mekong, River, 221
Mekran, 109
Melanesia, 223
Melanocroid, 4
Menam, 221
Menankerbau, 65, 237
Mentawei Islands, 237
Me Ping, 228
Merhart, G. v., 256
Meshed, 86, 89
Mesopotamia, 37, 38, 56, 79, 100 ff.
Messerschmidt, L., 253
Meyer, A. B., 259
Middle East, 85, 107 ff.
Migrations, 78, 87, 101, 235
Milne, L., 258
Mindanao, 242
Ming dynasty, 179, 185
Miocene, 76
Misery spots, 23
Mississippi, River, 39
Miyato, 207
Molucca Islands, 223, 224, 226
Mongol languages, 182
Mongolia, 148, 150, 177 ff., 198, 256
    Inner, 163, 180, 256
Mongolian fold, 61, 182
    plateau, 36
Monro, N. G., 257
Montandon, G., 210, 212, 256
Montefiore, J., 256
Morant, G. M., 12, 52, 143, 144, 161,
    162, 164, 170, 171, 181, 182, 215,
    230, 232, 238, 250, 255
Morgan, J., 258
Mousterian Period, 72, 73
Muller, Max, 124
Myres, J. L., 112, 252

Nan-Shan, 149, 152, 153, 178
Narbada, 39, 117
Nasal bones, 58
Neanderthal man, 75
Neolithic Period, 74, 158
New Britain, 20
New Guinea, 45, 145, 224, 242
Nias Islands, 44, 251
Nicobar Islands, 37
Nile, River, 38
Ning Hsia, 73
Nippon, 214, 215
Niya, 173

Obi, River, 39, 41, 192, 196, 201
Oceania, 33

Okayama, 209, 215, 216
Olekima, River, 198
Olgontorsky Cape, 196
Orbit, form of, 54
Ordos, 73, 149, 178, 179
Oust Kiakhta, 194

Pacific Islands, 33
Paissel, V. E., 175, 255
Palæoliths, 72 ff.
Palasan, 242
Palestine, 99
Pamirs, 35, 110, 169, 177
Panntetier, G., 232, 258
Parjakoff, 188
Parker, H., 254
Payne, C. H., 254
Peake, H. J. E., 93, 112, 252
Pearl, R., 251
Pearson, 7, 24, 250
Peking, 159, 235
Perak, 235
Perm, 201
Persepolis, 111
Persia, 37, 107, 253
Persian Gulf, 104
Philippine Islands, 45, 66, 145, 224,
    227, 259
    ethnology of, 241
Phœnicia, ancient remains in, 75
Pigmentation, 25 ff., 251
Pithecanthropus, 71, 74
Platycnemia, 206, 208
Platymeria, 208
Pliocene, 76
Poch, R., 253
Polynesia, 34
Porotov, M. T., 181, 182, 256
Potanin, G. N., 180
Probable errors, 10
Pumpelly, R., 72, 252
Punjab, 125, 126
Pure Races, 15

Quatrefages, J. L. de, 250, 259
Quetelet, A. de, 6, 250

Race, criteria of, 1 ff., 14 ff.
    fixity of, 16
Races of Asia, 32 ff.
Racial likeness, coefficient of, 11
    geography, 32
Rainfall, Western Asia, 85, 86
Rajputana, 125
Ramaprasad-Chanda, 129
Red River, 221
Reed, W. A., 259
Reicher, M., 20, 57, 182, 255
Retzius, A., 97, 250
Rhinoceros tichorhinus, 73
Richards, F. J., 136, 139, 254
Richards, L., 251

Richthoven, Freiherr von, 251
Rig Veda, 137
Ripley, W. Z., 6, 22, 23, 27, 28, 32, 45,
    49, 53, 55, 57, 63, 96, 104, 112,
    156, 250
Risley, Sir H. H., 45, 129, 140 ff.,
    254
    classification of Indian races, 124 ff.
Rivers of Asia, 37 ff.
Rivers, W. H. R., 254
Roberts, S. G., 253
Robertson, G. S., 254
Robinson, H. C., 258
Rockhill, W. W., 171, 255
Rose, A., 255
Roudenko, S., 201, 202, 256
Roux, P., 258
Roxby, P. M., 149
Russia, 85
Ryukyu Islands, 37, 257

Saghalien, 37, 43, 198, 205, 209
Salaman, R. N., 253
Samarqand, 169, 253
Santal Parganas, 118
San-tao Ho, 73
Sarasin, P. and F., 254, 259
Sardinia, 92
Sasva, River, 201
Satsuma, 215, 216
Savanna regions, 41
Savenkov, 252
Scandinavia, 50, 77
Scheube, B., 257
Schmidt, W., 143, 146, 254, 259
Schrenk, L. V., 195, 257
Scott, Sir G., 258
Seeland, Dr., 257
Selanga, River, 181, 256
Selection, natural, 24
Seligman, C. G., 105, 106, 253, 255
Semirechie, 173
Senart, E., 253
Sergi, G., 4, 88, 250
Shan States, 220, 221, 228
Shansi, 150, 157
Shantung, 150, 157, 163
Shensi, 150
Shikoku, 205
Shimada, K., 257
Shirokogoroff, S. M., 162 ff., 189, 190,
    199, 203, 255
Shi-tsui-tze, 73
Shrendrikovski, J. J., 256
Siam, 221, 258
Sian, 152
Siangyan, 152
Siberia, 36, 37, 39, 40, 179, 182, 187,
    192 ff., 251, 256, 257
    ancient man in, 72, 74
    archæology of, 194
    climate, 193

Siberia, ethnology, 195 ff.
Sikkim, 142, 171
Sinkiang, 148, 167 ff., 173, 255
Sino-Japanese area, 41
Siwalik, 76
Sjara Osso Gol, 73
Skeat, W. W., 258, 259
Skin-colour, 25, 26, 49, 60, 182
Smith, G. Elliot, 33, 44, 52 ff., 72, 88,
    102, 251
Smith, V. A., 253
Sollas, W. J., 82, 252
Spiller, G., 251
Standard deviation, 8, 130
Stature, 22, 49, 63, 158
Stavropol, 180
Stein, Sir A., 173, 255
Steppes, 40, 86, 138
Stratz, C. H., 259
Suchow, 169
Suez Canal, 34
Sulaiman Mountains, 109
Sullivan, L. R., 251, 259
Sumatra, 65, 68, 224, 225, 237, 242,
    259
Sumeria, 50
Sunda Islands, 224
Sung dynasty, 160
Susiana, 111
Swettenham, Sir F., 258, 259
Sygva, River, 201
Syr Daria, 114
Syria, 56, 85 ff., 99, 100, 251, 252
    palæoliths in, 72
Szechuan, 152, 155, 156

Tabriz, 86
Tachienlu, 168
Tagara masks, 194, 195
Taiwan, *see* Formosa
Taklamakan desert, 41, 178
Talko-Hryncewicz, J. D., 194, 256
Tapti, River, 39
Tarbagatai Mountains, 178, 180
Tarim basin, 35, 36, 149, 153, 169, 173
Tasmania, 34
Teheran, 89
Teilhard, P., 73, 252
Temperate forests, 40
Temple, Sir R. C. D., 258
Temporal muscles, 59
Tenasserim, 220, 221
Terai, 116
Testut, L., 82, 252
Thebaid, 50
Thessaly, 94
Thomson, A., 17 ff., 21, 69, 83, 250,
    255
Thurston, E., 129, 254
Tibet, 35, 40, 148, 149, 161, 167 ff.,
    169, 255
Tibeto-Yunnan plateau, 220

Tien-Shan, 149, 169, 178
Tientsin, 159
Tigris, 38
Tildesley, M. A., 230, 258
Tobolsk, 193, 196, 201
Tod, J., 254
Toldt, E., 257
Tomsk, 177, 196, 201
Tonkin, 258
Topinard, P., 4, 14, 18, 250
Torri, R., 187, 256
Tourensk, 201
Trade routes, 169, 178
Transbaikalia, 177, 193
Troll, J., 253
Tropical forests, 42
Troy, siege of, 93
Tsaidam, 168
Tsanpo, 167
Tsing Ling Mountains, 150, 152
Tsukumo, 207
Tsushima, 215
Tuck, H. N., 258
Tuen-heng-sien, 169
Tumen, River, 189
Tundra, 40
Tungting Lake, 155
Tunguska, 196, 198
Turan, plain of, 39, 41
Turania, 192
Turfan, 169, 173
Turkestan, 72, 114, 156, 169, 183, 252, 253, 256
Turkestan, Chinese, see Sinkiang
Turkey, 93
Turkish Empire, 85
Turkoman desert, 41
  republic, 85, 107
  steppes, 112
Turner, Sir W., 161, 170, 254, 255, 258, 259
Turukhansk, 196

Udaipur, 125
Ujfalvy, C. E., 112, 113, 188, 253, 256
Uliassetai, 178
United Provinces, 133
Ur, 101
Ural Mountains, 192, 197
Urga, 178
Urumchi, 169
Uzbeg Republic, 85, 107

Vegetation, Western Asia, 86

Verneau, R., 67, 229, 231, 233, 258
Vincent, G., 253
Virchow, R., 255, 256
Visher, S. S., 251
Vitamins, 23
Volga, River, 179, 180
Volkov, Th., 252
Volz, W., 237, 259

Wall, Great, of China, 35, 148, 150
Wei, River, 152
Weissenberg, J., 96, 97, 252, 253
Weldon, C., 7
Wells, J., 252
Western Ghats, 39, 118
White, Sir H. T., 228, 258
Winstedt, R. O., 235, 258
Woods, H. A., 157
Woolley, C. L., 101
Wuting, 157

Xanthoderms, 45

Yablonoi Mountains, 36, 40, 177
Yadrintseff, N. M., 174
Yajur Veda, 137
Yakutsk, 193
Yalu River, 189
Yamato, 215
Yana River, 193, 196
Yangtze Kiang, 36, 38, 117, 149, 150
Yarkand, 169
Yellow River, see Hwang Ho
Yellow Sea, 187
Yemen, 86, 105
Yenesei River, 39, 44, 192, 196, 201, 256
  valley, palæoliths in, 72
Yeneseisk, 177, 193
Yezo, see Hokkaido
Yinach'ang, 157
Yuan River, 155
Yu-feng-chiao, 73
Yuldur River, 169
Yule, G. Udney, 250
Yunnan, 149, 152, 155 ff., 231, 255

Zaborovski, S., 232, 258
Zammit, T., 34
Zayan Mountains, 177
Zichy, Count de, 253
Zumoffen, 75, 252
Zwaan, K. de, 44, 251

THE HISTORY OF CIVILIZATION

Titles in the series

Pre History	Language - A Linguistic Introduction to History	J Vendryes
	A Geographical Introduction to History	Lucien Febvre
	The Dawn of European Civilization	V Gordon Childe
	The Aryans	V Gordon Childe
	From Tribe to Empire	Moret & Davy
	Death Customs	Effie Bendann
	The Migration of Symbols	D Mackenzie
	The History of Witchcraft and Demonology	Montague Summers
	The History of Medicine	C G Cumston
	Money and Monetary Policy in Early Times	A R Burns
	Life and Work in Prehistoric Times	G Renard
	Social Organization	Rivers & Perry
Greek Civilization	The Ægean Civilization	G Glotz
	Ancient Greece at Work	G Glotz
	The Formation of the Greek People	A Jardé
	Art in Greece	de Ridder & Deonna
	Macedonian Imperialism	Pierre Jouguet
	Greek Thought and the Origins of the Scientific Spirit	Léon Robin
	The Greek City and its Institutions	G Glotz
Roman Civilization	Primitive Italy	Leon Homo
	Rome the Law-Giver	J Declareuil
	The Roman Spirit	Albert Grenier
	The Roman World	V Chapot
	Roman Political Institutions	Leon Homo
	The Economic Life of the Ancient World	J Toutain
Eastern Civilization	The Nile and Egyptian Civilization	A Moret
	The Peoples of Asia	L H Dudley Buxton
	Mesopotamia	L Delaporte
	A Thousand Years of the Tartars	E H Parker
	Ancient Persia and Iranian Civilization	Clement Huart
	Chinese Civilization	Marcel Granet
	The Life of Buddha	Edward J Thomas
	The History of Buddhist Thought	Edward J Thomas
	Ancient India and Indian Civilization	Masson-Oursel et al
	The Heroic Age of India	N K Sidhanta
Judaeo Christian Civilization		
	Israel	Adolphe Lods
	The Prophets and the Rise of Judaism	Adolphe Lods
	The Jewish World in the Time of Jesus	Charles Guignebert
	The History and Literature of Christianity	Pierre de Labriolle
European Civilization	The End of the Ancient World	Ferdinand Lot
	The Rise of the Celts	Henri Hubert
	The Greatness and Decline of the Celts	Henri Hubert
	Life and Work in Medieval Europe	P Boissonnade
	The Feudal Monarchy in France and England	C Petit-Dutaillis
	Travel and Travellers of the Middle Ages	Arthur Newton
	Chivalry	Edgar Prestage
	The Court of Burgundy	Otto Cartellieri
	Life and Work in Modern Europe	Renard & Weulersse
	China and Europe	Adolf Reichwein
	The American Indian Frontier	W Christie Macleod

For Product Safety Concerns and Information please contact our EU
representative GPSR@taylorandfrancis.com
Taylor & Francis Verlag GmbH, Kaufingerstraße 24, 80331 München, Germany

www.ingramcontent.com/pod-product-compliance
Lightning Source LLC
Chambersburg PA
CBHW060151280326
41932CB00012B/1719